Uncovering the Bible's Greatest Mysteries

Alton Gansky

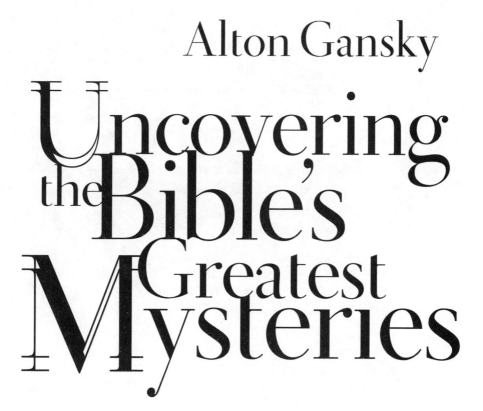

Uncovering the Bible's Greatest Mysteries

BROADMAN
&HOLMAN
PUBLISHERS

Nashville, Tennessee

0-8054-2499-7

Published by Broadman & Holman Publishers,
Nashville, Tennessee

Subject Heading: BIBLICAL STUDIES

1 2 3 4 5 6 7 8 9 10 06 05 04 03 02

To my mother-in-law, *Anna Jane Venosdel,*
who taught me the value of asking tough Bible questions,

and to my father-in-law, the *Reverend Don Venosdel,*
for his years of support and encouragement.

Contents

Preface

EARLY IN 2001, I was doing a radio interview to promote my latest novel. After a short break, the program host came back on and promptly reintroduced me. As he began, I heard the crescendo of some familiar music. "Our guest is novelist Alton Gansky, the author of *The Prodigy* and nine other novels. He writes Christian X-files."

X-files? Then I recognized the music as being the theme song to that very show. Christian X-files? I had never thought of myself as writing books that could be described that way, but after a few moments in thought, I could see how others would think so.

I confess to having a fascination with mysteries and the unexplained. I grew up reading books by mystery reporter Frank Edwards (*Stranger than Science*, for example) and other chroniclers of the unexplained. I consumed

The Jordan River near the Sea of Galilee

comic books and took in episodes of "Twilight Zone" and "Outer Limits." Perhaps I confess too much, but the unusual is my stock and trade.

But I do more than write books; I'm also a pastor who has spent the last two decades preaching and teaching the Bible. Each week I stand before a congregation of experienced Bible students and those brand new to the study of God's Word. For both, the Bible is a reservoir of amazing stories and events. Within its pages I find direction, peace, comfort, and mystery. That's right, mystery—not just any mystery, however, but such that boggles the mind and challenges the soul. In the Bible's sixty-six books are stories far stranger than the fiction created by television writers. The difference is the Bible stories are historical accounts and not fiction. Flesh and blood people saw events that defied explanation. Yet there they are.

Unfortunately, many of the billions of copies of the Bible spread across the world remain unread. Admittedly, parts of the Bible are difficult to grasp and intellectually demanding. Yet the Bible is a fascinating book filled with intrigue, action, romance, and the deepest spiritual truth the world will ever know. In its pages truth is defined, men and women are molded into the image of Christ, the past is revealed, and the future is foretold.

The study of the Bible is more than an academic exercise, more than yoga for the brain. It is an adventure that can capture the mind, heart, and soul. Through its pages we see the invisible God and are transported back to creation and forward to a new heaven and new earth. Included in all this is the miraculous, the puzzling, and the bewildering. But these insights do more than make us scratch our heads; they reveal the enormous power of God, the ultimate authority of Christ, and the intervention of the Holy Spirit.

To read the Bible with open eyes and a receptive mind is to plumb the depths of understanding.

In this book, I hope to explore some of the more enigmatic subjects of the Bible. This is not to say that other topics of Scripture are less important or even less interesting. All Scripture is beneficial to the reader, and no part of it should be dismissed as irrelevant. From Genesis to Revelation is inspired and worthy of study.

The Bible is a book unique among all the world's books in that it is a text that has its origin outside the normal reign of man. It begins with

God, points to God, speaks of God, reveals God, and displays Christ as the resurrected Savior of the world. What I hope to do is kindle excitement about the Word of God—to restore the adventure of reading the biblical text.

Years of study have shown me that the Bible is a well so deep that no man can fully understand it. Almost everyone knows something about the Bible; some know a great deal, and others even bear the title "expert." But no one knows everything about the Scripture. The Bible is like infinitely layered ground. The deeper we dig, the more we find; and when we think no further digging is possible, new gems come to light.

The Bible includes mysteries, questions that have yet to be fully explained. This book is designed to look at some of those enigmas. Not every answer will be new, and some will be incomplete. Biblical understanding is an ongoing process, but that should not be discouraging. It is the journey through time that matters; the journey and what we learn from our travels.

This is not an academic book. It has neither footnotes, nor extensive quotations from scholars. There is a place for such books, but there is also a place for a book written for the person who holds no degrees in theology. That person may be a medical doctor, auto mechanic, homemaker, insurance salesman, soldier, retiree, student—anyone who sits in the pew and wants to know more about the Bible.

My heart's desire is for this book to start a fire of curiosity and create a new, vital interest in the Scriptures.

The adventure waits. Let's get started.

> Make me know Your ways, O LORD;
> Teach me Your paths.
> Lead me in Your truth and teach me,
> For You are the God of my salvation;
> For You I wait all the day. (Psalm 25:4–5)

> It is the glory of God to conceal a matter,
> But the glory of kings is to search out a matter.
> (Proverbs 25:2)

How to Use This Book

The chapters are designed for the casual reader to be used in personal study, family study, or in church Bible classes. Chapters have Bible references so you the reader can examine the biblical text.

Each chapter is broken down into small sections to make study and teaching easier. At the end of each chapter dealing with a mystery is a series of questions meant to prompt thought and discussion.

I have also included a few chapters to help those new to the Scriptures understand some of the people and terms mentioned in the other chapters. These sections, called "A Bit of Background," are short and are meant to provide a better understanding of the stage upon which biblical accounts occur.

A few technical matters: I have chosen the New American Standard Updated version as the Bible translation for this book. I do this partly because of its faithfulness to the original languages and partly because it has been my companion for so long. For consistency, I have followed the translation choices for capitalization and other matters.

Let's open our Bibles and our minds and dive in. Mysteries are waiting!

An ancient millstone similar to those used in biblical times

There Be
Giants

IT HAD BEEN FORTY DAYS since the confrontation began. Forty days of listening to the ridicule, jabs, insults, and taunts from the terrifying man on the valley floor. Behind him, stationed on the slope of a hill, stood the Philistine army, ready to fight or ready to sit and wait. King Saul and his army were encamped on an opposing hill. It was a standoff, as neither army was willing to surrender the strategic position of higher ground. Whichever army was foolish enough to descend from their perch, cross the flat valley bed, and climb the next rise would be at the mercy of their enemy. It was a stalemate, but the Philistines, the persistent enemy of Saul, had an idea: Why not send their best warrior to fight the champion of Israel?

1 Samuel
17:1–58

Goliath made his way to the valley floor and issued a challenge: "Choose a man for yourselves and let him come down to me. If he is able to fight me and kill me, then we will become your servants; but if I prevail against him and kill him, then you shall become our servants and serve us."

There was logic in this. A one-on-one battle would save a great deal of bloodshed. Still, no one took Goliath's challenge—and for good reason. Goliath was no ordinary man. As he stood on the valley floor with the sun high overhead, glinting off the bullet-shaped helmet Philistine soldiers wore, he seemed a colossus. No one was willing to face him.

CHAPTER ONE

After all, the Bible describes him as standing six cubits and a span. A cubit was an inaccurate measure—the distance between a man's elbow and the tip of his middle finger. People come in different sizes, so the cubit varies in length from seventeen and one half inches to twenty-one inches. (Just imagine the difference between a cubit based on David's forearm and that of Goliath's.) For most purposes, eighteen inches serves as an average cubit. A span was the distance between the thumb and little finger when the hand is spread wide—about nine inches. This would make Goliath at least nine feet nine inches tall (if the long cubit is used, he would have towered over eleven feet).

Heights like that are hard to imagine. Even the tallest professional basketball player would seem small standing next to Goliath. In a modern home the standard door height is six feet eight inches from the unfinished floor. That means that Goliath would have to lower his head three feet eight inches just to walk into a house.

But he was more than just tall; he was powerful. The text describes his armor and weapons in detail. Converting the biblical weights of "shekels of iron" into modern terms (about forty shekels of iron to the pound), we learn that Goliath wore 125 pounds of scale-armor and carried a spear with a sixteen-pound head. This does not count the weight of his spear shaft (about seventeen pounds), helmet, or sword. Goliath, whose name means "splendor," would have been a frightening sight.

Did Goliath Have a Glandular Disorder?

Goliath may have suffered from one of several growth disorders such as acromegaly or gigantism. Acromegaly (from *acro,* meaning "height" or "extreme" and *mega,* meaning "large") is caused by a benign tumor on the pituitary gland and effects fifteen thousand Americans. This tumor causes an excessive release of growth hormone that leads to extreme height. The condition also causes medical problems such as thickening of the skin, spade-like hands, premature osteoarthritis, and weakness. It usually occurs in adults older than thirty, although it can begin in childhood. But it is doubtful that Goliath could have been a warrior with such a disease. Saul tells David that Goliath "has been a warrior from his youth." Acromegaly, while not incapacitating in itself, would have left Goliath unfit for his role as a titan of war.

Gigantism, a similar disorder, occurs at a much younger age and is caused by an overactive pituitary gland. The condition begins prior to adolescence, so the bones have not ossified (hardened), allowing for unusually great growth. Robert Pershing Wadlow of Alton, Illinois, grew to nearly nine feet (eight feet eleven inches) and weighed 491 pounds. But Goliath could not have suffered from this affliction either since it too brings muscular weakness.

What then was the cause of Goliath's great size? No one can say for certain, but he wasn't alone in his stature.

It Ran in the Family
2 Samuel 21:15–22

It may be surprising to learn that there is more than one giant mentioned in the Bible. Almost everyone knows of Goliath, but few realize that eleven other giants are discussed—four of them related to Goliath.

In 2 Samuel 21 the account of the four skirmishes between David and/or his men with these Philistines reports on the giants who died and the men who slew them. The first clash occurs between King David, now a much older man, and a giant by the name of Ishbi-benob. His height is not given, but the passage makes his size clear. We are told that his spear weighed three hundred shekels of bronze (about seven and a half pounds, less than half of Goliath's spear). It is also said that he carried a "new sword." The word sword is not in the original Hebrew. The phrase should be translated "a new thing." What was the new thing? No one knows. It may have been a weapon never before seen by David, or it may have been nothing more than an unused sword. The fact that it is mentioned is odd.

Ishbi-benob proved more than King David could handle. In hand-to-hand combat, David was no longer a youth with a sling, but a man well past middle age. Abishai, one of David's men, killed the Philistine giant and rescued his king. David's men refused to let him return to battle lest "the lamp of Israel" be snuffed out.

Another battle with the Philistines took place at Gob and again a giant was present. Saph (Sippai, in 1 Chronicles 20:4) faced off with and was killed by Sibbecai the Hushathite. As with Ishbi-benob, Saph's height is unknown. He, too, is referred to as a "descendant of the giant."

A third battle is recorded in this chapter—one that has brought much debate. The controversy centers on a giant by the name of Goliath, killed by a man named Elhanan (the son of Jaare-oregim the Bethlehemite). Does this account contradict the story of David and Goliath in 1 Samuel 17? Could there be two giants with the same name, each with a spear like a weaver's beam? Or could Elhanan be another name for David? Let's consider the possibilities. First, Goliath may have been a popular name in that era. Second, even though both had spears described as the size of a weaver's beam, the description does not necessarily indicate the same man. An Egyptian giant (whom we will talk about later) is also said to have had such a spear (1 Chronicles 11:22–23).

That both lived in Gath is to be expected, especially since the two were most likely related. This Goliath was also "born to the giant in Gath" (2 Samuel 21:22). The simplest and most probable answer is that there were two giants named Goliath, one decades older than the other. Sound like too much of a stretch? There are several people (some count five) in the Bible named Jesus (see Colossians 4:11 for an example).

The fourth giant in this passage is nameless but unique. All we are told of his height is that he was a man of "great stature." We are also told that he had "six fingers on each hand and six toes on each foot"! He was slain by David's nephew, Jonathan.

These giants have several things in common:
- They may have been a race unto themselves, but they shared one or more cities with the Philistines.
- They fought against God's chosen people.
- They were killed by servants of King David.
- They were remarkable enough to have their deaths recorded in Scripture.
- They were descendants of "the giant," literally, the Rapha.

This last point is curious. Who was the Rapha? The Rapha was the ancestor from whom these giants came. (Rapha is an eponym—a name that is the source of other related terms or names. For example, Rome is named after its mythical founder, Romulus. Romulus, therefore, is an eponym.) In 1 Chronicles 20:4, the writer uses the same Hebrew term Rapha but makes it plural—the Rephaim—a race distinguished from others living in the same area.

It is possible that these four giants were blood relatives of Goliath of Gath, whom David slew. Or there may be somewhere in the dark, unseen past a giant by the name of Rapha who was considered the progenitor of a race of giants. Either way, a genetic connection certainly existed.

Not every giant, however, was associated with the Philistines or lived during David's time.

The Odd Furniture of King Og
Deuteronomy 3:3–4

Long before David, in the days of Moses and Joshua, there was a powerful king by the name of Og. He ruled Bashan, a region east of the Sea of Chinnereth (known as the Sea of Galilee in Jesus' time). He was master of sixty cities, many of which were fortified with walls, gates, and bars. The extent of his power and the importance the Jews placed on his downfall is evident from the multiple mentions (twenty-two times) of his name in the Bible. King Og was utterly defeated by Moses and the Israelites because of God's intervention.

In addition to being a powerful king who went down in defeat, Og has another historical note of interest—his bed. "For only Og king of Bashan was left of the remnant of the Rephaim. Behold, his bedstead was an iron bedstead . . . . Its length was nine cubits and its width four cubits by ordinary cubit" (Deuteronomy 3:11). This would make his bed thirteen and a half feet long and six feet wide. For years all that remained of the last Rephaim giant in the land was his bed.

Taller Than Your Average Egyptian
1 Chronicles 11:22–23

Not all biblical giants are Canaanites or Philistines. First Chronicles relates the story of a mighty warrior named Benaiah who fought and killed an unnamed Egyptian of great stature. According to the Bible, the Egyptian soldier stood five cubits tall, about seven and a half feet. Compared to other biblical giants, he was short (Goliath would have towered over him by two feet). Also of interest is the comparison of his spear to a "weaver's beam." This phrase is used two other times: once to describe David's Goliath (1 Samuel 17:7) and once for Goliath the Gittite (2 Samuel 21:19). It was the Egyptian's bad luck to run up against Benaiah, who killed the big man with the Egyptian's own spear.

Like Father, Like Sons
Joshua 14:15; 15:13–14; 21:11, 21; Numbers 13:22–33;
Deuteronomy 9:2; Judges 1:10–12

Before the city of Hebron was named Hebron, it was called Kiriath-arba, the city of Arba. Arba was a man with two claims to fame: (1) he built a city and (2) he was the father of a giant named Anak and the grandfather of Ahiman, Sheshai, Talmai. The fact that he had four sons and grandsons total may explain why he was called Arba, since his name means "four." Each son became the head of a tribe.

Almost nothing is known of Anak. He is always mentioned as either being the ancestor of the Anakim or the son of Arba. Nothing more is revealed. The Anakim were the giants whose strength and stature so frightened ten of the twelve spies sent by Moses to assess the land of Canaan.

Ahiman, Sheshai, and Talmai are mentioned three times in the Bible and always together. Joshua and his army routed their descendants.

Land of the Giants

Giants were not unique in biblical days. In fact, the Bible records not only twelve individual giants, but also at least five races of mega-men. The exact number of races is difficult to determine because some of the terms seem to be local words for the same group of people. There also seems to be two types of giants: pre-flood and post-flood.

Nephilim
Genesis 6:1–4; Numbers 13:33

A hotly debated section of the Bible is Genesis 6:1–4. The passage has launched a torrent of opinions, all hinging on the identity of the "sons of God" (*B'nai ha-Elohim*) and where they came from. Various human origins have been suggested, such as the descendants of Seth, but the most reasonable (also the most provocative) answer assumes them to be nonhuman beings. Why nonhuman? Read on.

First, the phrase "sons of God" is consistently used for angels. The description occurs in Job 1:6; 2:1; and 38:7. Similar terms are used in Psalms 29:1 and 89:6. It is in keeping with Scripture to interpret this phrase the same as it is interpreted in other parts of the Old Testament.

Also the passage states the "sons of God" took whatever wives they chose. The wording is interesting, implying that the choice rested solely with them. The Hebrew word for "took" can mean "seize," although it is used also to mean "accept." It appears the women had little choice in the matter as the Nephilim had unrivaled authority and influence.

Third, the offspring are unusual. They are first described as Nephilim. Nephilim is the plural of *naphal*—a word that means "fallen" or "feller" (that is, one who causes others to fall). During the third and second centuries before Christ, the Old Testament was translated from its original Hebrew into Greek. That translation, called the Septuagint,

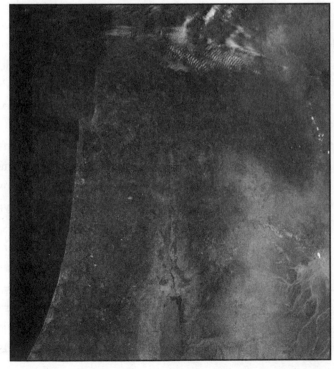

Moses led the children of Israel to the edge of the Promised Land, but their sin prevented them from entering. They feared the giants in the land.

translates Nephilim as *gigantes,* from which we get the word "giant." Genesis 6:4 calls these offspring "mighty men" (*gibbor*)—men of valor. In other words, they had a frightening reputation.

A fourth reason is found in the New Testament. In Jude 1:6 is this intriguing line: "And angels who did not keep their own domain, but abandoned their proper abode, He has kept in eternal bonds under darkness for the judgment of the great day." Jude wrote this as if his readers already knew who these wayward angels were. Their crime is listed twice in this one verse. The initial mention is that they did not keep their own domain. Literally, the verse reads "did not keep their first position." Then Jude goes on to say that they "abandoned their proper abode," meaning that they left their place of habitation, their dwelling place. The question is, Did they leave their domain to mate with humans on earth?

The apostle Peter mentions the same event in 2 Peter 2:4—"For if God did not spare angels when they sinned, but cast them into hell and committed them to pits of darkness, reserved for judgment." Again sinning angels are mentioned. If these are not the beings of Genesis 6, then what are they? Looking more closely at the verses of 2 Peter 2:4–6, we see that all his illustrations are from Genesis: angels who sinned and were condemned to the pits of darkness (Genesis 6); the ancient world destroyed by the flood (Genesis 6–9); and Sodom and Gomorrah destroyed by fire (Genesis 19). Clearly, Peter had the "sons of God" of Genesis 6 in mind when he wrote his book.

Ancient writings other than the Bible hold the view of nonhumans mating with human women. The *Book of Enoch* mentions the same event (69:4–6). The Jewish historian Josephus Flavius mentions it in his *Antiquities of the Jews.* Even early church fathers such as Justin Martyr and Irenaeus held the view of nonhuman/human cohabitation.

What about Jesus' teaching that angels neither give nor take in marriage? Some have maintained that this teaching proves an angel is incapable of physical relations. But is that what Jesus said? Consider Matthew 22:30: "For in the resurrection they neither marry nor are given in marriage, but are like angels in heaven." To understand this teaching we must understand the context. The Sadducees—a religious group who were distinguished more by what they didn't believe than what they did (they didn't believe in angels or the resurrection)—had asked Jesus a trick question. They had posed a hypothetic situation (a woman marries seven times and each time her husband dies) and asked Jesus whose wife she would be in the resurrection.

It's a slippery question, and the Sadducees must have felt that they had constructed a problem that not even Jesus could solve. They were wrong. "But Jesus answered and said to them, 'You are mistaken, not understanding the Scriptures nor the power of God. For in the resurrection they neither marry nor are given in marriage, but are like angels in heaven.'" Consequently, He says that angels neither give nor take in marriage. He does not say that angels are incapable of such things, merely that they don't. The point in this passage is not what angels can or cannot do, but the faulty doctrine of the Sadducees.

But the strongest proof that the "sons of God" were angels is found in their offspring. The sons of God had relations with the daughters of men (literally, "the daughters of Adam"), yielding unique children called "mighty men who were of old, men of renown." Their influence was truly global.

What happened to the mighty Nephilim? They were destroyed in the flood along with all humankind. Only Noah, his wife, his three sons, and their wives escaped. But here is a problem.

Long after the flood, about fourteen hundred years before Christ, Moses sent out twelve spies into Canaan, the land promised to the Israelites by God. Ten of those spies were frightened by what they saw and delivered a discouraging report, one meant to frighten the people:

> But the men who had gone up with him said, "We are not able to go up against the people, for they are too strong for us."
>
> So they gave out to the sons of Israel a bad report of the land which they had spied out, saying, "The land through which we have gone, in spying it out, is a land that devours its inhabitants; and all the people whom we saw in it are men of great size.

"There also we saw the Nephilim (the sons of Anak are part of the Nephilim); and we became like grasshoppers in our own sight, and so we were in their sight." (Numbers 13:31–33)

If all life on earth (besides Noah and kin) was destroyed by flood, how can the Nephilim be living in Canaan centuries after the flood? There are several possibilities. One, there was a reoccurrence of the Genesis 6 events, but we have no biblical record of that, and it seems unlikely that the first account would be mentioned and the second wouldn't be. Two, the Nephilim somehow survived the flood, but that is contrary to Scripture because the purpose of the flood was to destroy all flesh on earth. Third, the Nephilim of Canaan are not the Nephilim of Genesis 6.

How can this be? The answer is found in the overall context of the passage. Moses sent out twelve spies. For forty days they examined the land, its produce, and its people. They returned with the same observations but very different conclusions. Two spies, Joshua and Caleb, are ready to invade; the other ten are far more timid. In an effort to sway the people, the ten described the giants in the land first as the Anakim (the sons of Anak) and then stated that the Anakim were related to the Nephilim. This word so frightened the people that they all "lifted up their voices and cried, and the people wept that night" (Numbers 14:1).

Then they turned on Moses and Aaron and planned an overthrow. But God thwarted their revolt and condemned the adults to wander and die in the wilderness. Forty years later, Joshua led the attack that gave Canaan to the children of Israel, just as God had promised to Abraham so many years before.

Prior to his death, Moses spoke a dynamic message of promise and hope to the Israelites:

"Hear, O Israel! You are crossing over the Jordan today to go in to dispossess nations greater and mightier than you, great cities fortified to heaven,

a people great and tall, the sons of the Anakim, whom you know and of whom you have heard it said, 'Who can stand before the sons of Anak?'

"Know therefore today that it is the LORD your God who is crossing over before you as a consuming fire. He will destroy them and He will subdue them before you, so that you may drive them out and destroy them quickly, just as the LORD has spoken to you." (Deuteronomy 9:1–3)

Moses makes no mention of the Nephilim. Why? In no way does he soft-pedal the danger that awaits the Hebrews. Before them lay many battles and dangers. Moses goes so far as to mention the giant Anakim, why not the Nephilim? The reason can only be that no Nephilim existed.

Although the Nephilim were long gone, there were still giants in the land.

Rephaim
Genesis 14:5; 15:20; Deuteronomy 3:11, 13;
2 Samuel 5:17–20; 23:13

While the Nephilim were the result of the pairing of nonhuman fathers with human mothers, the Rephaim were most likely the result of something more natural. Rephaim means "lofty men"—a title no doubt inspired by their great height—and the term is used eighteen times in the Bible, eight of those referring to the Valley of Rephaim.

Genesis 14:5 describes their defeat at the hands of King Chedorlaomer, ruler of Elam. So, although apparently people of great size, the Rephaim were not invincible.

In His covenant with Abraham, God promises the land of the Rephaim to the patriarch and his descendants. Moses mentions the strange people in Deuteronomy. Deuteronomy means "second law" and is primarily a collection of Moses' speeches given in the last months of his life. The people who had spent their lives wandering in the wilderness were about to follow Joshua across the Jordan River when Moses reminds them of all that has occurred to their fathers. In his dialogue he mentions the Rephaim who used to live in the land, including the last of the tribe, Og, King of Bashan (he of the big bed), who was defeated under Moses.

Anakim

Deuteronomy 1:28; 2:10–11; Joshua 14:12, 15; Numbers 13:33

We have already met the Anakim. The Anakim were a race of giants, descended from Arba and Anak. It was the Anakim that so frightened the Israelites that they rebelled against God's commands. According to Moses, the Anakim were regarded as Rephaim. "The Emim lived there formerly, a people as great, numerous, and tall as the Anakim. Like the Anakim, they are also regarded as Rephaim, but the Moabites call them Emim" (Deuteronomy 2:10–11).

Emim

Genesis 14:5; Deuteronomy 2:10–11

Mentioned only twice, the Emim, whose name means "frightful ones," are the same as the Rephaim. Emim was the Moabite term for the giants.

Zamzummin

Genesis 14:5; Deuteronomy 2:20–21

Zamzummin ("plotters" or "mumblers") were a race of giants that lived east of the Jordan and were displaced by the Ammonites. Another group named Zuzim ("powerful ones" or "roving creatures") were most likely of the same group.

Modern Giants

To provide a basis of comparison, the tallest contemporary giants are
- Angus MacAskill (1823–63). He stood 7 feet 9 inches tall and weighed 420 pounds.
- Radhouane Charbib of Tunisia. He stands 7 feet, 8.9 inches tall.
- Zeng Jinlian (1964–82) of Yujiang, China, measured 8 feet, 1.68 inches.
- Romanian-born NBA star Gheorghe Muresan measures 7 feet 7 inches tall.

In a Nutshell

Some might challenge the reality of giants in biblical times, but their existence is clearly recorded in Scripture. Research by archaeologists may one day uncover scientific evidence for the existence of a race of giants, but for now we can take the Bible's word for it.

From biblical evidence, we know the following:

- A pre-flood race of giants was known as the Nephilim.
- Several groups of post-flood giants known by different names lived east of the Jordan.
- Twelve individual giants are listed in the Bible, some by name, some not.
- Some giants remained in the land until the day of David.
- People encountered giants during the times of Noah, Abraham, Moses, Joshua, and David.
- The giants mentioned in Scripture always stood in opposition to God's work.

More to Think About

1. Jesus said, "And just as it happened in the days of Noah, so it will be also in the days of the Son of Man" (Luke 17:26). Is it possible that the sons of God and the Nephilim are included in this statement?

2. As we approach the second coming of Christ, is it possible that an event similar to Genesis 6 could happen? If so, how would that happen?

3. Why do you suppose the giants in the Bible were always shown as enemies of Israel? Is there some spiritual significance in battles between Israel and the giants?

Strange Critters

IT'S HARD TO RESIST A MYSTERY, especially mysteries involving unknown animals. The Loch Ness monster, Bigfoot in the Pacific Northwest, the Yeti in the Himalayas, and other such enigmas capture our interest. Books have been written and films produced dealing with these unusual critters. There are an ever-growing number of people (called cryptozoologists) who hunt for proof of hidden, yet-to-be-defined animals.

Job 40:15–24; 41:1–34; others

Such studies seem foolish to some, but gain some respectability when we remember the panda and the gorilla were once thought to be mythical. And in 1938, near Madagascar, an unusual fish broke the ocean's surface and made history. Long thought extinct, the rough-looking coelacanth shocked the world by proving to be very much alive. It earned the oxymoronic nickname "the living fossil."

Strange creatures are not foreign to the Bible. The pages of Scripture mention four animals enigmatic enough to stir the interest of any cryptozoologist or any student of the Bible. The nature of these beasts has been debated for hundreds of years with no satisfactory conclusion reached. Yet there they are, undeniably recorded in the pages of the mysterious Bible.

CHAPTER TWO

Behemoth
Job 40:15–24

The Book of Job is the account of a man who had everything and lost it all. His family, wealth, and health were taken from him one after the other like a cascade of dominoes. Tortuously ill and weary of pain and anguish, Job verbally wrestles with God, and God answers back, rebuking Job for his prideful assumptions. As God speaks, He makes His point by using two animals as illustrations, animals that have caused centuries of discussion.

The first is called Behemoth, and even the meaning of his name is uncertain. It may come from the Hebrew word *behemah* that is usually translated "beast." Behemoth would then be the plural of *behemah*. Yet the passage describes the creature as one animal, so perhaps it is an individual animal with a plural name. This may be because the animal is so impressive and majestic.

Another possibility is that the word Behemoth comes from an Egyptian term meaning "water ox," but evidence to support that assumption is neither conclusive nor convincing. Whatever the origin of the term, the creature itself is described by God in amazing detail. In only ten verses, we learn that this animal is like no other known to man.

First we learn that, like Job, he is a created animal. "Behold now, Behemoth, which I made as well as you." God's point is that He is master of all creation, including the most powerful animals and the man Job.

Then comes a description of Behemoth's diet. "He eats grass like an ox." That makes the creature a herbivore. And even today, the world's largest animals—such as elephants and giraffes—are plant eaters. This was true of the largest dinosaurs too. Consider the Apatosaurus (formally known as Brontosaurus) and Diplodocus—those gargantuan creatures measured more than eighty feet in length. This kind of scientific detail indicates that the passage is speaking of an actual animal, not a mythological beast.

The text goes on to describe the animal's physical characteristics in detail. First we are told of his might: "His strength (*koach*) [is] in his loins and his power (*'own*) in the muscles of his belly." It's an odd description that might be paraphrased like this: "He is powerful inside and out." This may also be a reference to his reproductive ability.

The description of the tail has caused some controversy. Many scholars have stated that the animal described here is a hippopotamus that lived along the Jordan River, but the description of the tail just doesn't fit. God describes the animal as having a tail like a cedar tree. Cedars are mentioned frequently in the Bible. The tree could grow one hundred feet tall and reach fifty feet in circumference. No wonder it was a symbol of strength. Behemoth's tail is like a mighty cedar that he bends or sways. (A few have suggested that what is meant here is the trunk of an elephant, but that would require elephants to have lived in the land during the time of Job and God to confuse a trunk with a tail. Neither is likely.)

"The sinews of his thighs are knit together." This is a puzzling phrase. The term and the context indicate that this is a description of power, perhaps suggesting that the creature had the ability to move quickly or even leap. However, the literal translation can be taken to euphemistically refer to sexual organs.

What follows next is more description of his power. His bones are described as tubes of bronze. Bronze, an alloy made by blending copper with tin, was known for its strength and use in weaponry. If Behemoth's bones are like tubes of metal, and his limbs like hammered bars of iron, then he's solid power.

All this leaves us with a large, plant-eating animal with strong legs, a stiff tree-like tail, and an impressive skeletal structure. But there's more: Behemoth is also described as being "the first of the ways of God." It's a wonderfully cryptic line and can be rendered several ways, the most logical being "he is chief among God's animal creations." The phrase can even be understood to mean that Behemoth was God's first animal creation. Whatever the exact meaning, this animal is unique among all others.

The Bible even tells us about Behemoth's habitat—under the lotus plants and among the reeds and the marsh. Behemoth was semi-aquatic. The beast is unperturbed when the river rages and swirls around his mouth. The river and its banks are his home.

To all of this, God asks, "Can anyone capture him?" The implied answer is no.

So what was it?

Speculation about Behemoth has been far-reaching. Some choose to see the animal as something common—an ordinary creature made extraordinary by its portrayal. Behemoth seems much more than that. Animals that have been suggested to be Behemoth include the elephant, water bison, and the hippopotamus. Of these, the hippo is the most likely, but, like a badly tailored suit, the description doesn't fit on such points as the tail, the thighs, and the appellation of being "the first of the ways of God."

The flip side of this opinion is to make Behemoth quite a bit more than what is described. Several have suggested that Behemoth is a literal dinosaur. There are some problems with this idea as well. While the biblical description does describe an animal beyond the taming influence of man, there is nothing to indicate that Job or any other ancient biblical person ever saw a dinosaur. While paleontologists have shown that there were numerous types of dinosaurs that dwelt along lakes and rivers and that many were indeed plant eaters, it is hard to get such a creature to fit the description given in the Bible. The description of the tail makes sense, but it's hard to imagine such a dinosaur taking shade under a lotus tree (a small tree common in Africa and along riverbanks).

Something different is being described—something long extinct. Every year dozens of animal species die out, never to walk, or fly over, the planet again. By the same token, approximately one hundred new species of animal are discovered every year—mostly in the vast depths of the ocean. Behemoth was an animal familiar to the people in Job's day, but now lost to us. We are left to wonder about his exact nature. Perhaps more information will be discovered, but until then we can only speculate.

Leviathan
Job 41

If Behemoth is incredible then Leviathan is mind-boggling. There are five passages of Scripture that use the term Leviathan, and still we are left hungering to know more. No creature is so completely described and so terrifying in description. The entire forty-first chapter of Job is devoted to this enigmatic creature. As with Behemoth in chapter 40, God is speaking to Job, forcefully driving home that He is the Supreme Being who is omnipotent over all creation and therefore not to be second-guessed. In showing Job this truth, God once again mentions an animal that has no contemporary counterpart.

The passage contains sixteen rhetorical questions, such as "Can you draw out Leviathan with a fishhook?" The answer is no. The questions are intended to reinforce the point that humankind is seldom as great and powerful as it thinks.

This passage also demands that we take a stand on viewing the Bible either literally or figuratively. Is God using poetic language to make His point or is every detail to be taken as is?

The Bible should always be taken literally, but with the understanding that it uses very expressive language. The Bible contains passages that are clearly similes, metaphors, and hyperboles. Similes are comparisons that use the words "like" or "as" (the summer breeze was warm like a blanket). A metaphor compares by substitution ("All the world's a stage"). Hyperbole is exaggeration ("I've told you a million times to stay away from the cookie jar"). The Bible does indeed use all of these tools of language. God is said to be a rock, a fortress, a shield, and much more, but we do not believe He is made of stone or metal. The use of metaphors, similes, and hyperboles does not make a fact a falsehood. They are descriptive tools meant to heighten our understanding of reality. In other words, there is truth behind the poetry.

What kind of creature was Leviathan? His name gives us a clue. Our word Leviathan comes from the Hebrew term *livyathan,* which came from the root word *lawa,* meaning to bend or twist. We have then a bending, twisting creature.

The passage begins with a series of questions designed to show how weak and ineffective man was against that peculiar beast. The creature could not be hooked, tied, pierced, or led about like an ox. Nor does the creature bow to man. Leviathan couldn't be domesticated. His skin was immune to harpoons and fishing spears. "Do battle with him," God says, "and you'll never do it again."

So far the description could fit a number of animals. Many scholars believe the crocodile to be the creature described by God. Others think it was a whale. If we stopped after the first few verses of Job 41, then such conjectures might be acceptable or even reasonable. But the description is far from complete.

"I will not keep silence concerning his limbs, or his mighty strength, or his orderly frame," God says. He then goes on to list a set of physical qualities that stretch the imagination including:

- mighty strength
- double-mail armor
- teeth of terror
- skin composed of strong, airtight scales
- eyes that shine like sunrise
- a mouth that spews fire
- nostrils that release smoke
- a strong neck
- "a heart of stone"

God also says the terrifying, fearless creature is nearly impossible to kill with the weapons of that time and that he leaves a massive wake behind in the water. So Leviathan is definitely impressive, but what is he? Does he really breathe fire? Do his eyes truly glow like a sunrise? It's hard to say. The most popular belief of scholars is that God is speaking of a crocodile. The tough armor-like skin, strength, quickness in water, and fearlessness sounds like a crocodile.

Some types of crocodile, like the saltwater crocodile, grow to more than twenty feet and can weigh a ton. It is a fearless creature that is capable of crushing bones in its jaws. Still, just like the idea that Behemoth was a hippopotamus or an elephant, the notion that Leviathan was a simple river crocodile seems implausible.

The difficulty in all of this is determining how literally to take the passage. Clearly the expansive language of hyperbole is being used, but hyperbole is rooted in fact (and is an excellent teaching tool of the Bible in how it makes facts more memorable). Still, it is hyperbole. John the apostle states at the end of his Gospel, "And there are also many other things which Jesus did, which if they were written in detail, I suppose that even the world itself would not contain the books that would be written" (John 21:25). John didn't mean that the books would literally cover the earth, but that his Gospel was an abbreviated account of the life of Christ.

How much of this description of Leviathan should be taken as poetic speech is difficult to determine, but one thing is clear: Leviathan was no ordinary animal.

A recent sighting of a Leviathan-like creature occurred on July 30, 1915, when the German U-boat *U-28* sank the British ship *Iberian*. The ship sank stern-first, exploding as it did. In the wreckage was a "gigantic sea animal" resembling a sixty-foot crocodile. It sank moments after being spotted. Such tales are not unusual and span centuries. Certainly many of them are misidentification or even fanciful tales of bored sailors, but some may be based in fact.

The last century has seen the discovery of the mountain gorilla, the Okapi (forest giraffe), the megamouth shark, and the Komodo dragon. If there are animals unknown to us living today, then it's not too far a stretch to assume that there were animals unknown to us in Job's time four thousand years ago.

Dragons and Snakes

Leviathan may have been the source for the many dragon stories that permeate both Eastern and Western cultures. In the East, dragons were revered; in the West, they were despised. Many of Leviathan's attributes resonate with those of fire-breathing, scaled, fierce dragons. Almost every major culture has a dragon myth, including Babylonians, Chinese, Japanese, and Europeans. Tales of dragons attacking villages and decimating legions are found throughout the centuries.

English translations of the Bible use the term "dragon" to translate the Hebrew word *tanniyn* (sometimes *tanniym*) and the Greek word *drakon*. In the New Testament the word is used only in Revelation (where it serves as a representation of Satan). And through the centuries Christian art has portrayed Jesus standing on a dragon, symbolizing the Savior's victory over sin.

It's in the Old Testament where things get sticky. Modern translations have struggled with the specific translation of the word *tanniyn*.

While the King James Version routinely translates the word as "dragon," contemporary translations have rendered it "sea monster," "serpent," "jackal," or just plain "monster."

The word first appears in Genesis 1:21: "God created the great sea [*tanniyn*] monsters and every living creature that moves." This has caused some to assume that the ancient creature is a whale. But the next time we find the term is in Exodus 7:9, where God is giving instruction to Moses. He says, "When Pharaoh speaks to you, saying, 'Work a miracle,' then you shall say to Aaron, 'Take your staff and throw it down before Pharaoh, that it may become a serpent [*tanniyn*].'" The term is used to describe a snake or snake-like creature.

In other passages the word is translated as "jackal." When the word is used in conjunction with the sea, it becomes "sea monster."

Which is it?

Perhaps the best term to use is "monster" each of the twenty-eight times *tanniyn* is used.

Tanniyn is something different from a snake and from Leviathan. Isaiah 27:1 uses all three terms: "In that day the LORD will punish Leviathan (*livyahtan*) the fleeing serpent (*nachash*), with His fierce and

The Bible lists several strange animals, including serpents, that may have been more than they appeared.

great and mighty sword, even Leviathan the twisted serpent; and He will kill the dragon (*tanniyn*) who lives in the sea."

That *tanniyn* does not mean "snake" can be seen in accounts that are located very close together and recorded by the same author. Moses recounts his calling by God at Mount Horeb in Exodus 4:3—"Then [God] said, 'Throw [your staff] on the ground.' So [Moses] threw it on the ground, and it became a serpent; and Moses fled from it." The word for serpent is *nachash*. But, when Moses faces Pharaoh and does as God has commanded by having Aaron throw down his staff, the staff changes into a *tanniyn*, a different animal from a typical serpent. Remember, it is Moses' words under God's inspiration that records these events. Why he would use different terms is unknown.

What then is this creature? It is impossible to identify. The Bible gives no physical description as with Behemoth and Leviathan. In some passages (Genesis 1:21; Job 7:12; Psalms 74:13; 148:7; Isaiah 27:1) it may mean a sea monster, while other references (Exodus 7:9; Psalm 91:13; Isaiah 35:7) clearly mean a land animal. The Genesis 1 account speaks of a "great" *tanniyn*, while the animal that is transformed from Aaron's rod seems much smaller. The *tanniyn* then refers to an animal that is somehow unusual (large like a whale, vicious like a snake, unwanted like a jackal). It is not a single creature, but a type. Just like we refer to various insects by the inclusive title of "bugs," so the Bible uses *tanniyn* to describe any kind of monster.

What *tanniyn* is not, is a dragon, at least as the modern world thinks of a dragon. That term would be better applied to Leviathan.

Rahab

Job 9:13; 26:12; Psalm 87:4; 89:10; Isaiah 30:7; 51:9

There are two famous Rahabs in the Bible. One is the harlot who aids the children of Israel by hiding two of their spies. Her heroic decision earned her a place in "Faith's Hall of Fame" in Hebrews 11.

But there's another Rahab—a nonhuman Rahab. The Bible mentions a creature by that name in a negative way in Job 9:13 and 26:12, Psalms 87:4 and 89:10, and Isaiah 30:7.

The Hebrew word *rahab* means "proud, boastful, and arrogant" and is used as a symbol for Egypt. But in two passages a strange creature is meant. The creature itself is not described, but Jewish tradition holds that it was a sea monster representing chaos. In Isaiah 51:9, Rahab is described as a dragon (*tanniyn*). Nothing more is known. The creature remains enigmatic, shielded by centuries of history.

Real or Symbolic?

Many creatures described in the Bible are symbolic. This is especially true in prophetic books like Isaiah and Revelation. However, it is not too far a stretch to think that some of the animals mentioned were very real in their day. In our scientific society we tend to dismiss anything that doesn't fit life as we understand it. So when the Bible describes Leviathan, Behemoth, sea monsters, and more, there is an urge to say, "Well, they were an ancient people caught up in myth." It is true that some animals come to represent countries like Egypt or judgments passed by God. But while God uses poetic language, He does so with images familiar to the reader. Behemoth, Leviathan, and *tanniyn* were creatures whose very existence inspired fright. Their power became symbols of the power of God over His creation.

Perhaps someday science will uncover definitive proof of the existence of these strange critters, but until then we'll have to take the Bible's word on it.

More to Think About

1. Cultures around the world have stories of strange beasts. Myths from centuries past include descriptions of bizarre creatures. Is it possible that some of these stories are rooted in biblical accounts of Behemoth, Leviathan, and others?

2. Critics of the Bible often cite the passages about Leviathan and Behemoth as proof that the Bible is not a historical work. What could be some responses to this criticism?

3. What impact would the discovery of Leviathan or Behemoth remains have on Christians and the world? Would such a find make a difference to you?

The Divine
Alchemist

IN THE MIDDLE AGES IT WAS BELIEVED that common metals could be turned into something far more valuable. Alchemy, the study of converting base metals into gold, consumed some of the finest imaginations in history. Even the great physicist and mathematician Isaac Newton believed that gold could be made from something far less valuable like lead.

Making something from nothing is hard; actually, it's impossible. The early alchemist learned that lesson through trial and error. Humans live in a physical world governed by immutable laws. The cosmos dances and sways according to the music of those laws, and nothing we do will ever change that. God, however, is not limited by those laws.

God has done what men can only dream of doing: He can convert one substance into another and create something from nothing. These are special miracles, miracles that show that unique power of God over His creation. In that sense, He is the Divine Alchemist.

Instant Wine
John 2:1–11

Jesus' first miracle took place in an out-of-the-way village called Cana in Galilee. The city no longer exists but is believed to have been a small town about eight miles north of Nazareth. It is the hometown of Nathanael, one of the disciples. Jesus had traveled back to His hometown after His baptism in the Jordan and then further north to Cana to attend a wedding. The passage mentions a special detail: The event took place on the third day. This may refer to the third day of the wedding feast. Ancient Jewish weddings usually consisted of the ceremony itself followed by seven days of feasting. On the third day of the week-long celebration, a crisis happens. The host runs out of wine.

In a day long before supermarkets, this was an embarrassing situation. Jesus is there with His first few disciples (Andrew, Peter, Philip, and Nathanael) and his mother, Mary.

Because Mary is so central to the account and seems to have some authority in the situation, it is very likely that Mary was related to someone in the wedding party. It is possible that the bride could even be a younger sister of Jesus or perhaps a cousin.

The crowd had gathered for another day of festivities and fellowship. Spirits were high; it was a time of joy. Then word came to the steward, the man in charge of serving the guests, that there was no more wine. It was a social disaster. Ancient custom dictated that the guests be cared for in every possible way. Not to do so could haunt a family for years.

Mary somehow is aware of the problem and brings the need to Jesus. Why? Did Mary expect Jesus to perform a miracle? There is no biblical record that Mary had ever seen Jesus work a miracle (although there are many traditions that say she did). Still, she knew who He was and what He was capable of doing.

Jesus' response puzzles many modern readers. At first reading, it seems that He is being aloof and maybe even rude. "Woman, what does that have to do with us? My hour has not yet come." But was He really being short with her? No.

The term "woman" was a kind and respectful address. Jesus uses the same term six times, including the poignant moment on the cross when he assigned to the disciple John the responsibility of caring for His mother. "Woman," he said, "behold, your son" (John 19:26). He also used the term when addressing Mary Magdalene after His resurrection (John 20:15).

At first, Jesus seems to back away from the request, mentioning that His hour—the beginning of his public ministry—had not yet arrived. The real clue to this is Mary's response to Jesus' remark. Turning to the servants, she says, "Whatever He says to you, do it." Clearly Mary was convinced that Jesus was going to take matters into His own hands.

Here the story takes an interesting but often overlooked turn. Nearby, probably just outside the house where the feast was being held, sat six stone water pots. These pots held between 20 to 30 gallons each. The water in the pots was used for the Jewish rite of purification. The Jews of Jesus' day customarily washed before eating, thoroughly cleansing their hands according to a specific traditional pattern. Many feasting guests would require a large amount of water, hence the need for 120 to 180 gallons. The fact that Jesus says, "Fill the water pots with water," indicates that they were not full since the guests had already arrived and washed.

The servants do as they are instructed, filling each pot to the brim. Why would Scripture record that fact? Because no claim can be made that Jesus worked some prestidigitation by adding something to the water. Any additional fluid or solid substance added to the jars would cause them to overflow, something that would not be overlooked by the servants or disciples.

Jesus performed His first miracle in the city of Cana by turning water to wine. The change took place in jars similar to this one.

There is no further action. No special words were said. Nothing more was brought to the scene. One moment there are six jars of water; the next there are six jars of wine.

Jesus' next command is for a servant to take some of the water-now-wine to the steward for an ancient taste test. The steward, a man who certainly knew his wine, pronounced it better than anything yet served. Tradition was that a host served the good wine first and the lesser-grade wine later. This appeared to the steward as a welcome reversal of custom.

This is the first of thirty-five recorded miracles that Jesus performs, and it is described in exquisite detail. For example, Jesus never touches the pots or the water contained in them, nor does He personally take the sample to the steward. The only people who touch the containers are the servants. There is a reason for this, and it refers to Jesus' remark that His hour had not come. This was a "secret" miracle; secret in the sense that Jesus limits those who know of it. John goes so far as to record that the steward did not know where the wine had come from. Only the servants, the disciples, and Mary knew what the Lord had done. This miracle caused the disciples to believe in Him. They began to understand that Jesus was more than an itinerant rabbi.

But what had Jesus actually done? There is more to this miracle than preventing social embarrassment—much more. First, consider the remarkable transformation. Water literally became wine. This is remarkable since there is nothing in the water to naturally produce wine.

Wine had been around for four thousand years before Christ. Every culture from China to Egypt made wine. The first thing Noah did after coming off the ark was to plant a vineyard and make wine. In Jesus' day, wine was an important drink, second only to water.

The making of wine requires a sugary fruit, usually grapes, to be pressed until its juice is free. Wine yeast converts the fruit sugar into alcohol. This process takes about fourteen days. But Jesus turned water with no added ingredients into something that impressed the palate of the steward—and did it without lifting a finger in no time at all. Of the thirty-five recorded miracles, nine deal with power over nature and only one of those involves making something out of nothing. This is it.

Is there some significance to the fact that the wine was made in jars designed to hold water for purification rites? Absolutely. Nothing is in Scripture by accident. Everything in its pages is meant to document the work of God and edify the reader. This is certainly true in this case. Jesus, who made object lessons out of fig trees, the temple, life-threatening storms, and much more, converts this into a lesson for believers.

First note the number of water pots: six. Anytime a specific number is listed in the Bible, we should ask why. Numbers are very important and convey additional meaning when they appear in Scripture. Certain numbers are representative of concepts: the number three usually refers to deity, the number seven to completion, twelve to Israel, and forty to testing and judgment. Six is the number of man and carries the idea of incompleteness. The fact that Jesus uses six stone jars to work His miracle says something about the original purpose of pots.

In Jesus' day, it was customary for Jews to purify their hands and cooking utensils before use. This practice came not from the Bible, but from tradition: "The Pharisees and all the Jews do not eat unless they carefully wash their hands, thus observing the traditions of the elders" (Mark 7:3). So prevalent was the practice that Jesus endures scorn and ridicule because He and His disciples choose not to follow the custom (Mark 7:1–13).

The religious leaders were fixated on this practice for several reasons. One belief of the day was that demons rested on the hands, so eating with hands that were not ceremonially washed from fingertip to elbow allowed a demon into the body. Another reason was rooted in racial prejudice. Israel was occupied by a Gentile nation. It was also situated along important trade routes. It was impossible not to come in contact with Gentiles. The concern was that one might accidentally touch the clothing of a Gentile and thereby be defiled. To many of the religious leaders, not washing before eating was as severe a sin as sexual immorality. In that sense, the water pots represent sin and the water a means of removing transgression.

Jesus' use of the water pots was no accident. Surely there would have been plenty of empty wine containers around; why not use them? Jesus had a point to make: Sin was not dealt with by water or ritual; it could only be abolished by a Savior.

Some Quick Math

The Gospel of John gives wonderful details on this miracle, even including the capacity of the pots, saying that each held twenty to thirty gallons. Why a range of volume? Most likely, the pots were of different sizes. Since this was a wedding, a great many people (probably the whole town of Cana) were moving in and out of the house. Additional pots would be needed to provide for the large number of guests. These containers may have been borrowed from different families and therefore were not a matched set.

If we do a little math, we can see that together the pots held between 120 and 180 gallons of water. This is equivalent to 480 to 720 quarts. Taking it one step further and using the larger number of gallons, Jesus made enough wine to fill 2,880 eight-ounce glasses of wine. Why so much? There were still four days left in the marriage feast. Jesus always provides in abundance.

A Secret Processional Miracle

Another unique aspect of this miracle is that it is done in stages. It is a processional miracle. Jesus gives commands, and the servants carry out His orders. Most miracles by Jesus are done instantaneously. Usually no time lag exists between Jesus' decision to act and the miracle's occurrence. Here, however, several steps are taken. First, the pots are filled to the brim. Next, a ladle full of the water-now-wine is taken to the steward. The wine is then declared superior to any that had been served before it.

Jesus appears to do nothing other than provide directions. He doesn't touch the pots or the water. He doesn't make a statement, raise His hand, or ask that anything be done to the water. So why doesn't He do something?

The reason is found in the timing of Jesus' ministry. This miracle was not part of His plan. His mother makes a request; Jesus sees the need and intervenes, but not to draw attention to Himself. His public ministry will start a short time later when He cleanses the temple. This miracle was not meant to garner attention, announce His ministry, or authenticate His message. It was a simple act of courtesy and respect.

Transformations

Several things were changed that day. First, and most obvious, was the plain water that was transformed into spectacular wine. While the main ingredients of wine are water, sugar, and alcohol, more than 400 known compounds give wine its unique aroma, taste, and color. The wine that Jesus made was superior to any that had ever been made.

To the Jewish mind, wine was synonymous with joy (Psalm 104:15). To run out of wine at such an important event would have been a social disaster seen as a bad omen for the newly married couple. In that sense, not only was water turned into wine, but tragedy into joy.

Something else was changed that day in Cana, a ritual that signified impurity was replaced by grace. Water cannot wash away sin, but Christ can. He can and does convert past sin into present forgiveness.

The disciples, who only numbered four at this point, were also changed. John 2:11 tells us that "His disciples believed in Him." It was in Cana that the first disciples began to understand that Jesus was more than an average man—He was a miracle worker. What impressed the disciples so was the nature of the miracle. Only God makes something from nothing, so Jesus, their new teacher, must be much more than a man.

They were right.

Miraculous Lunch Times Two
Matthew 14:15–21; Mark 6:35–44; Luke 9:12–17; John 6:6–13

As Jesus entered the final year of His earthly ministry, His popularity rose dramatically. The disciples had spread word of the Savior and accounts of His healing miracles were opening the floodgates of interest. Crowds amassed around Jesus, so much so that even walking became difficult. Often Jesus would slip away, taking His disciples to a quiet place for rest and prayer. But at times, that didn't work.

On one occasion, Jesus and the disciples, seeking seclusion, sail for the town of Bethsaida on the northwest shore of the Sea of Galilee, but a large crowd follows them around the lake and meets them when they land. Jesus, instead of feeling frustration, is overcome with compassion, seeing that they are sheep without a shepherd. He teaches them, but the day grows late and it becomes clear that there is no food in the area to feed them.

It is then that Jesus works a miracle so impressive, so important that it is mentioned in all four Gospels—the only one of Jesus' thirty-five recorded miracles that can make that claim.

Several things make this event so monumental. First is the sheer size of the event. The Gospels tell us that five thousand men were present. Women and children were not included in that count, but if they were, the number might swell to fifteen thousand people—the size of a small city. When asked about providing bread for such a large group, Philip (who was from the area) responds, "two hundred denarii worth of bread is not sufficient for them, for everyone to receive a little" (John 6:7). A denarius was equal to one day's wage. Two hundred denarii would be the equivalent of eight month's wages. The need was overwhelming.

Andrew comes back with a boy's lunch—five loaves of bread and two fish. The disciples might make a meager meal out of this for themselves, but it would do nothing for the thousands at the base of the hill.

Then, in what must have appeared to be an act of madness, the Divine Alchemist offers thanks to God and begins handing out food to the disciples. The crowd, who had been arranged in groups of fifty and one hundred, are fed to their satisfaction. So much food was provided that the disciples picked up the remains, which filled twelve baskets.

Amazing as this is, the miracle is repeated at a different place before a different crowd but with similar results (Matthew 15:32–38; Mark 8:1–9).

The Same Thing Twice

Jesus converts what *is* into more of what *was*. Starting with bread and fish, He multiplies the supply until all are fed and satisfied. As with the wine, He provided more than what was needed. He gave abundance.

The two loaves-and-fish miracles have many similarities in that they both
- begin with crowds eager to be near Jesus
- occur in the country

- stir up compassion in Jesus
- involve fish and bread
- begin in doubt but end in glory
- involve the disciples distributing food
- show Jesus giving thanks for the food
- multiplied a little to a lot
- had leftovers that were gathered by the disciples

The Difference That Makes All the Difference

While the two events share many similarities, it is their differences that tell the real story:

- Five thousand men are fed in the first event; four thousand men in the second.
- They take place in different parts of the country (the first event occurs on the northeast side of the Sea of Galilee; the second on the southeast shore).
- The amount of food used for the miracles is different (five fish and two loaves in the first event; seven loaves and a "few small fish" in the second).
- The amount of "leftovers" differs (twelve baskets in the first; seven baskets in the second).
- The terms used for basket are different (*kophinos* for the first; *spuris* for the second).
- The nationalities of the crowd differ (primarily Jewish in the first; but largely Gentile in the second).

This last point—the ethnic aspect—is the most revealing and sheds the most light on the miracles. While the need is the same and the solution nearly identical in both miracles, the crowds were very different. Let's take a closer look.

The Jewish Version. One of the most provocative elements of the feeding of the five thousand is what happens after the crowd has eaten. Bread is collected in baskets. These baskets were commonly carried by Jews just as students today carry backpacks. Often used to hold provisions while traveling, the baskets were relatively small compared to other such devices.

Why twelve baskets? Twelve is a number usually associated with the nation of Israel (based on the twelve tribes of Israel). It is a Jewish audience, so having twelve baskets of bread left over is appropriate.

Why bother picking up the pieces of bread? Bread was considered a gift of God not to be wasted. It was customary to pick up any bread that may have fallen and to do so out of respect for God's provision. Not to do so was seen as ingratitude toward God.

The meaning of the miracle is simple: Jesus is the Messiah to the Jews. Just as Moses fed the children of Israel, so Jesus fed them that day.

The Gentile Version. The feeding of the four thousand took place in the region known as the Decapolis ("ten cities"). It was an area of Greek cities. In short, it was primarily Gentile territory.

The most noticeable difference in this miracle is found in the number of baskets retrieved at the end. Even the term for basket is different. For the feeding of the five thousand, *kophinos* is used for "basket" and refers to something carried by the individual. Both Matthew and Mark use a different term for the feeding of the four thousand—*spuris. Spuris* is a hamper-size basket—much larger than the ones used by the disciples at the first feeding. These baskets could be made large enough to hold a man. (And, in fact, one did! The Book of Acts tells how Paul escaped would-be killers in Damascus by being lowered through a hole in the city wall. He was lowered in a basket—*spuris*—and then made his way to safety.)

While the disciples may have gathered up fewer baskets of remains, the baskets were so much larger that they may have picked up more fish and bread than they had at the first miracle.

The real kicker is in the number of baskets collected. In the feeding of the five thousand, twelve baskets (representing Israel) were taken up. At the Decapolis event, seven baskets were gathered. To understand what the number seven refers to, we have to go back in time another fourteen hundred years to the days of Joshua.

Moses had led the children of Israel out of Egypt and through forty years of wandering in the wilderness. The time to cross over the Jordan into the Promised Land had at last arrived. Leading the charge after Moses' death was Joshua. God used the great Hebrew general to drive out the pagan nations that occupied the land, sending them into the region that would later be referred to as the Decapolis. In Deuteronomy, we read their names: Hittites, Girgashites, Amorites, Canaanites, Perizzites, Hivites, and the Jebusites. Seven names for the seven pagan nations.

Just as the meaning of the Jewish version of the miracle was that Christ was the Messiah to Israel, so Jesus repeats the miracle for the Gentiles to make the same statement. Jesus was not the Messiah for just Jews, but for the whole world, and He proved it as the Divine Alchemist.

The Ultimate Something from Nothing

There was a time when there was no time—a place where there was no place. The Bible is filled with miracles involving control over nature, but the greatest miracle of all—the one that overshadows the rest—is creation. Calling the universe and all that is in it into being is the ultimate act of the Divine Alchemist—the making of everything from nothing.

There are several interconnected creation accounts in the Bible; the longest and best known is found in the early chapters of Genesis. There creation is described in detail, listing six days of creation and the results of each.

It begins with a simple yet profound statement: "In the beginning God created the heavens and the earth" (Genesis 1:1). That's it—just a simple statement of fact. There is no discussion of God's origin or how He called the universe into being. The words are presented in such a way as to dismiss any argument. Yet in that statement is stunning truth: God called "what is" from "what was not." In an instant there were materials, elements, and energy. Then God gets to work.

Day one brings the creation of light. Life is dependent upon light.

Day two brings an atmosphere and, like day one, it comes by the simple desire and command of God. Nothing else is involved—just God impressing His will on the physical world.

In day three, God causes dry land to appear and the seas to be gathered into place. All of this is necessary for life. But in day three, we see a change in the way God causes life to originate: He commands the earth to bring forth plant life. Plant life is extremely complex and structured, yet by simple command the earth responds.

In day four we again see the formula, "Let there be . . ." and sun, moon, and stars become visible. Now there is a means of telling seasons and time.

Day five brings sea creatures and birds of every kind. Now life is abundant on the planet and that life is giving birth to new life.

Land animals appear on day six and like the emergence of sea animals and birds, these come to be by divine order. Nothing more is needed. It is also on day six that God takes a different approach with a special creation. Unlike the sea animals, land animals, and birds, Adam was not called into being—he was made by hand. The arrival of the first man was unique in the entire universe, so God formed him from the dust of the earth, shaped him in His own image, and personally blew into his nostrils the breath of life.

All that we see and all that we are is the result of God as the Divine Alchemist working His will. But the New Testament fleshes out this miracle by teaching that the universe was created by and holds together because of Christ. John 1:3 says that "all things came into being through Him, and apart from Him nothing came into being that has come into being." The apostle Paul says the same thing in Colossians 1:16–17: "For by Him all things were created, both in the heavens and on earth, visible and invisible, whether thrones or dominions or rulers or authorities—all things have been created through Him and for Him. He is before all things, and in Him all things hold together."

All of this reminds us that nature is subject to its Creator and that the miracles Jesus worked were additional proof of his deity. He was and remains the Lord of all creation.

Other Amazing Transformations

Other accounts of one thing being turned into another are in the Bible. Most are associated with Moses, Elijah, or Elisha. The following is a sample of such miracles:

- Moses sees a staff transformed into a serpent and then back into a staff (Exodus 4:2–5).
- During the plagues of Egypt, water turns to blood, dust into gnats, and light into darkness.

- During the wilderness wanderings, Moses turns bitter water into sweet and draws water from a rock, and dew turns into manna.
- During Elijah's ministry, a widow's food is multiplied (1 Kings 17:8–16).
- Elisha, who followed Elijah in prophetic ministry, changes toxic water into potable water (2 Kings 2:19–22).
- Elisha multiplies a widow's oil so that it can be sold to pay her debt (2 Kings 4:1–7).
- Elisha multiplies loaves of bread so that one hundred men could be fed (2 Kings 4:42–44).

Those accounts are just a taste of what God can do. Although scientists study distant stars and earthly microscopic life, and the surface of the earth is mapped, analyzed, and utilized; we are only a part of God's creation. While we can exert some control over our environment through technology, it remains superior to us. We are the slaves of immutable scientific laws. God, however, is not. Nature remains in the control of the Divine Alchemist.

More to Think About

1. Jesus did not go to the wedding at Cana to perform a miracle. What do you think was the ultimate reason for His decision to convert the water into wine?

2. Mary plays an important role in the water-to-wine miracle. What does the passage teach you about the relationship between Jesus and Mary?

3. Do you suppose Jesus worked miracles before the first recorded miracle at Cana?

4. Do you think that Mary may have witnessed previous miracles, motivating her to ask Jesus to do what He did?

5. Do you think the five thousand and four thousand understood the significance of Jesus' power to feed them? The number of baskets of leftovers was related to the ethnic background of the crowd. Was this done for the crowds' benefit or the disciples' or ours?

6. The Bible shows a pattern in the way God created the universe. What does the order of creation teach you about God? Could God have created in a different order?

Call Me
Barabbas

THE SPRING SUN HAD JUST CRESTED the Judean hills, flooding the streets of Jerusalem with golden light. The city was scarred by long black shadows cast by walls and buildings. A breeze still cold from the night swirled through alleys and byways and into the open windows of a hundred homes. A new day had cut through the darkness of evening, and Jerusalem, the holy city, was coming alive.

Matthew 27:16–26; Mark 15:7–15; Luke 23:17–25; John 18:39–40

The houses and inns were threatening to burst at the seams as observant Jews, who had traveled from the corners of the known world to Jerusalem to celebrate Passover, occupied every bed and filled every room. Today the people would bring doves and lambs to be sacrificed at the temple. It was a family time—a time to rejoice that sins could be forgiven. It was a holy day.

The sun, while successful at pushing back the gloom of night, found a darkness it could not shed, a blackness it could not eliminate. A shadow of hatred and conspiracy hung just outside the entry to the Antonia fortress, a stout building cobbled together with thick stones, situated just to the north of the temple.

An impressive structure, the fortress was constructed by the Maccabeans many years before and rebuilt by Herod the Great, the man who slaughtered the children of Bethlehem in hopes of killing the Christ child. He named the structure after the Roman general and statesman Mark Anthony. During most of the year, a Roman cohort of six hundred soldiers was headquartered in the building, but during Passover the numbers swelled. With the population of the city multiplied many times over for the holiday, an already explosive situation could easily get out of hand.

In the shadow of the fortress stood Jesus, His clothing still laced with the delicate perfume of olive trees and grass, as well as stained with sweat from His agonizing prayer in the garden of Gethsemane. Surrounding Him was an assortment of elders, religious leaders, and temple guards. The ruling body known as the Sanhedrin had pronounced its judgment: Jesus was guilty of blasphemy for claiming to be God. The penalty was death, but there was a problem. Only Rome could put someone to death, and as much as the Jewish leaders hated it, they were a nation in the unyielding grip of mighty Rome. If Jesus were to die, then a high-ranking Roman official must decree it—and one had come to town.

Inside the fortress Antonia was the Roman military governor, Pontius Pilate. Pilate ruled not from Jerusalem, but from the coastal city of Caesarea (northwest of Jerusalem), a city snuggled along the shore of the Mediterranean Sea. As governor of Judea, he was in Jerusalem to see

A model of the Fortress Antonia where Jesus was tried by Pontius Pilate

that the crowds remained orderly and peaceful and to quickly dispense Roman justice. But Pilate was a harsh man hated by the Jews. On three occasions he angered the people to near revolt.

First, he brought Roman shields into the fortress, shields that bore the image of Caesar, a man who claimed to be God. These standards were in full sight of the temple, and the people bitterly complained, traveling to Caesarea to plead their case before the governor himself. Pilate made them wait a week before he would hear them. Then he sent in his guards to intimidate the crowd. So incensed were the Jews that they lay upon the ground and exposed their throats to the soldiers, taunting the guards to kill them. Only after it was clear that a revolt was imminent did Pilate recant and order that the shields be brought back to Caesarea.

In another heartless incident, he appropriated money from the temple to build an aqueduct. To the Jewish mind, that money was reserved for God and no one else. When they protested, Pilate sent in his troops, stabbing and slashing both protesters and innocent alike.

He then wiped out a village of Samaritans who were following a man they believed to be a prophet. He had promised the Samaritans a viewing of the ancient vessels of the wilderness tabernacle but killed them instead. Pilate used his army to kill many, doing so without reservation or remorse.

Scores of Jews and others lay in their graves because of Pontius Pilate. It was to this man that the Jewish leaders brought Jesus.

Jesus stood in the early dawn waiting for the next scene to unfold. Already He had portrayed His death to His disciples through the Last Supper, prayed with great emotion in a nearby garden of olive trees, been betrayed by Judas, and endured several mock trials. Now, with His face swollen from the beatings received at the hands of temple guards, the Savior waited, knowing everything that was to happen. His accusers waited with Him, unwilling to defile themselves by stepping one foot in what they considered a pagan palace.

Someone else was in the building. Not a man wearing the official purple of Rome, but a commoner; a man often overlooked in the trial and crucifixion of Jesus. His name was Barabbas.

Locked away in a stone prison cell was a man of mystery. History tells us nothing of him, and the legends and myths that followed his life are doubtful. What we do know leaves us with more questions than answers. Yet he is one of the most unique men in the Bible.

Each of the four Gospels mentions him by name. He is described as a notorious prisoner, an insurrectionist, a robber, and a murderer. Hardly the kind of man you wanted for a neighbor.

Barabbas was a representative figure in the Bible. He had only one moment of importance, but that moment branded his name in the pages of history.

Pilate heard the complaints of the Sanhedrin against Jesus and found them groundless. He had no concern for what he considered myth and legend, but the leaders played a hand that Pilate couldn't ignore. When they tried Jesus, they did so on religious grounds; but when they presented Christ before Pilate, they took a different tact, saying, "We found this man misleading our nation and forbidding to pay taxes to Caesar, and saying that He Himself is Christ, a King" (Luke 23:2). This was an accusation Pilate could not ignore. There could be no king but Caesar. By law he was compelled to hear the complaint and to pass judgment. Already on precarious ground with Rome, Pilate had no choice but to try Jesus in his court.

Still, Pilate found no reason to put Jesus to death and offered to have him beaten, then released. Certainly that would have satisfied their self-righteous hunger. It didn't. A crowd orchestrated by the religious leaders had gathered. Pilate, as was the custom for the holidays, offered to free one prisoner and gave the crowd a choice between Jesus the Christ and a known thief and murderer.

The crowd chose Barabbas and called for Jesus to be crucified.

Two Named Jesus?

Barabbas is an Aramaic name. The Jews of Jesus' day spoke Aramaic, a language similar to Hebrew, as their everyday language. Greek was the business language, and Latin the political language. Barabbas is a compound word knitting *bar* (son) with *abba* (father). Therefore, Barabbas's name means "son of the father." How symbolic it was that Pilate stood between two prisoners—one whose name meant "son of the father," and one who was the Son of the Father.

The ironies didn't end there. There are several manuscripts (Greek, Latin, Syriac, Armenian, and others) that state that Barabbas's first name was Jesus. Most modern translations omit this, but there is sufficient manuscript evidence to believe it is true.

Jesus is the Greek form of the Hebrew name Joshua and was a popular name. Joshua means "Jehovah is salvation." The New Testament mentions several men named Jesus in the Bible, so it is probable that Barabbas may have also bore the name. What makes it so interesting is the provocative coincidence. The prisoner we call Barabbas is named "Jehovah is salvation" and "son of the father." The fact that Barabbas was named Jesus may account for the somewhat awkward way Pilate asks the crowd whom they want released. He said, "Whom do you want me to release for you? Barabbas, or Jesus who is called Christ?" (Matthew 27:17). Why does Pilate add the title Christ in his reference to the Savior? One reason is to distinguish one man called Jesus from another.

The Same Charge

Barabbas was charged with insurrection—a crime requiring death under Roman law. He was also said to have been a murderer and a robber. There are no details of the insurrection, the murder, or the robbery, but the Bible indicated that the charges were true.

Ironically, Jesus was also accused of insurrection. This was a calculated charge. Pilate could not be compelled to execute a Jewish man simply because other Jewish men didn't like his thinking. A revolutionary was a different matter. All threats to Rome were taken seriously and handled with speed and cruelty.

So Pilate stood between two men—both Jews, both with followers, both named Jesus, and both accused of insurrection. One of the men would be going to the cross. Pilate preferred to release Jesus, finding no fault in Him, but the people pressed their will upon the governor even though Jesus was innocent of all charges. If He was guilty of anything, it was in stating the truth of His nature and mission. He was (and is) the Messiah, the Christ, and the Anointed One. As such, He is King, but His kingdom is not an earthly one. Jesus made this clear when He said, "My kingdom is not of this world. If My kingdom were of this world, then My servants would be fighting so that I would not be handed over to the Jews; but as it is, My kingdom is not of this realm" (John 18:36).

Pilate, quick to jump on what Jesus has said, asks, "So You are a king?"

Jesus replies, "You say correctly that I am a king. For this I have been born, and for this I have come into the world, to testify to the truth. Everyone who is of the truth hears My voice" (John 18:37).

Jesus made it clear that His spiritual kingdom was no threat to Rome's political standing, at least not in such a way as to be classified as insurrection. Barabbas was a different matter; he was legally arrested for crimes he committed. Yet Jesus would die in his place.

There is the lesson: Jesus the innocent went to the cross for the guilty. A murderer murdered Jesus so that a murderer could go free.

The Choice

Both men stood before a crowd that had gathered that morning outside the fortress. In the custom of releasing a prisoner at Passover, the governor offered Barabbas and Jesus to the crowd. To Pilate, the choice was simple. Surely the crowd would ask for their "king" back and not a criminal. He was wrong.

Pilate had had trouble with crowds before. They made demands and he reacted, often violently. Now, as before, a gathering of Jews stood before him, telling him what to do. No matter what he said or tried, the crowd could not be swayed. They wanted Barabbas, and when asked what to do with Jesus called the Christ, they chanted, "Crucify Him!"

The crowd made a choice. They chose the lesser over the greater, the sinner over the sinless, and the guilty over the innocent. No one suspected the gravity of the choice made that cold morning. Of course, the decision did not surprise Jesus. He had come to die and had on several occasions taught His disciples that this very event would occur.

One wonders what went through Barabbas's mind as the crowd chanted his name, their words rebounding through the cool morning. He had some followers, but not so many as to make up the large crowd that stood outside. Why were they chanting his name? We know the religious leaders incited the crowd, but did Barabbas know it? Did he understand the decision that was being made?

Many similarities existed between Jesus the Son of God and Jesus Barabbas, but there were also many contrasts. Both offered kingdoms—Barabbas, a political one; Jesus, a spiritual one. Each offered the shedding of blood—Barabbas shed the blood of Romans; Jesus offered to shed His own. One offered political redemption; the other, redemption from sin. Barabbas was motivated by hatred; Jesus, by love. Barabbas loved his people, but hated the Romans; Jesus loved them all. Barabbas would fail; Jesus would triumph. Both were beaten—Barabbas for his crimes; Jesus for His innocence.

Pilate had Jesus beaten. The Savior endured blows from the guards and a whipping that had been known to kill other men. While this scourging took place, while the sound of the whip against Jesus' back echoed off the dark stones of the fortress, Barabbas walked from the building and into freedom. Another man had taken his place.

We Are Barabbas

Nothing more is known of Barabbas. If he continued his insurrection, history ignored it. The man disappears from all record. Still, we can't help wondering about him. Did he attend the Crucifixion later that day? Did he stand in the shadow of the cross, surrounded by some of the people who chanted for his release? Did he look up at the battered Jesus and realize that He hung in Barabbas's place?

Crucifixion was not unusual in that day and would become all the more frequent in the years ahead. Certainly Barabbas had seen men hang from crosses, their breath becoming more shallow with each inhalation. This time must have been different. It was no ordinary cross upon which Jesus hung—it was a cross intended for Barabbas. The man who hung from it was a substitute. Barabbas had come within hours of execution, but now he stood a free man.

In truth, we are all Barabbas. Jesus hung on that cross not just for the insurrectionist, but for the crowd that called for His execution, for the religious leaders who orchestrated the conspiracy, for Pontius Pilate, for His disciples, and for each of us.

Like Barabbas, we too are "sons of the father." Regardless of our gender, we are the end result of God's creative act. But the relationship goes beyond that; through Christ, we become true children of God, adopted into the family by Jesus' great sacrifice and our decision to follow Him.

Like Barabbas, we are guilty of sin. Our crimes may not be of the magnitude of insurrection and murder, but none of us stand innocent. All have sinned. These would be dark words if not for the light of Christ. And Barabbas's mission failed. Rome continued to thrive despite his efforts. Jesus, however, succeeded, and that made the eternal difference. Compelled by love, not swayed by fear or pain, Jesus took our place so that we might walk free.

Barabbas is a man whose deeds before and after the crucifixion of Christ will forever remain shrouded in mystery. One thing is certain—he is the perfect representation of mankind in need of a Savior.

Parallels and Contrasts

CHRIST	BARABBAS
Jesus	Jesus
("Jehovah is salvation")	("Jehovah is salvation")
Is the Son of the Father	Name means "son of the father"
"Insurrection" (Falsely)	Insurrection (Accurately)
Sentenced to death by crucifixion	Sentenced to death by crucifixion
Tried by Pontius Pilate	Tried by Pontius Pilate
Died on cross	Went free
Innocent	Guilty
Gave His life for others	Took the life of others
Motivated by love	Motivated by hate
Bore a cross meant for Barabbas	Bore no cross
Innocent but condemned by the guilty	Guilty but freed by the innocent
Wanted to free all men	Wanted to free Jews
Rejected by the crowd	Received by the crowd
Greatest Person in history	Lost in history
Achieved His goal	Failed his goal
Died for the guilty	Freed by the guilty

More to Think About

1. Many parallels and contrasts exist between Jesus and Barabbas. Did this happen by coincidence or was it planned? If planned, then what is the silent message behind the strange juxtaposition of Jesus the Christ and Jesus Barabbas?

2. How many ways does Barabbas represent the world as a whole? In how many ways does he represent us as individuals?

3. The story of Barabbas is a silent sermon. What is the core message of that sermon?

4. What's the importance in the fact that Barabbas was already a prisoner when Pilate tried Jesus?

5. If Barabbas represents the sinner in need of a perfect Savior, then whom does the crowd represent?

6. Is Pilate symbolic of anything or anyone or is he just a player on the scene?

7. We are not told what happened to Barabbas, but tradition says that he became Christian. Does this seem possible to you? Do you think he saw Jesus crucified?

Background

Languages of the Bible

The Bible has been translated into nearly every language on earth
(although there are about three thousand languages that have yet
to see a word of Scripture). Yet, it's easy to forget that the Bible
has a language of its own. At times we are tempted to think that
the Bible was written in English, but it wasn't. When we read the
Bible, we are reading words that have come to us through very
ancient languages that have been skillfully translated by highly
trained people.

The Bible is a composite of three languages, each with its own
special advantages. Most of the Old Testament was written in ancient
Hebrew, with small portions being recorded in Aramaic.

Aramaic is an ancient and widespread Semitic language. Ancient Aramaic
inscriptions have been found in China and Egypt. The language is similar to
Hebrew and became the daily language of the Jews. The language has been
around since at least 2000 B.C. Small sections of Daniel were written in
Aramaic. It even appears in the New Testament. Jesus' Aramaic words are
recorded in Mark 5:41 (*talitha, kum*—"little girl, get up") and Mark 7:34
(*ephphatha*—"be opened").

In the Old Testament a few passages are in Aramaic: Ezra 4:8–6:18 and
7:11–26; Daniel 2:4–7:28; and Genesis 31:47.

Hebrew is the primary language of the Old Testament and the religious
language of Jesus' day. This is no accident. Hebrew has many qualities that
make it the perfect language for transmitting God's thoughts. In addition to
being an ancient language, it is extremely poetic and personal. Things can be
said in Hebrew that would lack color and clarity in any other language. No
wonder it has lasted so long. What many do not realize is that Jesus and His
disciples (as well as others in His day) may have spoken four languages:
Hebrew, the religious language; Aramaic, the day-to-day language; Greek, the
business language; and Latin, the language of Rome.

The New Testament was written in Greek—Koine Greek. Koine means "common" or "shared." Until a little over a century ago, it was considered a heavenly language or even the language of the Holy Spirit. Research has shown that while it is different from classical Greek, it was the common, everyday language. Like Hebrew, Greek is ideally suited for recording Scripture. Whereas Hebrew is very poetic, Greek is very precise, often having multiple words for an idea where English has only one. Love is a good example. In English, we have one word for love and a few words to describe something similar, like affection and fondness. Greek has *agape* (God-motivated love), *eros* (sexual love), and *philos* (friendship love).

In the Bible we have two primary languages that give us beauty, poetry, and precision: Hebrew and Koine Greek. Each was perfectly designed to carry the nuances of God's Word.

In 1947 a shepherd boy discovered long lost manuscripts in a cave in Qumran.

That
Brass Thing

IN EL MONTE, CALIFORNIA, more than thirty-five hundred people traveled to see a cross shining in a bathroom window of an apartment building. Crowds became so large that police were forced to barricade the street. They began arriving at 10 A.M., and hundreds remained after 9:00 P.M. Interestingly, this was the second "cross sighting" in a week. Similar events have happened in the Philippines, in a Baptist church in Knoxville, Tennessee, in Altadena, California, and in other cities around the world. Crowds swarmed at each.

*Numbers
21:4–9*

It is amazing to see what people will bow to in worship. Both history and the present show humankind can make a god out of anything. Several cultures worship nature; others worship objects; and many more worship myths.

Humans have a basic need to worship. Those who do not know what to worship create gods. The apostle Paul said, "Professing to be wise, they became fools, and exchanged the glory of the incorruptible God for an image in the form of corruptible man and of birds and four-footed animals and crawling creatures" (Romans 1:22–23).

In the Old Testament there is a clear and fascinating example of worshiping man-made materials. In three passages, separated from one another by seven hundred years and covering a span of fourteen hundred years, we see what happens when a tool is turned into an icon.

CHAPTER FIVE

The Story in Three Acts

Few people like snakes. For most, the creatures are frightening and repulsive. Snakes, of course, have a place in God's creation and provide a valuable service in the balance of nature, but in the Western world, the snake carries an evil stigma. In other cultures, however, the lowly reptile is revered as a powerful religious symbol.

The Aztecs worshiped Quetzalcoatl, the "Feathered Serpent," as the "Master of Life." Some African cultures worship the rock python. Aborigines in Australia see the giant rainbow serpent as the creator of all life. Even the caduceus, the symbol of the physician, has two snakes wrapped around a staff.

The serpent was an icon for ancient people. In Egypt, snakes were associated with the restoration of life, and serpent amulets were often placed upon mummies. Even the living wore images of snakes around their necks to ward off evil. Hebrew altars have the image of a snake etched into the stone. In Mesopotamia the serpent was a fertility symbol. Snakes have left their mark on history.

In the Book of Numbers we have the unusual account of snakes as tools of judgment and the image of a snake as a tool of forgiveness.

A Bad Trip Made . . . Bad

The Bible starts the tale by stating, "Then they set out from Mount Hor by the way of the Red Sea, to go around the land of Edom; and the people became impatient because of the journey."

The Israelites, who had been freed from Egypt, were wandering the wilderness. It was a difficult journey made all the more arduous by their sin and negative attitude. Moses was charged with leading them, which was no easy task. During their journey, Moses led his people into the desolate plains of Edom. The trip was uncomfortable and unwanted. The phrase "the people became impatient" reads literally as "the spirit of the people became short." That's far more descriptive. The people Moses led had a history of being "short-spirited." In this episode, they came to Moses with their usual load of biting criticism. "Why have you brought us up out of Egypt to die in the wilderness? For there is no food and no water, and we loathe this miserable food."

Not only did they not like the direction they were taking, but they also found fault with the provisions God had given. Their complaint is not only directed at Moses, but at God. This was not unusual for them. For example, when Moses was on Mount Sinai receiving direction from God, the Israelites became impatient and turned to Aaron, saying, "Come, make us a god who will go before us; as for this Moses, the man who brought us up from the land of Egypt, we do not know what has become of him" (Exodus 32:1). They were looking for a replacement not only for Moses, but also for the God who led them out of Egypt.

Another case is recorded in Numbers 14:2–4: "All the sons of Israel grumbled against Moses and Aaron; and the whole congregation said to them, 'Would that we had died in the land of Egypt! Or would that we had died in this wilderness! Why is the LORD bringing us into this land, to fall by the sword? Our wives and our little ones will become plunder; would it not be better for us to return to Egypt?' So they said to one another, 'Let us appoint a leader and return to Egypt.'"

So Moses had heard complaints before. The word "miserable" used in Numbers 21:5 means "contemptible, worthless." This was what they called God's provision!

They complained to Moses, but God also heard.

Things Could Be Worse

According to Sir Isaac Newton, every action has an opposite and equal reaction. This is true in physics. It's also true in the spiritual life. The people were unhappy with God; He wasn't thrilled with them. "The LORD sent fiery serpents among the people and they bit the people, so that many people of Israel died" (Numbers 21:6).

No one knows what kind of snakes these were. They're described as "fiery," a term that probably describes the burning effects of the venom. It is possible, however, that the designation refers to the physical appearance of the snakes. Perhaps their scales were shiny or brass-colored. (It is interesting to note that the plural of the word used here is "seraphim," the term Isaiah uses in to describe the winged, angelic beings he sees in his vision in Isaiah 6.)

The discontent of the people starts the process of sin. It's a cascade effect. One hard feeling leads to another, which ultimately leads to sin. Not much different from today, is it? Note the following steps of the process.

First, the people became impatient. As was said earlier, their "spirits became short" and they grumbled against God and Moses. This is the natural outcome of impatience. Impatience seldom remains silent.

Next, they called God's provision worthless. God had been providing for their needs for decades, yet they remained unsatisfied and discontent. None had died from starvation or thirst, but many had died from sin and rebellion. God gave them what they needed, but they wanted more.

Judgment then came in the form of snakes—deadly snakes. These creatures were supernaturally sent and therefore had to be dealt with spiritually. No explanation was made as to why God used snakes.

Artist rendering of Moses and the bronze serpent

The punishment was a persistent one; the serpents arrived and remained for some time. The condition became unbearable to the people, so they finally sought help from Moses—the very person they had complained about earlier.

As expected, the people repented and pleaded for help. People change for one of four catalysts: new information, force, discontent, or pain. Some will change when presented with enough information. This is the noblest reason for change. We are presented with the facts of a situation, see the truth of the matter, and change our behavior accordingly. Unfortunately, few people change for this cause.

The second reason people change is force. We're driving faster than the speed limit. A blue light appears in our rearview mirror. We pull to the side of the road. Why? It's not because we want to, but because we are forced to by the power of the law.

Discontent is another reason change takes place. It was discontent that made the people accuse God and Moses of ill treatment.

Pain is the primary reason people change things in their lives. We will alter our behavior if it becomes too painful to remain the same. This is what happens to the Israelites. Their sin brought a painful punishment and that initiated a change in their attitude.

How Do You Spell Relief?

"Then the LORD said to Moses, 'Make a fiery serpent, and set it on a standard; and it shall come about, that everyone who is bitten, when he looks at it, he will live.' And Moses made a bronze serpent and set it on the standard; and it came about, that if a serpent bit any man, when he looked to the bronze serpent, he lived" (Numbers 21:8–9).

What an unusual solution. Why not just get rid of the snakes? It seems simple enough. Send snakes as punishment; remove them after repentance. If there are no snakes, then there can be no snakebites. It's logical but not what God had in mind. Instead of removing the problem, God provides a cure. The snakes remain. Puzzling as this is, there is a reason for it and a great spiritual truth within it.

To understand God's solution we must first understand that much of the Old Testament is revealed in the New Testament. There is an old saying: "The New Testament is in the Old concealed; the Old Testament is in the New revealed." To understand what happened in Moses' day, we must skip ahead to the time of Christ. But before we get there, we must first make another stop along the timeline.

All mention of the bronze snake disappears until seven hundred years later.

Hezekiah's Reform

The history of Hebrew kings is a roller-coaster affair with dramatic inclines and precipitous falls. A good king would ascend to power only to be followed by an evil king. In Judah, the southern kingdom, a spiritual and determined young man takes the throne. His name is Hezekiah.

"Now it came about in the third year of Hoshea, the son of Elah king of Israel, that Hezekiah the son of Ahaz king of Judah became king. He was twenty-five years old when he became king, and he reigned twenty-nine years in Jerusalem; and his mother's name was Abi the daughter of Zechariah" (2 Kings 18:1–6).

The kingdom of the Jews had been divided for many years. Israel to the north had become extremely pagan and had been conquered by a foreign kingdom. Only the southern kingdom of Judah remained. Ahaz, Hezekiah's father, was a poor leader who encouraged pagan worship. Despite the proverb "Like father, like son," Hezekiah undertook great spiritual reforms. In a brave effort to clean up the idolatrous mess his father had left, Hezekiah began a purification of the land. He was a man of devotion and a noble leader who achieved much for his people and for God. The Bible says that "he did right in the sight of the LORD" (2 Kings 18:3). There is no higher praise.

Hezekiah's campaign of cleansing was a serious one: "He removed the high places and broke down the sacred pillars and cut down the Asherah. He also broke in pieces the bronze serpent that Moses had made, for until those days the sons of Israel burned incense to it; and it was called Nehushtan."

Hezekiah's plan of action takes four decisive steps. First he "removed the high places." The Hebrew word for removed means to set outside, to set aside, and to reject. High places were hills or other elevated areas dedicated to idol worship. Statues of gods were erected there. Hezekiah cleared off the hilltops, removing all things dealing with idol worship.

Next, he broke down the "pillars." Pillars were artifacts of idol worship. The Hebrew word for broke is more violent and means to shatter or crush. Hezekiah did his work with extreme prejudice. Not only did the king remove the idols and other items from their high places, but he also had them destroyed.

Then he cut down the Asherah. Asherahs were wood poles dedicated to the Canaanite goddess Asherah, the "mother of all gods." Hezekiah ordered that an axe be taken to the wood idols and had them chopped down like trees. The people saw this as an act of violence against their gods. They were right.

But Hezekiah wasn't done. He also broke the bronze serpent in pieces. The word for "broke" here means to beat, to hammer, and to grind to dust. Now here's the surprise: The bronze serpent that Moses had made seven hundred years before had become an idol, and the people of Hezekiah's day were burning incense before it. What had once been a symbol of God's redemption had become a cultic icon worshiped by the descendants of those who first saw it.

Nehushtan, the name of the bronze serpent, appears only here in the Bible and seems to be an ingenious combination of two similar Hebrew words. Nehushtan is similar to the Hebrew word *nachash*, which suggests a serpent, but is also very similar to *nechushbah*, which means bronze. It may also be an insult hurled by King Hezekiah at the object that had become a cultic icon. The king is calling it "that brass thing," belittling it before the people.

Nehushtan was also a proper name, as the people had christened their icon before elevating it to idol status.

Seven centuries had passed since Moses had raised the bronze serpent for the dying Israelites to gaze upon. Now that serpent had become an object of idol worship no different from the other idols that sat upon the shelves of people's homes. The people had made it into something it was never intended to be. No longer grounded in the faith of God, but instead surrounded by the daily idolatry encouraged by Ahaz, the people had made an idol out of a tool of grace.

Unfortunately, despite Hezekiah's great work, cultic practices resumed soon after his death. Purity, faithfulness, love, and worship cannot be legislated. They must always come from changed hearts, not changed behaviors. A great man attempted a great thing and he was successful for a time. But evil never gives up.

Now let's take another seven hundred-year leap forward to the time of Christ.

Reclamation

Right before the most famous passage of Scripture (John 3:16), the Nehushtan is mentioned again and by none other than Jesus in His conversation with Nicodemus, a religious leader: "As Moses lifted up the serpent in the wilderness, even so must the Son of Man be lifted up; so that whoever believes will in Him have eternal life. For God so loved the world, that He gave His only begotten Son, that whoever believes in Him shall not perish, but have eternal life. For God did not send the Son into the world to judge the world, but that the world might be saved through Him" (John 3:14–17).

The Nehushtan was an ancient portrayal of Christ on the cross. As people looked to the raised serpent to save their lives, so people look to the raised Christ to save their souls.

On several occasions the Bible records certain objects and people that represent or foreshadow Jesus. The Old Testament's Joseph had a life that foreshadowed Christ's life, as did Joshua and others. Also, the ark of the covenant, Noah's ark, the tabernacle, and the temple were all "types" of Christ. A type is a symbolic representation of what will come later. The Nehushtan was an object that portrayed Christ on the cross and the salvation that faith in His sacrifice would bring.

As the serpents in the wilderness surrounded and afflicted the people in Moses' day, so sin surrounds us. A major theme of the Bible is the problem of sin. "All have sinned and fall short of the glory of God" (Romans 3:23). "If we say that we have not sinned, we make Him a liar and His word is not in us" (1 John 1:10). Verse after verse reminds us of the problem of ever-present sin. Life itself bears out this truth. Very few people would be so brash and arrogant as to say, "I am not a sinner."

Sin comes with a price. It separates us from God, damages our self-esteem, harms those around us, pirates away our joy and happiness, and keeps us from becoming all that we can be. Jesus is the solution: On the cross, He became the sacrifice for our sin. "He made Him who knew no sin to be sin on our behalf, so that we might become the righteousness of God in Him" (2 Corinthians 5:21). The Nehushtan prefigured this scenario when, in the desolate regions of Edom, Moses held up the brass serpent so that any afflicted person could see it and be healed. Today Christ is the one to whom we look.

More to Think About

1. Looking back, it seems silly that anyone would worship an object like a brass snake, but don't people do similar things today?

2. Why is history filled with examples of people creating their gods? What compels a person to make a god?

3. In John 3, Nicodemus asks a probing question about the means of salvation. What does his question reveal about him? What is revealed about Jesus?

4. What might be other Old Testament symbols of Jesus?

5. Does it seem odd that an image of a serpent becomes a symbol of Christ?

6. How is it that by simply looking at the bronze serpent, snake-bitten people could be healed?

The Glow

A DESERTED MOUNTAINSIDE. A disembodied voice. Glowing people. The walking dead. The reappearance of a man who vanished 850 years earlier. And a mysterious, glowing cloud. Sounds like an episode of the *X-Files*, but the event was as real as the morning paper.

Matthew 17:1–13; Mark 9:1–13; Luke 9:28–36

It is the late summer of A.D. 29, and Jesus is in the last stages of His earthly ministry. His opposition had become vocal; the crowds that followed had grown in number; and the Crucifixion loomed just beyond the dark horizon. Questions about Jesus abounded; rumors spread like the wind. Even among His disciples, there was confusion.

In Matthew 16, Jesus asks the disciples who people thought He was. They reply, "Some say John the Baptist; and others, Elijah; but still others, Jeremiah, or one of the prophets."

Interestingly enough, they all suggest dead people! The crowd had looked upon Jesus, heard His teaching, witnessed His miracles, and concluded that He must be a resurrected prophet of old. They were missing the point.

Jesus asks another question—a far more pointed inquiry: "Who do you say that I am?"

After a moment's silence, Peter, always ready to launch out into the deep, blurts out, "You are the Christ, the Son of the living God."

A smile, broad and beaming, crosses the Savior's face as He says, "Blessed are you, Simon Barjonah, for flesh and blood did not reveal this to you, but My Father who is in heaven."

But the point of Jesus' identity still needed to be driven home. Six days later, Jesus leads three of the disciples—Peter, James, and John—to nearby Mount Hermon for an event they would never forget (see Matthew 17:1–13, Mark 9:1–13, and Luke 9:28–36). Mount Hermon is a twenty-mile-long mountain that rises ninety-two hundred feet above sea level at the highest of its three peaks. Once the place of pagan sacrifices, it became the stage for one of the most mysterious and supernatural events in the Bible. Now a vacation site for skiers for its almost year-round snow, Mount Hermon, whose name means "sacred mountain," was once the scene of a soul-shaking event.

Somewhere on Mount Hermon, three men receive a preview of the life to come. They see what no living person has witnessed before or since. They see Jesus fully glorified.

The Scene

Away from the pressing crowds, away from the nagging critics, Jesus leads Peter, James, and John up the slopes of the mountain. A breeze, cooled by the remaining snow not evaporated by the summer sun, washes over them. It has been a week since Jesus asked the decisive question of His identity. The journey has been made on foot, and the disciples are weary from the trek. Somewhere on the slopes of the great mountain, Jesus pauses to pray. The disciples use the break to rest. The air is thin, and the climb has been taxing. Luke states that the men were sleeping when the event began, but sleep soon left them.

Through eyes still bleary from napping, Peter and the others see that Jesus has changed. Jesus, the man with whom they had spent every day and night of the last three years, was now remarkably different. His face shone like the sun. We get our word lamp from the term (lampo) Matthew uses to describe the altered Jesus. Luke says His face was different, altered in some way not described. His clothes changed too. Matthew states that Jesus' garments became white as light, but Mark goes further, stating that white was whiter than any launderer "on earth can whiten." Luke uses the word *exastrapto* that means "to shine forth" or "to be dazzling." The change the disciples see is in both Jesus' person and the very clothing on His back.

Yet, as astonishing as that was, there were still bigger surprises coming.

Jesus was no longer alone; two men had joined Him. Just how the three followers of Christ recognized the strangers as Moses and Elijah, we are not told. Luke, however, states that Jesus, Elijah, and Moses were discussing "His departure which He was about to accomplish at Jerusalem." Most likely, the disciples heard some of this conversation.

What a startling pair to see. Moses had died and been buried by God fourteen hundred years before. Yet, there he was, carrying on a conversation with the Lord. A promise is fulfilled here and connections made. It had been promised to Moses that he would see the Promised Land. See it he did, but because of a rebellious act, he was not permitted to cross over into the land that God set aside for Abraham and his descendants. At least, he didn't cross over with his people. But God is faithful about His promises. There on the Mount of Transfiguration, Moses sets foot on the land just as promised by God so long ago.

There's another interesting connection here. When Luke wrote about "His departure which He was about to accomplish at Jerusalem," he used a special Greek word for departure. It's the word for exodus. Moses, of course, is known for leading the exodus of Hebrews from their captivity in Egypt. Jesus, by His death and resurrection, would be leading an exodus of believers from their bondage to sin and death to life. It is an exodus that ends in heaven.

What about Elijah? He also is unique in the annals of history: He is the Old Testament prophet who never tasted death. Elijah left this world alive, having been taken up to heaven in a fiery chariot and whirlwind (2 Kings 2:11). Now he, for a short time, was back on earth.

There, before the eyes of the disciples, stood Jesus the Savior, Moses the lawgiver, and Elijah the prophet. Peter is overcome by the sight and offers to build three tabernacles. A tabernacle was a temporary structure usually made from branches. The ancient Jewish celebration of the Feast of Tabernacles (often called the Feast of Booths) was a short time away.

Peter has that in mind. The tabernacles represented the time the Jews, led by Moses, spent wandering in the wilderness—again, another connection to Moses and his ministry.

While Peter is making his offer, a cloud appears and overshadows the group. The immediate response of the disciples was fear. Who can blame them? Luke says that "they" entered the cloud. He may have meant Jesus, Elijah, and Moses, or he may have meant all six individuals. The cloud is important. It harkens back to Moses' experience on Mount Sinai. Another person is now on the scene, yet this one cannot be seen. He can, however, be heard. God says, "This is My beloved Son, listen to Him!" Now the number at the mount is a perfect seven—three disciples, Jesus, Moses, Elijah, and God.

The Point of It All

Decades later, Peter would write about the event saying, "For we did not follow cleverly devised tales when we made known to you the power and coming of our Lord Jesus Christ, but we were eyewitnesses of His majesty. For when He received honor and glory from God the Father, such an utterance as this was made to Him by the Majestic Glory, 'This is My beloved Son with whom I am well-pleased'—and we ourselves heard this utterance made from heaven when we were with Him on the holy mountain" (2 Peter 1:16–18).

What did the Transfiguration prove? What difference does it make to twenty-first-century people?

First, the Transfiguration provided evidence of life after death. Many books discuss near-death events in which a person apparently crosses from this life to the next, only to return by medical intervention. Some dismiss these cases as fantasy, while others cling to them as proof that death is not an end. Scripture, from beginning to end, shows that we were meant to live eternally. The oldest book in the Bible is Job (Genesis covers a time long before Job but was actually written after Job), and the subject of that book is a man who experienced the worst that life could offer. Yet he says, "As for me, I know that my Redeemer lives, and at the last He will take His stand on the earth. Even after my skin is destroyed, *yet from my flesh I shall see God;* whom I myself shall behold, and whom my eyes will see and not another" (Job 19:25–27, italics mine). Job understood that death was not an end but a transition. For the believer, it is a homecoming, a blessed event that should be anticipated with joy. The appearance of Moses and Elijah proves that life continues on for those who die in the Lord and those whom He takes before death.

Moses experienced a physical death, yet he appears in bodily form, is aware of his surroundings, and carries on a conversation. Death did not diminish him, but enhanced him in every way.

The fact that the great lawgiver stood on Mount Hermon in the Promised Land is a reminder that God is faithful in His promises not

On Mount Hermon a cloud descended upon six very special people. From it came the voice of God.

only in this life, but also in the next. We don't miss out because of death; indeed, we are enriched by it.

But what of Elijah? He never died. Most conservative scholars believe that there will come a time when the church will be called from this world. Generally referred to as the Rapture, it will come unexpectedly and as quickly as the twinkling of an eye. Paul writes about it in one of his letters to the church at Thessalonica: "For the Lord Himself will descend from heaven with a shout, with the voice of the archangel and with the trumpet of God, and the dead in Christ will rise first. Then we who are alive and remain will be caught up together with them in the clouds to meet the Lord in the air, and so we shall always be with the Lord. Therefore comfort one another with these words" (1 Thessalonians 4:16–18).

When that remarkable event happens, then the number of people who have not died will grow from two to untold millions. Elijah represents these. There is a place in heaven for every believer.

The events of the Transfiguration are a demonstration that life continues on; that faith in God through Christ throws open the doors of eternity. It also shows that the new life is in many ways similar to the old. Not only were Moses and Elijah aware and able to communicate, but they were also recognizable. Peter, James, and John didn't see angels or disembodied spirits; they saw people—people like we will be.

The Glorified Jesus

They also saw Jesus as never before. They had observed Jesus in every possible situation: alone and in large crowds, eating and sleeping, teaching and listening. They had walked uncounted miles with Him and had seen Him perform miracles and challenge religious leaders. But this was something different. For a short time, Jesus let slip the drab dressing of humanity and allowed His deity to shine. So glorious was this transformation that it even affected His clothing. It was an unforgettable sight, and it is something that all believers will experience.

Have you ever wondered what Jesus will look like when you see Him? The apostle Paul wrote: "In the future there is laid up for me the crown of righteousness, which the Lord, the righteous Judge, will award to me on that day; and not only to me, but also to all who have loved His appearing" (2 Timothy 4:8). What a promise! A crown placed on our heads, not by an angel or a martyred saint but by the King of Glory Himself. And He may very well look like He did on Mount Hermon.

The light, the cloud, the mountain, and the presence of Elijah and Moses are all proofs of Jesus' deity. The fact that Jesus was shining brilliantly reminds us that God appeared as light in the Old Testament. The term *shekinah* was later applied to those events when God manifested Himself as a cloud or as light. Such appearances occurred over the temple, over the mercy seat of the ark of the covenant, and other places. Jesus is indeed God in the flesh.

A few days before, Jesus had asked His disciples who they believed Him to be. Elijah had been suggested, as were other prophets. Now the truth was known without contradiction. They had seen both Jesus and Elijah. Jesus was unique. Peter had been right: Jesus was the Christ, the Son of the living God.

Coming down the mountain, we can only wonder what thoughts they held about the sight they had just seen. Jesus was more than they could imagine; beyond what they could comprehend. There is great joy in this. There is more to Jesus than we know. There is more yet to learn and to experience. We have just begun our journey down the path of knowledge.

More to Think About

1. Why have someone who died (Moses) and someone who never died (Elijah) on the Mount of Transfiguration?

2. Why did Jesus take His disciples with Him? What did He want them to learn?

3. After Jesus was resurrected, several people had trouble recognizing Him. Is there a connection between the way Jesus looked on the Mount of Transfiguration and the way He looked after the resurrection?

4. How did this event change Peter, James, and John? How would it change you?

5. Moses, who had died centuries before, appeared in physical form on the Mount of Transfiguration. What is the significance of that? What does it say about the afterlife?

A Sinful Stretch
for the Sky

IF WE COULD STAND ON a magical mountain and peer back to the horizon of human history, our attention would be drawn to the exquisitely crafted remains of stone structures. Wars have come and gone; buildings have been erected then destroyed by time; and entire nations have sprouted into existence, flowered in their day, and then faded.

*Genesis
11:1–9*

Cultures have worked hard to be remembered by those who would follow. From Stonehenge in England to the Great Pyramid at Giza in Egypt come the ancient voices whispering, "Don't forget us." As impressive as these structures are, an older and more mysterious structure captures the attention—the tower of Babel.

No one knows how much time had passed between the flood and the events in Genesis 11—perhaps one thousand years or more. The children of Noah had blossomed into a substantial population, capable of undertaking major construction projects that would certainly take years to finish. One such project brought disgrace and humiliation. From the moment of God's judgment on the tower, the name Babel has been equated with arrogance and sinful pride.

Sandwiched between the Table of Nations in Genesis 10 and the introduction of Abraham in the latter part of Genesis 11 is the story of a people who discovered that self-glorification has consequences.

The first eleven chapters of Genesis follow a pattern: Success comes first, but is soon followed by a tremendous failure and judgment. The

CHAPTER SEVEN

negative always follows the positive. The universe is created and God declares it good, then Adam and Eve sin and are expelled from the garden. God receives sacrifices from Cain and Abel, accepting Abel's but rejecting Cain's; then Cain kills Abel. Humanity grows and thrives; then humankind is contaminated by the intermarriage of the divine beings called the sons of God with the human daughters of men, leading to the corruption of mankind and the flood. Noah and his family follow God's specific instructions and survive the flood, then Noah becomes drunk and curses Canaan. And the thriving descendants of Noah settle in a fertile region only to once again disobey God.

The account of the tower of Babel is the last great judgment to befall mankind. Future judgments will come against nations and cities (Israel and Sodom and Gomorrah, to mention a few) but none of them to the extent of what occurs in the first eleven chapters of Genesis.

Just One Lip
Genesis 11:1–9

"Now the whole earth used the same language and the same words" (Genesis 11:1). The Hebrew of this verse literally reads "of one lip and one kind of words." Only one language and only one dialect existed. The natural question is, What language was it? No one knows. It was probably a Semitic language and very likely a form of Hebrew. The key is found in the names used in Genesis 10 and 11. The names of places and people make sense only in Hebrew. Either someone like Moses (the writer of Genesis) translated the names from the original language into Hebrew, or Hebrew was itself the native tongue.

Whatever the original language, it was the only one known to the people. This is not surprising since the entire population could trace its lineage back to Noah and his sons. Even if a millennium had passed, the language would remain largely unchanged.

A New Home

"It came about as they journeyed east, that they found a plain in the land of Shinar and settled there" (Genesis 11:2). The King James Version and Revised Standard Version translate the direction of migration as "from the east." All other translations follow the New American Standard as "journeyed east." Since Mount Ararat (where the ark ran aground) is west of the Plain of Shinar, this translation is probably correct. Today we would say they left Turkey and traveled south then east into Iraq.

The Plain of Shinar would be a natural place to settle. Found in Mesopotamia (a word that means "between the rivers") the area is deep in the Fertile Crescent. The two rivers are known today as the Tigris and Euphrates—the same names as two of the four rivers that flowed out of Eden (the Pishon and Gihon being the other two). The people carried with them a memory of the past. Finding a land with rich soil, adequate water, and other necessities, they settled down. Perhaps they wanted to rebuild Eden.

It was in this rich area that the Sumerians flourished. Some of the earliest writings known were found there. It was the Sumerians who invented cuneiform writing that would later become the basis for other forms of writing. Some consider the area the cradle of civilization.

Nothing Says "Home" Like Construction

"They said to one another, 'Come, let us make bricks and burn them thoroughly.' And they used brick for stone, and they used tar for mortar" (Genesis 11:3).

Before moving on, let's meet a key character: Nimrod. The great-grandson of Noah (Genesis 10:8), Nimrod's name is built upon the Hebrew verb *marad,* which means "we will rebel" or "come, let us rebel." He is credited with starting nine city-states: Babel, Erech, Accad, Calneh, Nineveh, Rehoboth-Ir, Calah, and Resen (Genesis 10:10–12). Generally associated with Babylon, the southern region of Mesopotamia, Nimrod is also mentioned as being connected with Assyria in the north (Micah 5:6). In short, he was a powerful man with a wide area of influence. And it is Nimrod the mighty hunter who leads the people into this act of rebellion. (Interestingly, many of the centers Nimrod is said to have founded became some of the greatest enemies faced by Israel.)

Back to the building: They made bricks, but not just any bricks. Moses, the author of Genesis, knew something about brick making. It was during his time in Egypt that the sons of Israel were required to make bricks for buildings. Those bricks were sun-dried, but here Moses makes special note that the tower of Babel was made of *oven*-baked brick, a far better technique, but one that is expensive and time-consuming. This was no hastily-thrown-together effort. They planned to stay forever.

Scripture says they used "brick for stone." Unlike Egypt and other countries, the Plain of Shinar lacks the kind of stone that can be quarried and used to make large buildings. This little phrase that is so easy to gloss over shows the incredible accuracy of the Bible. Add to that the archaeological finds of kiln-fired brick and asphalt construction in the area, and we see how historically precise the Bible is.

They used tar for mortar. The King James Version uses the word "slime." Better words would be "asphalt" or "bitumen." The substance is very common in Mesopotamia, an oil-rich area. Exposing crude oil to air can make this type of asphalt. The combination of tar and the very porous kiln-fired brick made for extremely sturdy structures. Centuries later, natives of the region would remove the brick to build their own homes and other structures.

Partially reconstructed ziggurat at Ur

A City Right Here, Right Now

"They said, 'Come, let us build for ourselves a city, and a tower whose top will reach into heaven, and let us make for ourselves a name, otherwise we will be scattered abroad over the face of the whole earth'" (Genesis 11:4).

A point of contention among scholars is the word "tower." Babylon is well-known for pyramid structures called ziggurats. Ziggurat comes from an Assyro-Babylonian word, *ziqquratu*. *Zaqaru* is the root of the word and means "to be high or raise up." The word could also refer to mountains. These ziggurats could be high and impressive. One such construction stood 297 feet from ground to pinnacle and was named Etemenanki. The title means "the building of the foundation of heaven and earth." Archaeologists have found more than two dozen similar structures.

The tower of Babel was the prototype—the first pyramid. These structures were more like stepped pyramids than towers (as we think of them) and were similar in shape and style to ancient Aztec buildings found in Mexico. The Mexico pyramids, however, were made of stone. Ziggurats were rectangular and built in stages—like that of a wedding cake—with three to eight levels. Each level was smaller than the one below it. A long staircase or ramp ascended each side to a temple at the top. The Hebrew word for such a structure is *migdal* and describes a military or observation tower, hence the name, the tower of Babel. (Interestingly, tourists are told to avoid the ziggurat at Borsippa, which is about seven miles southwest of the ruins of Babylon. It is called Birs Nemrod. Those who visit the site, or so tradition states, run the risk of losing their memories just as the original inhabitants lost their memory of their original language.)

Why would a civilization decide to build such a tower? The people had certain goals. The first was to secure a unified place of existence. In many ways, the people were looking to urbanize and stabilize their nomadic life. Settling and building a city would not necessarily short-circuit God's will. Even if the descendants of Noah had settled there in southern Mesopotamia, expansion would certainly have continued.

The real problem was their second goal: to ascend to a place they should not go. Of course, they could not literally build a tower to the heavens, but their arrogance could grow into a massive structure of sin.

They're not the first to have this problem. In the Book of Isaiah is an interesting passage that most conservative scholars see as an account of Satan's fall. Take a close look at Lucifer's motivation:

> "How you have fallen from heaven,
> O star of the morning, son of the dawn!
> You have been cut down to the earth,
> You who have weakened the nations!
> "But you said in your heart,
> 'I will ascend to heaven;
> I will raise my throne above the stars of God,
> And I will sit on the mount of assembly
> In the recesses of the north.
> 'I will ascend above the heights of the clouds;
> I will make myself like the Most High.'
> "Nevertheless you will be thrust down to Sheol,
> To the recesses of the pit." (Isaiah 14:12–15)

The arrogance of Satan is clear, and it led to his downfall. "I will ascend to heaven." Isaiah's words could be cut out and pasted in Genesis 11.

The grave sin of Nimrod and his people was to be found not in the way they built a city and a tower, but in their arrogant motivation. Their pride told them they could ascend to a place where they did not belong. Their error was thinking that God would do nothing about it.

A Visit from God

The first four verses of Genesis 11 were written from the people's point of view. Then God steps in and we hear His perspective: "The LORD came down to see the city and the tower which the sons of men had built."

It's an unusual verse. Many scholars have struggled over the phrase, "The LORD came down." Anthropomorphism—attributing human qualities to God—is the general suggestion that is made. I want to suggest something else. This turn of phrase is used three other times in the Bible, and each time it is used to show God's superiority to a human. In Exodus 19:20 the Lord comes down to Mount Sinai to meet with Moses; in Numbers 11:25 the Lord comes down and empowers the seventy men commissioned to help Moses; and, in Numbers 12:5 the Lord comes down to defend Moses against the accusations of Miriam and Aaron. In each of these cases, Moses was either present or the subject of God's act. Why then use this phrase at the tower of Babel?

There is a trace of sarcasm in the words—the irony is in the fact that man is building a tower to reach the heavens and God has to descend to see it. As Isaiah said, "It is He who sits above the circle of the earth, and its inhabitants are like grasshoppers, who stretches out the heavens like a curtain and spreads them out like a tent to dwell in" (Isaiah 40:22).

It's impossible to be greater than the Almighty.

The Etemenanki ziggurat of Babylon is thought by some to be the original tower of Babel. It was a brick structure that rested on a platform that measured 1,500 feet by 1,360 feet, comprising a surface area of more than two million square feet. That's the equivalent of forty-one football fields. Three structures the size of Noah's ark could be laid end to end along the long side. The ziggurat itself was three hundred feet square and rose to about three hundred feet in height. It had three flights of stairs.

The ancient Greek historian Herodotus (460 B.C.) mentions the structure and describes it as having eight towers and seven stages with a temple at the top:

> In the middle of the precinct there was a tower of solid
> masonry, a furlong in length (roughly 607 feet) and breadth,
> upon which was raised a second tower, and on that a third,
> and so on up to eight. The ascent to the top is on the outside,
> by a path which winds round all the towers. When one is

about halfway up, one finds a resting place and seats, where persons are wont to sit some time on their way to the summit. On the topmost tower there is a spacious temple, and inside the temple stands a couch of unusual size, richly adorned, with a golden table by its side. There is no statue of any kind set up in the place, nor is the chamber occupied of nights by any one but a single native woman, who, as the Chaldaeans, the priests of this god, affirm, is chosen for himself by the deity out of all the women of the land.

For us the tower would be impressive. For God it was a trivial thing.

So What's the Problem?

"The LORD said, 'Behold, they are one people, and they all have the same language. And this is what they began to do, and now nothing which they purpose to do will be impossible for them'" (Genesis 11:6).

The people were unified under a single language and a single purpose. This, by itself, was not bad. It was, after all, God's original design. Coupled with their arrogance and disobedience, the situation became an opportunity for sin.

This verse may sound familiar as it resembles another pronouncement by God made back in the garden of Eden: "Then the LORD God said, 'Behold, the man has become like one of Us, knowing good and evil; and now, he might stretch out his hand, and take also from the tree of life, and eat, and live forever'—therefore the LORD God sent him out from the garden of Eden, to cultivate the ground from which he was taken. So He drove the man out; and at the east of the garden of Eden He stationed the cherubim and the flaming sword which turned every direction to guard the way to the tree of life" (Genesis 3:22–24).

In the garden of Eden, man was driven out to protect himself from himself. Could the same thing be happening in Genesis 11? Could God be scattering the people so that they do not multiply their sin? Yes. Unchecked, the sin of the people could grow beyond imagination. Once again, God must protect the people from themselves.

Language School

"Come, let Us go down and there confuse their language, so that they will not understand one another's speech" (Genesis 11:7).

This is the last time the plural phrase—"let Us"—appears as it relates to God. It was used once before at the creation of man: "Let Us make man in Our image." Now it is used again here.

Notice that in Genesis 11:3–4, the people repeatedly use the phrase "let us." "Let us build a city (and tower)." "Let us make bricks." "Let us build a name for ourselves." God has a response: "Let Us confuse their language." God's words mimic theirs. The difference is this: God will achieve what He sets out to do.

Just how does the Lord confuse the language? Is it a miracle that works on the mind? Do the people stand around talking the same language one moment, only to be utterly confused the next? Perhaps. The text certainly allows for it.

Some think that God scatters the people, and then the languages diverge from their common source. But that explanation doesn't work with Genesis 11:8: "they stopped building the city." It implies an abrupt change. Most likely, the confusion takes place first, which in turn leads to the scattering of the people.

Forced Relocation

"So the LORD scattered them abroad from there over the face of the whole earth; and they stopped building the city." Many scholars think that "whole earth" is figurative. The phrase is used figuratively elsewhere in the Bible (Jeremiah 51:41; Psalm 48:2). Hebrew is a poetic and visually descriptive language. It is not uncommon to see hyperbole used to make a point. But it may also be literal. The Lord may have physically transported the people to different locations. Too hard to believe? Let's take note of a few things before dismissing the idea.

First, the Hebrew allows it. In fact, it's stated twice, once in Genesis 11:8 but also in verse 9. The word "scattered" is from the Hebrew *puwts* and is used sixty-five times in the Old Testament. The word carries a violent connotation and can be translated "dash" or "shatter." Imagine that someone throws a drinking glass onto a concrete walk. The glass does not impact the ground then slowly divide into shards that, over time, move away from the point of impact. Instead, the glass explodes in all directions.

Also, this verse and the one that follows include a small, frequently used word, *kowl*. It means "all" or "the whole of something." The idea is that God scattered the group and had the people placed across the globe.

Second, it's interesting to note similar stories from other ancient cultures. Consider the Aztecs. If the Franciscan monk Diego de Duran is to be believed, then a very interesting piece of evidence is added to the case. He chronicled many of the beliefs of the Aztecs. In 1585, he visited Cholula where he interviewed an elderly man. The man told him this story about the making of the great pyramid of Cholula:

> In the beginning, before the light of the sun had been cre-
> ated, this place, Cholula, was in obscurity and darkness; all
> was a plain, without hill or elevation, encircled in every part by
> water, without tree or created thing. Immediately after the light
> and the sun arose in the east there appeared gigantic men of
> deformed stature who possessed the land. Enamored of the
> light and beauty of the sun they determined to build a tower so
> high that its summit should reach the sky. Having collected
> materials for the purpose they found a very adhesive clay and
> bitumen with which they speedily commenced to build the
> tower . . . And having reared it to the greatest possible altitude,
> so that it reached the sky, the Lord of the Heavens, enraged,
> said to the inhabitants of the sky, "Have you observed how
> they of the earth have built a high and haughty tower to mount
> hither, being enamored of the light of the sun and his beauty?
> Come and confound them, because it is not right that they of
> the earth, living in the flesh, should mingle with us."
> Immediately the inhabitants of the sky sallied forth like flashes
> of lighting; they destroyed the edifice and divided and scattered
> its builders to all parts of the earth.

In the Babylonian creation account known as the *Enuma Elish* (the title comes from the first words of the creation account, "When on high . . .") are these words:

> 'Let us build a throne, a recess for his abode!
> On the day that we arrive we shall repose in it.'
> When Marduk heard this,
> Brightly glowed his features, like the day:
> 'Like that of lofty Babylon, whose building you have requested,
> Let its brickwork be fashioned. You shall name it "The
>   Sanctuary."'
> The Anunnaki applied the implement;
> For one whole year they molded bricks.
> When the second year arrived, they raised high the head of
>   Esagila equaling Apsu.
> Having built a stage-tower as high as Apsu.

Do these two accounts sound familiar? How do we explain the Aztec legends that so closely mirror the truth recorded in the Bible? And the Aztecs are not the only ones who harbor such tales. From the Incas to the Chinese, there are accounts that can only be rooted in Scripture. Clearly, these tales are tied to a common memory.

It is reasonable to believe that God's judgment not only included the confusing of the language (that is, creating new languages) but the transplantation of some of the people to distant lands. How distant, no one knows.

What's in a Name?

"Therefore its name was called Babel, because there the LORD confused the language of the whole earth; and from there the LORD scattered them abroad over the face of the whole earth" (Genesis 11:9).

The ancient Babylonian name called the city *babilu*, which meant "God's gate." From that comes the Hebrew word *babel*, which is closely related to the Hebrew word *balal*, "to confuse."

What happened to the tower itself? We don't know. A Jewish tradition holds that the tower was split in two by fire that fell from heaven. Whatever the details, the people of Babel never achieved their goal. God, however, achieved His.

The Lesson in It All

A careless reading of this passage would have us see God as a spoiled child who knocks down the sandcastle of helpless humans. Such is not the case. The real problem is not in the building of the great structure, but in the demolishing of a great spiritual relationship. The builders of the tower had three sins that brought about God's judgment.

First, they had a pride that wouldn't submit. What was their real sin? Was it the tower? The city? For millennia, the tower of Babel has been a symbol of man's pride and rebellion. It is clear that the flood could wipe out sinful men, but that the man's sinful nature remained. They were given a fresh start, but sin permeated society again. Proverbs 11:2 reads: "When pride comes, then comes dishonor, but with the humble is wisdom." It was a lesson the people of Babel needed to understand; it is a lesson for us today.

Undertaking a great task is acceptable in the eyes of God. Think of David building up Jerusalem and Solomon building the temple. What matters to God is not the size of the task, but the size of the heart and focus of the mind.

The apostle Paul reminds us that our attitude and gratitude is what should be at the center of all that we do. He said, "Let all that you do be done in love" (1 Corinthians 16:14). He also reminded us, "Whether, then, you eat or drink or whatever you do, do all to the glory of God" (1 Corinthians 10:31). Work in love and work to the glory of God. Those two actions make all the difference.

There was another problem: Their work on the city and tower was contrary to God's revealed will. It's as if they said, "We are tired of doing it God's way. From now on, it's our way or nothing." It turned out to be nothing.

To this day, Babylon represents evil, selfishness, and ungodliness. The early church used the name to refer to the evil Roman empire

(1 Peter 5:13). Why we do something can be as important as how we do it. That is the lesson of the tower of Babel. The builders wanted to make a name for themselves, not for God.

These temptations are just as powerful today as they were in the days of Nimrod. Each of us must decide if we have set pride aside, if our goal is a godly one, and if our motivation is pure.

More to Think About

1. The following passages each have something to do with language. How do they relate to the account of the tower of Babel? Will God ever unify language again? See Zephaniah 3:9 and Acts 2:6–11.

2. History shows that every major culture has built large and enduring monuments. Is there a connection between the tower of Babel and these other large buildings?

3. What would the world be like today if there were only one language? Would such a situation be positive or negative?

Up in the Sky

NOTHING IS MORE NOTICEABLE than something new in the night sky.

Today, many live in areas where the evening sky is marred by the glow of streetlights and buildings—what astronomers call light pollution. Not so in the ancient world. Every night, unless screened by clouds, the stars were visible like chips of diamonds sparkling on black cloth. Then as now, the night sky held a deep fascination for those willing to direct their gaze upward. To some, however, it was more than entertainment—it was a job. It was to a group of those stargazers that a silent announcement came. A new star appeared—one that heralded a significant event that they were waiting for.

Matthew 2:1–12

For decades, greeting card companies have used the image of the wise men traveling by camel, their attention riveted to a glowing object in the sky. Every child knows the story, every church relates the account, and many homes have nativity scenes showing the robed Magi bowing before the infant Jesus.

Yet, as familiar as the story is, there remains mystery. Exactly what did the wise men see? What was it that hung in the dark sky more than two thousand years ago? Let's see what Matthew 2:1–12 tells us.

Mysterious Magi

We cannot understand the star without understanding the star watchers. Who were these men that would undertake a long, arduous, expensive journey simply because they saw something new in the sky? Oddly, the Bible gives very few specifics and history leaves no clear record. However, we do have some information about them.

First, they were Gentiles, probably from ancient Persia. They were astronomers, familiar with all that went on in the expanse of the black dome of sky. Some scholars have claimed that the magi were astrologers, but that is unlikely since astrology is condemned in Scripture (Deuteronomy 18:10–14). The word Magi comes from the Greek *magoi* and is used seven times in the New Testament—four times in reference to the wise men and twice in reference to a magician/sorcerer named Elymus (Bar-Jesus in Hebrew).

It is also possible that they were Jewish converts, or at least, sympathetic with Jewish belief. The fact that they recognized the meaning of the star tells us that they were anticipating the event. How? Most likely through the teachings of a man who had lived in the region more than five hundred years before: Daniel. The Book of Daniel relates the story of a young man who rises to prominence in Babylon. In Daniel 4:9, he is referred to as the "chief of the magicians." It is possible that the influence of Daniel percolated down through the centuries. If so, then these Magi would have a distinct advantage in anticipating the coming Messiah.

In Daniel 9 is a timeline predicting the coming of the Messiah. If these men were aware of that prophecy, then they would have the necessary knowledge to understand its stellar announcement.

It seems the Magi knew something of the Jewish Scriptures. Taking the Daniel 9 passage and knitting it with a statement made by the prophet Balaam recorded in Numbers 24:17 ("A star shall come forth from Jacob, a scepter shall rise from Israel"), the ancient sages would be able to make a connection. And their knowledge is detailed. After traveling a great distance, they don't ask, "Where is he who is to be born?" but "Where is He who is born King of the Jews?"

We cannot know the depth of their knowledge, but we can say that they knew enough to start a long and arduous journey. For at least six months, maybe as much as two years, the dedicated Magi traveled a well-worn trade route, arriving not at the manger as is so often portrayed, but at the home of Joseph, Mary, and Jesus. We cannot know the exact time the Magi arrived, but the context of the passage indicates that a number of weeks had passed, and very likely, several months.

More Astounding Facts

These men were "king makers." Magi often had a hand in selecting the rulers in their land. This makes King Herod's agitation (literally, "stirred up") understandable. The Magi ask, "Where is He who is born King of the Jews." As a reigning king duly appointed by Rome, the natural response for Herod would have been "I am the king of the Jews."

At this point, the Magi have taken their lives in their hands. Herod was a man intent on holding tightly to his throne. Although in his older years, he was not quick to turn the reigns of leadership over to someone else.

Stone manger similar to what Jesus may have been lain in in Bethlehem

Herod the Great was born in 73 B.C. Appointed king by Mark Anthony, he served from 40 B.C. until his death in 4 B.C. He was an effective leader but cruel and paranoid. In a fit of rage, he had his wife executed. In 7 B.C. he had two of his sons killed because he felt they were a threat to his throne. He would do the same to a third son for the same reason. In short, he was not a nice man.

When the Magi asked about the one born King of the Jews, they insulted Herod. Herod was appointed to the job, not born to it. He reigned as king and was recognized as such by Rome and reluctantly by the people, yet this group of foreigners dared to question his position. Still, he did not challenge them. That alone showed the influence of these mysterious travelers. Herod recognized their power and authority. It is also worth noting that Herod does not doubt them. The Jews of his day were looking for a coming Savior. Herod must have known that it could happen in his lifetime.

The Magi arrive with a clear message, a message that comes in the form of a question: "Where is He who is born King of the Jews?" In these few words is a huge statement about Herod, how the world views him, and more important, how God sees him.

The end result was an extremely disturbed king.

Is This Any Way for a Star to Act?

The most intriguing part of the story is the star itself. The English word star is translated from the Greek *aster* and is used for any light in the sky. Ancient cultures viewed stars, comets, and other heavenly objects as heralds of special events. This star, however, was unique. In fact, other than appearing in the sky, it doesn't act much like a star at all.

First, it appears suddenly. Piercing the darkness, its light shines down in Mesopotamia, the land of the Magi. They recognize it as a sign that a new king has been born. Yet no such star is recorded in history apart from the passage in Matthew. In fact, it seems that no one in Jerusalem knew anything about it. The message of the Magi comes as a surprise to Herod and his court. When he sends the Magi out, Herod says, "Go and search carefully for the Child; and when you have found Him, report to me, so that I too may come and worship Him" (Matthew 2:8). Why would Herod himself not simply follow the star?

There is another unusual facet of the star: It seems to have disappeared. How long it was visible, we can only guess, but the fact that the Magi go to Herod to seek final directions tells us that the star was no longer visible to them. Only after they leave Herod's presence does the star reappear.

The star also moves. The text states the star "went on before them" (*proago*). The word means "to lead forth." In other words, the star appears and then moves in a fashion the Magi can follow. This is revealing. A star high overhead would be difficult to follow, and even more difficult to use to pinpoint a spot as small as a house. Is it possible the star was lower in the night sky?

The star stops. The account clearly contrasts these two points. Matthew uses the typical term for "stand" (*histemi*). The term is better translated as "made to stand." He also uses a compound word (*epano*) that combines the Greek terms for "over" and "above."

So here is a star that appears, disappears, reappears, moves, and comes to a complete stop over a specific location. What other star can make that claim? It is because of these unusual actions that many have trouble with this passage. And when we try to make typical the atypical star, we do run into rough water. If we begin by assuming that the star is like none other and that it is the result of some special act of God, then the stop-and-go heavenly body makes sense. It is simply fulfilling its purpose. But if we try to make it like a common star that appears suddenly, then we are neck-deep in difficulty. Such assumptions have led to some unbelievable ideas.

What It Wasn't

Through the centuries, people have suggested natural explanations for the appearance of the star. Each explains some aspect of the star's appearance but falls short of matching the biblical text.

For example, many have suggested that the star was a conjunction of the planets. A conjunction occurs when planets appear to come near one another in the sky. To the observer, it looks as if they are close to merging. Such conjunctions happen with regularity. Jupiter and Saturn aligned in 7 B.C.; Jupiter, Saturn, and Mars did the same in 6 B.C.; and another such conjunction between Jupiter and Venus happened in 3 B.C. At first this seems a possibility for the Bethlehem star. It is the popular explanation given at planetariums. Still, despite the popularity of the idea, it simply doesn't measure up.

Conjunctions are not rare. Three such conjunctions occurred between 7 B.C. and 3 B.C. The Magi were keen and experienced observers of the night sky. A new conjunction would hardly be a reason for launching a long, expensive, difficult trip.

Another problem: Planetary alignments do not occur on cue, nor do they move and stop in the sky. Also, such an alignment would be seen from Jerusalem as well as from the land of the Magi. The final blow to this idea is the most obvious one: The Bible mentions a single star; a conjunction involves two or more planets.

Others have suggested a comet. Such a thing would be noticeable and, depending on the size of it, significant. But this idea suffers from the same shortcomings as the planetary conjunction idea: Comets, while rare, were not unheard of. Comets appeared in 5 B.C. and 4 B.C. The appearance, disappearance, travel, and timely stopping of the star knocks this idea out of contention too.

Another popular idea is that the star was a nova. A nova is a star blowing up, releasing tremendous amounts of energy that can be seen at great distances. A nova grows bright in the sky and then fades over a period of months (sometimes years). What about the star's reappearance? It has been suggested that an oscillating nova—one that grows bright, dims, and then grows bright again—would explain the disappearance and reappearance of the star. It's an intriguing, provocative idea, but still misses the mark. The Magi were able to follow the star when it was moving and when it stood still. And, like the other examples, a nova would have been visible in much of the world.

These suggestions have some credibility, but others lack even that. Other ideas for the source of the star have been Satan ("angel of light") and UFOs. (It seems the latter could have been more helpful by offering the Magi a ride and saving them the long journey.)

If the star was none of these things, then what might it have been? What can meet all the criteria?

God in Star Clothing

Since star (*aster*) is used for any light in the sky, there is no way to distinguish its use. It can be used to describe novas, planets, or traditional stars. The word appears twelve times in the New Testament: Matthew uses it four times in his account of Christ's birth; Paul uses it twice in one verse in his letter to the Corinthians in reference to the Resurrection; Peter uses "morning star" as a reference to Christ (2 Peter 1:19); and John uses the word five times—twice as a reference to Christ and three times to describe objects that fall from the sky. The plural "stars" is used thirteen times to represent not only heavenly bodies but also symbols of angels. Bottom line: The word is used in a variety of ways allowing elbowroom in our understanding.

Light is frequently mentioned in the Bible (224 times). God is often represented by light. He is shown as the creator of light (Genesis 1:3) and is even equated with light: "This is the message we have heard from Him and announce to you, that God is Light, and in Him there is no darkness at all" (1 John 1:5). James calls him the "Father of lights." In the Old Testament, Moses and the people are led by a "pillar of fire." The list is long, but the conclusion is clear: God has many times in the past revealed Himself as light.

The same can be said of Jesus, who said of Himself, "I am the Light of the world; he who follows Me will not walk in the darkness, but will have the Light of life" (John 8:12). Jesus uses light to describe the purpose of His ministry: "I have come as Light into the world, so that everyone who believes in Me will not remain in darkness" (John 12:46).

The list goes on. Paul's conversion experience on the road to Damascus begins with a blinding light (Acts 9:3). Paul would later describe it as a daytime light from heaven "brighter than the sun" (Acts 26:13). When an angel appeared to Peter to release him from prison, he was bathed in light (Acts 12:7).

Light is the tool of God as well as a representation of His deity. At the Mount of Transfiguration, Christ is literally transformed before the eyes of Peter, James, and John. Jesus' face "shone like the sun, and His garments became as white as light." Also a "bright cloud" descends upon them and the voice of God is heard to say, "This is My beloved Son, with whom I am well-pleased; listen to Him!" (Matthew 17:5).

Could the star of Bethlehem have been a manifestation of God? The Light had come into the world, and God made it known in several ways, including angels who spoke to shepherds and a star that appeared to Magi.

God is omnipresent, so there is no place in the universe that isn't occupied by Him. However, God often makes Himself known through a visual manifestation: the burning bush for Moses; visions for Ezekiel, Isaiah, and others; a glowing cloud; and a dozen other ways. Could it be that God manifested Himself as something described as a star? It would be fitting and consistent with other manifestations of God.

Another Possibility

Another possibility is that the star is a miraculous work of God. That He in His wisdom chose to make the star and give it the ability to shine high in the night sky or close enough to earth to guide the Magi. If such is the case, then the star is a unique creation made to be a holy beacon for the Son of God.

What We Know

The birth of Christ is more than a tale of a child's birth; it is the chronicle of God appearing in flesh for the purpose of our salvation. It is an act of great love and sacrifice. History balances on that moment when God dressed in human form. It is an event that should be recalled in every history book and recited in every heart.

The birth was humble in circumstance, but not in announcement. Angels told the shepherds who told others, and in the east, Magi waited for a sign—the sign of the star.

The star is God's birth announcement to the world. It was a personal and public announcement for the coming of the "bright and morning star," which shines in our hearts.

More to Think About

1. Why does God use a star to announce His Son's birth?

2. Did the fact that the Magi were Gentiles have anything to do with the star?

3. Is there a reason the star is never mentioned anywhere else in the New Testament?

4. Various suggestions explain the star's appearance as a natural event. Why is there such reluctance to believe in the supernatural nature of the star? If the star proved to be a comet or nova, would that change our understanding of Christ's birth?

Background

Defining the Basics

Doctors have a language all their own. So do carpenters, seamstresses, mechanics, attorneys, and just about everyone else. It's not unusual to get a little lost when listening to someone speak about a field with which we are unfamiliar. Many people feel the same way when they listen to Christians talk in church-speak. Here are some Bible-related terms that you're likely to encounter, described so as to distinguish them from each other.

Bible. Everyone knows what the Bible is, right? Right, except it has a more precise meaning than most people are aware of. The word Bible comes from the name of a Phoenician coastal city called Byblos (Gebal in the Old Testament). The name of the city referred to a reed that

Some of the Bible's most ancient manuscripts are kept in the Shrine of the Book Museum in Jerusalem. The museum studies the Dead Sea Scrolls.

was harvested in the area and used to make papyrus, a type of paper. So the word refers to the material upon which a person would write. Here is the important distinction: The word referred to the material that was written upon and not the writing itself. Technically, when someone says, "Did you bring your Bible with you to church?" they are asking if you brought the actual book and pages. Bible refers to the physical book, not what the book contains.

Scripture. On the other hand, Scripture refers to what is actually written, not the material that is written upon. Our English word Scripture comes from the Greek word *graphe* (from which we get our words graph and graphite). Scripture is what is written. Although we use "Bible" and "Scripture" interchangeably, there is a subtle difference: The Bible contains the Scriptures.

Word of God. This is a phrase that sometimes refers to Christ but is used more often to refer to a message given by God. The apostle Paul said: "Of this church I was made a minister according to the stewardship from God bestowed on me for your benefit, so that I might fully carry out the preaching of the word of God" (Colossians 1:25). The phrase is used the same way in the Old Testament.

Canon. This word does not appear in the Bible but comes to us through history. Originally, the word meant a measuring device like a yardstick; it was something by which something else was measured. The Bible is a collection of sixty-six books. The sixty-six books that make up the canon of Scripture were selected by certain criteria. Those books that "measured up" became part of the canon. Those that did not were rejected. Later the word canon came to mean a collection of things, like the complete works of Dickens or the writings that make up the laws of a land. Canon, therefore, simply means those sixty-six books that make up the Protestant Bible.

Inspiration. Basically, inspiration refers to the act of God in which He moves human writers to record what He wants recorded. In a letter to Timothy, Paul wrote: "All Scripture is inspired by God and profitable for teaching, for reproof, for correction, for training in righteousness; so that the man of God may be adequate, equipped for every good work" (2 Timothy 3:16–17). The word Paul used for inspiration is *theospneustos*. Like many words, this is a compound of two smaller terms, *theos* (God) and *pneustos* (wind or breath). So the word literally means "God-breathed." That is, the Scripture came from the mouth of God. The idea is simple: God gave it; man received and recorded it. That's inspiration.

Revelation. Revelation is more than the name of the last book of the Bible. It means to "lay bare" or to "uncover." Revelation is the act of God whereby He makes known what would otherwise be unknowable.

The following table summarizes the aforementioned terms and their interconnection.

God unveils = Revelation

Man receives = Inspiration

Man records = Scripture

Man collects = Bible

Man prayerfully compares = Canonization

Earthquakes, Darkness, Open Graves, and a Big Rip

THE ACTION HAD BEGUN EARLY that Friday morning. Outside the walls of Jerusalem a crowd had gathered. The disk of the sun was still crawling up the sky, casting long shadows on the cool spring morning. They knew the place well; they had been there before. The crowd was an eclectic assembly of dignitaries, religious leaders, Roman guards, and common folk. They were there for the same reason: Three men were about to die. Some had come to mourn, others to grant comfort, many more to mock, and some to kill. For some, crucifixion was a job they had to do; for others, it was entertainment; and for a few, it was a soul-scarring injury.

Crucifixions were common, and no one expected this one to be any different—but it was. The crowd was larger, swollen by the elders, scribes, and religious leaders. It was Passover time, and the population of Jerusalem, inflated by pilgrims who had traveled to celebrate the holy day, was near the breaking point. Consequently, more Roman guards were in the city, and some of them stood at the feet of the three men. Hundreds had died the same death before that day and thousands more would follow.

Still, this one was very different.

CHAPTER NINE

Hanging between two convicted criminals, on a cross that was meant for a terrorist named Jesus Barabbas, was the Savior of the world. Beaten beyond recognition, the flesh of His back shredded by the cat-o'-nine-tails wielded by a calloused Roman, hung Jesus bar-Joseph, son of Mary, Son of God, deity wrapped in flesh. He was there because on this Passover day—the day when lambs would be sacrificed in remembrance of the time in Egypt when the angel of death passed over the Hebrews, leaving their firstborn alive and well—He would be the Lamb sacrificed for the sins of the world.

It is the most poignant moment in history. Innocence, sinlessness, and righteousness—all nailed to a cross. The sacrifice was heroic at every turn: The perfect dying for the flawed.

"Father forgive them, for they know not what they do," Jesus prayed. It was an accurate statement. No one that morning fully understood what they beheld. They missed both nuance and big picture. But the event did not go unnoticed. God saw it all.

The strange happened that day; the unusual, the unexplained, and the supernatural took center stage, and all of it was recorded in just a few lines in the Bible.

The universe changed that Friday, never to be the same. History found its focal point, and the reverberation rattled through nature. Four miracles, frightening and significant, happened that dark day: an earthquake, supernatural darkness, resurrected dead, and the ripping of the most important curtain in the world.

Earthquakes

Few things are as frightening as an earthquake. Those who have lived through major quakes speak of the terror and sense of helplessness. The dependable earth suddenly becomes untrustworthy, betraying all those who take solid ground for granted. First there is a deep rumble, then a chattering, and then the jarring movement. The earth rolls and pitches, vibrating with such power that windows break, gas and water lines rupture, and buildings sway and often collapse. People begin to run, but fleeing is impossible on ground that refuses to be still. It only lasts for a few seconds, in the worst case a minute or two, but it is enough. Terror floods the area like a tsunami.

In ancient days, it was worse. Most buildings were incapable of withstanding the fury of an angry earth. Large structures were made of stone blocks fitted tightly together, but without the binding of mortar. It was not unusual for entire towns to crumble in a moment.

Josephus, the historian who lived shortly after Christ's time, wrote of an earthquake that took place in 31 B.C.: "In the seventh year of the reign of Herod there was an earthquake in Judea, such a one as had not happened at any other time, and which earthquake brought a great destruction upon the cattle in that country. About ten thousand men also perished by the fall of houses."

Earthquakes are common around the globe. The Holy Land is not exempt. The Hebrew word for earthquake is *raash* and means a vibration, or shaking. The New Testament Greek term is *sesmios,* from which we get our words seismology and seismograph.

The day Christ died, the earth shook violently. Interestingly, both the historian Josephus and the Talmud mention an earthquake that fits the time Christ was crucified. The Talmud dates it forty years before the destruction of the temple. Rome tore down the temple in A.D. 70, so the earthquake took place around A.D. 30. Was this the same earthquake of the cross? Most likely, yes.

The first earthquake mentioned in the Bible goes back to the days of the prophet Amos who lived and prophesied in the material heyday of Judah (Amos 1:1). The prophet received visions from God, visions he dates in general and specific ways. First he mentions the visions occurred in the days when Uzziah was king (792–740 B.C.), then he nails it down by adding "two years before the earthquake." The same earthquake is mentioned in Zechariah 14:5—nearly 250 years later! We are not told the extent of the destruction, but it was powerful enough for the memory to last centuries.

Earthquakes are sometimes the result of God's judgment. Fourteen hundred years before Christ, Moses struggled with the arduous task of leading the Israelites in the wilderness. A man by the name of Korah had complaints and, with several other conspirators, challenged the authority of Moses and Aaron. It was the wrong thing to do. Moses was God's handpicked leader. Publicly accusing him of wrongdoing and conspiring against him was not only unwise, it was fatal. God's anger burned against Korah and the people that sided with his cause. Numbers 16:31–33 tells the end of the matter: The ground split open directly beneath Korah and his men, and they plummeted to their deaths. As if to put the final seal on their execution, the earth closed over them.

Other supernatural earthquakes are mentioned in the Bible. Sometimes tremors are associated with the presence of the Lord. Elijah, the great prophet, depressed and fleeing the wicked Queen Jezebel, finds himself on Mount Horeb where God is making himself known. Through a spectacular display of God's power comes a wind strong enough to pick up rocks and dash them to the ground, a fire that blazed brightly on the mountainside, and the seismic shaking of the mountain. God was revealing Himself. The passage goes on to tell us that God is big enough to cause those natural disasters, but they do not define Him. Instead, He is found in the "sound of a gentle blowing" (1 Kings 19:11–12).

God's control of the earth was clearly seen when Jonathan, the son of King Saul, decided to challenge the Philistines, the perennial enemies of Israel. Taking matters into his own hands, he and his armor bearer undertook a secret mission, making their way to enemy lines where they engage and kill about twenty men. The situation was impossible: hundreds of Philistines versus two young men. But Jonathan knew that God had delivered the enemy into his hand, so the two waded into the thick of battle. It was then that "the earth quaked so that it became a great trembling." It was a spectacular intervention of God that made the few greater than the many (1 Samuel 14:1–15).

Miracle earthquakes are not always tools of destruction. Sometimes they highlight a major event, serving as an exclamation point to a miracle. The most dramatic example of this occurred nearly two thousand years ago in Jerusalem. The earth quaked at the death of Christ, but it also shook at His resurrection. The body of Jesus had been hastily prepared for burial by Joseph of Arimathea and Nicodemus and then laid in a borrowed tomb (John 19:38–42). Once in the tomb, a large stone was rolled in front of the opening, sealing it tight. Inside lay the lifeless body of the Savior, and so the situation remained for three days. On Sunday, the present and future were forever changed.

"And behold, a severe earthquake had occurred, for an angel of the Lord descended from heaven and came and rolled away the stone and sat upon it" (Matthew 28:2).

A severe earthquake, literally a "mega earthquake," shook the region again. This was not a simple release of tectonic pressure; it was an unmistakable statement. Both quakes, the one Friday afternoon at the cross and the one Sunday morning at the tomb, were powerful. The first was described with the phrase "and the rocks were split" (Matthew 27:51), the latter as a "mega shaking." These could not be overlooked.

Yet the quakes were controlled since the tremors had their origins in the will and power of God. No great destruction is recorded about this time. The walls of Jerusalem remained intact, the temple stayed on its foundation, and no deaths are mentioned. A natural quake would not be so discriminating. This can only be by the grace of God.

Natural earthquakes are the result of mindless forces. Miracle quakes have a purpose. The apostle Paul could testify to this. While on his second missionary journey, Paul finds himself in a Philippian jail with his fellow worker, Silas. Having been threatened by a mob, beaten with rods, cast into the inner prison (a high-security place often used for torture), and shackled in stocks, Paul and Silas were praying and singing (Acts 16:22–30). In the middle of their impromptu worship service, "there came a great earthquake." The foundation of the prison was shaken, jail doors were opened, and "everyone's chains were unfastened" (not only does God show His power over great things like the shifting earth itself, but also small things like the locks on manacles). They were set free, just as we were set free from sin after the earthquakes at Christ's death and resurrection.

As Jesus, weighed down with this sin of the world, died on the cross, an earthquake stamped the event as important. When He walked from the cold confines of a stone, hand-tooled tomb, rumbling of the earth marked it. When Christ comes again, that event, too, will be marked by an earthquake.

The apostle John saw the future quake in his revelation: "And there were flashes of lightning and sounds and peals of thunder; and there was a great earthquake, such as there had not been since man came to be upon the earth, so great an earthquake was it, and so mighty. The great city was split into three parts, and the cities of the nations fell. Babylon the great was remembered before God, to give her the cup of the wine of His fierce wrath. And every island fled away, and the mountains were not found" (Revelation 16:18–20).

Twenty-five hundred years ago, the ancient prophet Zechariah documents the return of Christ: "In that day His feet will stand on the Mount of Olives, which is in front of Jerusalem on the east; and the Mount of Olives will be split in its middle from east to west by a very large valley, so that half of the mountain will move toward the north and the other half toward the south" (Zechariah 14:4).

Although the earth is constantly changing and seismic activity has been happening since creation, God is the master of His creation and even the ground obeys His commands. In Old Testament days, at the cross, at the Resurrection, and in the early Church, God used the solid ground to make His point. What better way to say, "Pay attention, this is important"?

Darkness

Just an earthquake taking place at the cross would be remarkable enough, but there was more—much more. An inexplicable darkness covered the area. We are even told the time it began and when it ended. The event is recorded in three of the four Gospels and each describes a darkness that overshadows the region from the sixth hour (noon) until the ninth hour (3:00 P.M.). Each account uses the phrase "over the whole of the land" to describe the extent of the darkness. Luke goes a little further and reveals, "the sun was obscured" (Luke 23:45). This is a crucial detail, but one that has led many to jump to the wrong conclusion.

It is tempting to assume that a solar eclipse caused the unexpected gloom, but an eclipse is out of the question. Jesus was crucified during Passover and Passover occurred at the full moon. For the moon to be full, it must be on the side of the Earth farthest from the sun. A solar eclipse requires the moon to travel between the sun and the Earth. The moon can then cast a shadow on the Earth's surface. Since the moon was in the opposite position, no solar eclipse was possible.

The darkness of Crucifixion day was something far more unique than the shadow of the moon. We know it lasted three hours and occurred in the middle of the day. We know that it was one of several unusual events that were centered around Christ's death. Still, the exact nature of the darkness remains unknown. Luke tells us that the sun was obscured, but by what? A cloud? A swarm of insects? A dust storm? While such things have happened in history, none of these fit the situation. If the darkness was caused by anything as common as clouds, dust storms, or insects, then the Gospel writers could easily have recorded the cause. The context and tone of the three Gospel passages show that the event was puzzling to the observers. Any attempt to rationalize the darkness as a natural event misunderstands the text and demeans the authors. While the people of Jesus' day were technologically primitive by twenty-first-century standards, they were not ignorant or prone to superstition.

Jesus foreshadowed the darkness at the time of His arrest. A mob, which included religious leaders, servants, Roman guards, temple guards, and more, had come to seize Him. Jesus tells them that "this

The cross of Christ is the keystone of all history.

hour and the *power of darkness* are yours" (Luke 22:53, italics mine). The power of darkness. The word "power" (*exousia*) means "right of choice" or "the freedom of action." The mob was acting with evil intent and doing so by choice. Blame for the conspiracy rested squarely and fully on their shoulders. This was their moment, but it was a moment that came from dark hearts and evil plans. They came under the shelter of darkness to arrest Jesus, but their deeds came to light.

The apostle John spoke of a darkness that covers the heart: "But the one who hates his brother is in the darkness and walks in the darkness, and does not know where he is going because the darkness has blinded his eyes" (1 John 2:11). He also mentions it in the Gospel that bears his name: "This is the judgment, that the Light has come into the world, and men loved the darkness rather than the Light, for their deeds were evil" (John 3:19). The men who came to seize Jesus were filled with this kind of darkness.

Symbolically, that darkness becomes real and tangible as the man they arrest hangs dying on the cross. It is as though the darkness that was within them spewed out like a geyser and covered the sun. Yet they are not responsible for the darkness at the cross; they are responsible for the "darkness" that led to the cross.

The phenomenon at the cross was a manifestation of God's displeasure. Men of darkness had put the Light on the cross. Now they were to be covered by the dark. From 12:00 P.M. to 3:00 P.M. on the Friday when Christ died, an unusual, unexplained darkness covered Jerusalem and the surrounding region, but its complete nature will remain forever unknown.

Egypt

The supernatural darkness at the cross was not the first such event in the Bible. Going back nearly fifteen hundred years prior to the cross, we find another peculiar shadow. Moses is commanded by God to tell Pharaoh to release the children of Israel. Pharaoh refuses so "Moses stretched out his hand toward the sky, and there was thick darkness in all the land of Egypt for three days. They did not see one another, nor did anyone rise from his place for three days, but all the sons of Israel had light in their dwellings" (Exodus 10:22–23). The gloom is described as "a darkness which may be felt."

The passage is remarkable on several levels. The idea of a palpable darkness is hard to imagine. What does darkness feel like? This was not just a dimming of the light from the sun, nor is it, as some suggest, darkness from windblown sand. Although Egypt is subject to high winds that carry sand, sandstorms are something Pharaoh and his people would understand and would hardly find intimidating.

The darkness is persistent (lasting three days), complete (one person could not see another), and intimidating (the Egyptians could not leave their own homes). Yet the sons of Israel had light in their dwellings. The darkness was selective.

What kind of darkness can match this description? Certainly not an eclipse or shadows cast by clouds. No act of nature could cover Egypt in stygian gloom to the extent that not even the flame of lamps could dispel it, yet still allow a particular group of people like the Hebrews to be unaffected. Only the Author of the laws of physics could rewrite those principles to allow the supernatural to happen.

God in Darkness

Odd as it sounds, darkness is associated with God. "God is light," the apostle John tells us, but He is no stranger to darkness. Exodus 20:21 says, "So the people stood at a distance, while Moses approached the thick cloud where God was." The term "thick cloud" is better translated as "thick darkness." The same terms are used in 1 Kings 8:12: "Then Solomon said, 'The LORD has said that He would dwell in the thick cloud.'" The psalmist agrees: "Clouds and thick darkness surround Him; righteousness and justice are the foundation of His throne" (Psalm 97:2).

It is not God who is dark. His motives are pure, His actions direct, and His ways blameless. The darkness associated with God is something that shields frail humans from His incomprehensible glory, serving as a filter that allowed the presence of God to be seen in a limited way.

Resurrections

One of the most mysterious miracles surrounding the cross is the resurrection of a number of saints. Matthew describes the event: "The tombs were opened, and many bodies of the saints who had fallen asleep were raised; and coming out of the tombs after His resurrection they entered the holy city and appeared to many" (Matthew 27:52–53).

This passage is problematic and amazing. First, tombs in a Jerusalem cemetery are opened. Most tombs were either hewed from rock or were caves converted for the purpose of burial. Those who could afford to do so had tombs made from blocks of stone. Many tombs had "rolling stones"—large, circular stones that sealed off the opening to the vault. The earthquake that shook the area while Christ was on the cross most likely opened the sepulchers, allowing the raised dead to exit. No specific count is given, but the text states that "many" saints were raised.

Who were these formerly-dead-but-now-alive people? The passage calls them "saints." The word saints (*hagios*) means "holy" or "consecrated." It carries the idea of separation for a purpose. In the temple certain objects were considered holy—separated for God's use. They could not be used for anything else. The Bible refers to Christians by the same term. For example, Paul writes to a church in Ephesus and begins with the greeting: "Paul, an apostle of Christ Jesus by the will of God, to the saints who are at Ephesus and who are faithful in Christ Jesus" (Ephesians 1:1). The raised saints in Matthew are believers from a time prior or during Christ's ministry. We know nothing else of their identity.

A Little Quibbling

Were these unnamed saints truly resurrected? That depends on what is meant by "resurrection." Did they rise from the dead? Yes. This is no myth or fairy tale. A number of lifeless individuals are literally brought back from the dead. In that sense they are resurrected, but we must make a distinction between that resurrection and the one Jesus experienced.

The apostle Paul said, "But now Christ has been raised from the dead, the first fruits of those who are asleep" (1 Corinthians 15:20). "First fruits of the dead." Does that mean that Jesus is the first person resurrected? Yes and no. A distinction needs to be made between resurrection in the Christian sense and resuscitation.

The Bible has many accounts of the dead being brought back to life. Elijah raised the widow's son (1 Kings 17:20–24), and his successor, Elisha, does a similar thing (2 Kings 4:32–35). In both cases, the reviving of the dead child is very physical. Elijah lays himself across the boy three times as he utters prayers. Elisha performs what could be mistaken for cardiopulmonary resuscitation, lying across the child and putting "his mouth on his mouth and his eyes on his eyes and his hands on his hands" until the child sneezes seven times and opens his eyes.

By far the strangest case occurred when a group of men were in the process of burying a man only to be frightened away by a group of marauders. In their haste, they threw (literally, "thrust") the dead body into the tomb of Elisha. Ancient Jews did not use coffins as we do today. The deceased was wrapped in cloth and set in a tomb. The unburied body, hastily tossed in Elisha's grave, came in contact with the bones of the dead prophet. That contact brought the dead man back to life. He was revived and stood (2 Kings 13:21).

The New Testament has several accounts of the deceased being miraculously brought back to life. Jesus brought several dead back to life, including Jairus' little daughter (Mark 5:39–42) and Jesus' friend Lazarus, who had been dead for four days (John 11:39–44). Jesus also raised the son of a widow from the town of Nain (Luke 7:11–15), actually interrupting the funeral procession to do so.

God also raised the dead through the apostle Peter, who, while in Joppa, raised the dead woman Tabitha (also known as Dorcus; Acts 9:39–40). And the apostle Paul revived Eutychus, who had fallen to his death from a third-floor window (Acts 20:9–12).

The largest number of resurrections is found in Ezekiel 37:1–14, often referred to as the valley of dry bones, in which an entire army is raised from sun-bleached bones. There is debate as to whether Ezekiel is experiencing a vision or if the resurrection was a physical event.

The quibbling point is, Were the resurrections just mentioned true resurrections? What is a true resurrection? Jesus is indeed the first to experience a resurrection. What of the others? Their revival is better viewed as resuscitation. Jesus was resurrected, never to die again. He is the only One who can make that claim. All the others—Lazarus, Tabitha, Eutychus, and the rest—would one day die again. While they were brought back from the dead in a literal and physical way, they would ultimately pass through the gates of death a second time.

The resurrection of Jesus is different in that regard. Death can never claim Him again. The Christian has the same promise. The future resurrection is an eternal one in which dying is a thing of the past.

The dead saints who were revived from their tombs while Christ was on the cross were, strictly speaking, resuscitated. Like those raised by miracle before them, they, too, would die again . . . maybe.

Maybe? The Jerusalem saints' resurrection is different from the others in that they were raised in conjunction with Christ's death. In fact, that is the biggest mystery of this miracle.

A Timing Problem

Notice the timing of the events: "The tombs were opened, and many bodies of the saints who had fallen asleep were raised; and *coming out of the tombs after His resurrection* they entered the holy city and appeared to many" (Matthew 27:52–53, italics mine).

The miracle has its beginning while Jesus is still on the cross, but the saints do not come out of their tombs until after Jesus' resurrection. What would keep people in the area from resealing the tombs? Would they really allow tombs to remain open? The answer is yes and here's why. The Sabbath was just hours away and no work could be done on the Sabbath until nightfall the next day. Very little work could be done in a cemetery after dark. The next opportunity, therefore, would be after sunrise Sunday morning—the day Christ arose. Christ rises first, then the saints.

Another timing issue involves the raised saints themselves. Did they remain in Jerusalem? Other resuscitated individuals did, but they were raised prior to Christ's victory over death. And if the saints did continue to live on in the city, why are they never mentioned in the Book of Acts?

Some Guesswork

The work of Christ on the cross and His resurrection changed everything. Those two events, which are really two parts of the same event, are the fulcrum of history. Consequently, Scripture focuses on that event, and rightly so. Everything else stands in the shadow of the cross and Resurrection.

What we know of the event is this: During the Crucifixion, an earthquake rocks the area. Tombs are opened, but not just any tombs. Select tombs of chosen saints are opened to the inrush of fresh air and remain open with their lifeless bodies of long-dead believers remaining in place. So they remain until Sunday morning when Christ is raised from the dead. Then they go into the city of Jerusalem where they are recognized. This is a clue that the raised had died within recent memory of the people. Jesus continues His ministry for forty days in His resurrected body and then ascends into heaven from the Mount of Olives.

Did the raised saints ascend also? Enoch, the Bible tells us, ascended bodily into heaven. Could the same be said of these unnamed saints? No one can say with certainty. It is possible that, like Lazarus, they simply died again.

If they did ascend to heaven with their resurrected bodies, then they would be the "second fruits" of the resurrection and an example to all believers of the eternal resurrection to come.

Tearing Things Up

The last physical miracle of the cross requires a shift in location from the Crucifixion mount outside the walls of Jerusalem to the inner area of the temple.

The temple in Jerusalem was one of the world's great wonders. Expanded by King Herod, the main structure and surrounding courtyards were nothing short of amazing. Beginning in 19 B.C., workers finished the main building in ten years, but work would continue on the complex until A.D. 64. Six years later, the Romans would utterly destroy it.

The temple itself was the focal point of Jerusalem. Set on a hill, the structure dominated the skyline. Made with marble and decorated with gold, it was a source of pride for all who lived in the city. The main structure was fifteen stories high, 150 feet wide, and divided into two major sections: the Holy Place and the Holy of Holies (sometimes called the Most Holy Place). The priests did much of their work in the Holy Place, but only once a year on the Day of Atonement did the high priest enter the Holy of Holies. The Holy Place was sixty feet long and thirty feet wide and contained the golden altar of incense, the gold candelabrum known as the menorah, and the golden table for the bread offering. The room was paneled in cedar. Ninety feet above the floor hovered the ceiling.

The Holy of Holies was much smaller—thirty feet square. Unlike Solomon's temple a thousand years earlier, the Holy of Holies was empty. It was in this room that God was believed to dwell.

Close to one thousand priests and Levites were required to deal with the temple's daily rituals. During the pilgrim festivals of Passover, Weeks, and Booths, that number would swell to eighteen thousand temple workers.

Dividing the two rooms was a heavy curtain sixty feet long and thirty feet wide. This veil screened the Holy of Holies from view. According to the rabbinical writing, the veil was a handbreadth (about nine inches) thick, woven of seventy-two twisted plaits, each of which was made of twenty-four threads.

The significance of this miracle shines neon bright. In Jewish thinking, God dwelt behind the veil. The massive curtain separated the perfect God from sinful men: God over there; us right here—always separate, always distinct. Christ's death on the cross forever changed that. No longer would man's access to God require the work of a priest. No longer would the high priest be required to sprinkle the blood of an animal in the Holy of Holies. Instead, the barrier between man and God was torn from top to bottom, indicating that it was an act of God, not of man.

The veil would have been torn at the time a priest was making an incense offering. The Altar of Incense was situated directly in front of the veil. What a sight that must have been. We can only imagine what the priest thought.

God made His point through the miracles of the cross: The day grew dark, the earth shook, graves opened, and the veil tears.

What Does It All Mean?

The miracles were real in every sense, and each should be taken literally. Yet, each miracle is symbolic as well.

The earthquake shows us the judgment of God. Sin was being judged. Christ bore that sin. No other act in history is more important.

The perfect died for the faulty; the righteous suffered for the sinner; God on a cross for man on the ground. This was truly an earthshaking achievement.

The darkness represented sin itself. Jerusalem was filled that day with every possible negative emotion. Hatred, fear, and pride—all became conspiracy, but it was a conspiracy that had been seen before the foundation of the world was set. Jesus bore our sin; the Light was covered in our darkness.

Some graves opened then to remind us that all who place their trust in Jesus would indeed be resurrected. We live eternally, not as disembodied spirits, but as resurrected physical beings. Those saints who were raised the Sunday following Christ's death were promises to those of us who would follow.

The cross was about so much more than we can ever realize.

More to Think About

1. The miracles that surrounded the cross were impossible to miss. What do you think the people at the foot of the cross thought when the earth shook and the sky grew dark?

2. Those who had conspired to bring Christ to the cross had seen the results of several miracles, yet they remained unconvinced and uncommitted to Christ. Are miracles efficient tools for bringing the unbeliever to faith? If so, then why did so many religious leaders refuse to believe?

3. If the miracles of the cross were to happen again in your community, how do you think your neighbors and community leaders would respond?

4. What do you think happened to the resurrected dead who came out of their tombs?

Communication
Devices

TODAY IT IS NOT UNCOMMON to see people with cell phones pressed to their ears. Much of our communication takes place over devices like phones, radios, and even the Internet. We are accustomed to using devices to converse. God has spoken or made His will known through the use of devices too. Not electronic devices, but symbolic ones. Some are quite mysterious, puzzling scholars to this day.

Urim and Thummim

No such "device" is more mysterious than two objects called the Urim and Thummim. Much speculation has circulated about these two objects, but the truth is, we know very little about them. Still, we do know a few things.

The word Urim comes form the Hebrew *ur,* meaning "light." The "im" ending makes the word plural. So the word Urim means "lights." Thummim means "perfections." Thus, the Urim and Thummim mean "lights and perfections." However, there is a very good chance that Thummim comes from a Hebrew root meaning "dark" or "concealed." If that is true, then the terms would translate "lights and darkness."

The Urim and Thummim first pop up in Exodus 28:30 with no explanation, as if everyone involved already knew of the objects. Although we get no description or indication of how they worked, we do find out that they were used to determine God's will.

CHAPTER TEN

The high priest wore very specific garments. Exodus 28 described them in amazing detail. The description mentions an unusual breastpiece (sometimes called a breastplate). It was to be made with gold, blue, purple, and scarlet thread and connected to the ephod (an apron-like garment) with gold chains. On the breastpiece were gemstones arranged in four rows of three gems. Each gem had the name of one of the twelve tribes of Israel etched into it. The breastpiece had a pouch to hold the Urim and Thummim.

Later Jewish writings make the Urim and Thummim the same as the gems on the priest's breastpiece. A better understanding is that they were something entirely different.

How they were used is a mystery, but a few events give us some clues. Several key people other than the high priest made use of the stones: Joshua, King Saul, King David, and various high priests. On several occasions the Bible speaks of the people "inquiring of the Lord." These were times when the people turned to the Urim and Thummim for guidance.

Since the Bible doesn't tell us how the devices were consulted, theories have abounded. One popular view is that the Urim and Thummim were dice-like stones that were cast to determine God's will. In this view the stones would be marked with the Hebrew equivalent of yes and no. The inquirer would ask a question, toss the stones, and read a yes or no answer. This concept is beautifully simple, but doesn't match the biblical text.

For example, in 1 Samuel 28:6 we read, "When Saul inquired of the LORD, the LORD did not answer him, either by dreams or by Urim or by prophets." (A similar denial of response can be found in 1 Samuel 14:37.) How can a yes-no device yield no answer? Well, it's possible if the Urim and Thummim are consulted together. Imagine two flat stones, each with a 1 marked on one side and 0 marked on the other. (The ancient Hebrews did not have numerals, but used letters to represent quantities. The numbers mention here are only for illustration.) Now imagine shaking the stones in your hand and then gently dropping them on the ground. Three possible combinations arise: 1-1, 1-0 (or the equivalent 0-1), or 0-0. If 1-1 equals "yes," then 1-0/0-1 could represent "no." If that is the case, then 0-0 could represent no answer. That is, God has chosen to be silent.

Still, the tossing of the Urim and Thummim as lots does not fit the biblical description. While direct questions are asked that require only yes and no answers, the answers are often much longer. Consider the time that David seeks advice from God. "Then David said to Abiathar the priest, the son of Ahimelech, 'Please bring me the ephod.' So Abiathar brought the ephod to David. David inquired of the LORD, saying, 'Shall I pursue this band? Shall I overtake them?' And He said to him, 'Pursue, for you will surely overtake them, and you will surely rescue all'" (1 Samuel 30:7–8).

God's answer is much longer than a yes or no response and gives unexpected details. This is typical of those times when God spoke through the Urim and Thummim.

Some Theories

Flavius Josephus was a historian from around the time of Christ. He wrote that the Urim and Thummim would glow in the presence of God's glory.

Some sources, like the Talmud, speak of the engraved letters of the names of the twelve tribes of Israel on the stones on the ephod flashing in sequence to spell out words. The problem here is that even with every name of the twelve tribes of Israel spelled out, there is not a complete Hebrew alphabet. The ancient scholars adjusted for this problem by assuming that additional names—Abraham, Isaac, and Jacob—were somehow also present.

And one ancient scholar taught that the letters of words etched into the stones on the breastplate would actually move to form other words until an entire sentence was given.

Still, most scholars today view the Urim and Thummim as divine lots that were tossed like dice. This has several basic problems since, as already stated, the answers given to the questions asked are much more than yes and no answers.

So What Were They?

Unfortunately, the only accurate answer is one that doesn't satisfy the curious. The answer is, no one knows. The Bible never makes clear how the devices were used. What we do know is important:

- The Urim and Thummim were used from the time of Moses to the days of Ezra and Nehemiah—a time span of more than one thousand years. (The historian Josephus states that they were used until about two hundred years before he wrote *Antiquities*—that would be 150 B.C. or so.)
- The items drop from sight from the time of David to the days of Ezra and Nehemiah and then disappear again. The interim time was the age of prophets and God spoke through select inspired men, thus the Urim and Thummim were not needed.
- Generally, they were used in time of national crisis or war. David did inquire of the Lord during times of personal danger from Saul.
- The mechanism of communication involved a person asking questions and then receiving a response from the Urim and Thummim.
- The answers listed in Scripture were always longer than yes or no, ruling out the idea that the Urim and Thummim were just stones cast like lots.
- The Urim and Thummim pre-existed the tabernacle, priest system, and even the exodus itself. Exodus 28:30 shows that they were already in existence. Unlike the tabernacle, the priest's garb, and the ark of the covenant, God gives no direction on how to make the Urim and Thummim. They seem to be already in hand. How far the Urim and Thummim predate Moses is unknown.
- What happened to the Urim and Thummim remains unknown.

The Lot

The casting of lots is an ancient practice found in almost every culture. "That's just my lot in life" comes from the days when lots were used to make significant decisions. Also, in real estate we buy houses that are built on lots because property was often divided by lot casting.

The Bible is filled with examples of people using lots to determine God's will and of God using lots to communicate. Seventy-seven times the term is used: seventy times in the Old Testament and seven times in the New Testament.

The first biblical reference to the use of lots comes from God Himself: "Aaron shall cast lots for the two goats, one lot for the LORD and the other lot for the scapegoat. Then Aaron shall offer the goat on which the lot for the LORD fell, and make it a sin offering" (Leviticus 16:8–9).

The ancients believed that God could control the outcome of the random act of casting lots. It's even mentioned in Proverbs: "The lot is cast into the lap, but its every decision is from the LORD" (Proverbs 16:33).

The story of Jonah also illustrates lot casting. Jonah, in an effort to flee God's call, pays for passage by boat to Tarshish. God has other ideas. The ship is besieged by a sudden, severe storm. The crew, all experienced sailors, are frightened for their lives. They rightly assume that someone on board is the cause for the supernatural storm and cast lots to determine who the culprit is. The lot accurately fell on Jonah (Jonah 1).

Not every use of lots in the Bible is legitimate. In the Book of Esther, an evil man named Haman casts a lot to wipe out the Jews: "For Haman the son of Hammedatha, the Agagite, the adversary of all the Jews, had schemed against the Jews to destroy them and had cast Pur, that is the lot, to disturb them and destroy them" (Esther 9:24). As it turns out, Haman dies instead.

The most poignant use of lots by unbelievers is found at the foot of the cross. As Jesus hung from the cross, His clothing was given away after the casting of lots. The new owner won his "prize" because the lot fell to him (John 19:24).

Back to the legitimate lot casting, it was God who initiated the lot with Aaron, a practice followed by high priests through the years. It was by lot that temple officers and places of service were decided—all with God's implicit blessing (1 Chronicles 25:8).

Even the disciples turned to lot casting when they filled the vacancy left in their ranks by Judas. Interestingly, Acts 1:26 states that the disciples "drew" lots. Normally, lots were cast, not drawn. Perhaps the disciples did something similar to drawing straws as opposed to tossing dice-like stones. The lot fell to a man named Matthias, whom we never hear from again. Later another man comes on the scene—Paul. Paul was God's choice to make the twelfth apostle.

How were lots cast? This, too, remains a mystery. No details about technique are given. This is probably by design. Casting lots is very near to the kind of divination the Bible prohibits (Deuteronomy 18:10). Casting of lots was not meant to be the normal manner of communicating with God. It was confined to rare occasions and people of special standing such as the priests. Proverbs 16:33 is not teaching lot casting as means of getting direction from God. Instead it teaches that God can control life's little things, even lots.

Still, it would be nearsighted not to notice that God did indeed guide a few people through the use of lots. One such case involved the father of John the Baptist. Zacharias received news of his wife's pending pregnancy while he was attending his priestly duties. The privilege of burning incense in the temple fell to him. That privilege came by lot (Luke 1:8–9). It was through God's providence that the lot fell to

Herod's temple. In earlier versions of the temple, the ark of the covenant was kept inside the Holy of Holies.

Zacharias, allowing him to be in the temple and at the Altar of Incense that stood near the Holy of Holies. Zacharias was to receive a special message; God made sure the priest was in the right place to hear it.

The Inside/Outside God

What about today? Should Christians be casting lots, listening for the audible voice of God, and seeking their own Urim and Thummim? The answer to that rests in an understanding of the difference between "then" and "now."

In Old Testament times, God was always seen as existing on the outside of the person. He was a God that was real, powerful, and worthy of obedience and worship, but He was still outside the person. Christians stand on a different side of the time line. We live in an age of grace made possible by the work, death, and resurrection of Christ. God is no longer on the outside; He's on the inside. Christ and the spirit of God dwell within us (Romans 8:9–10).

With the Holy Spirit on the inside, we do not require a device on the outside to commune with God. The Holy Spirit serves as our guide and prayer is our connection.

The use of lots or other devices is not encouraged anywhere in the New Testament. We are, however, encouraged to know the Bible (2 Timothy 3:16–17). The Bible is the inspired Word of God, and it is perfectly designed by the designer Himself to reveal huge quantities of spiritual knowledge, so much so that a single lifetime of study is inadequate to understand it all.

In many ways, the contemporary Christian has been blessed far above the saints of the Old Testament. The mysteries of the Old Testament have been revealed in the New (Romans 16:25–27). Seeking God's will is a simple function of faithful prayer and diligent Bible study. The only device necessary is an open, obedient heart.

More to Think About

1. The Bible shows the godly seeking God's direction through lots and the Urim and Thummim. How has that changed since the coming of Christ?

2. What role does the Bible play in our communication with God? Is it fair to say that the Bible has replaced lots and the Urim and Thummim?

3. What advice would you give someone who says, "I don't know what God wants me to do. How can I know His will?"

4. What do you suppose would happen if the Urim and Thummim were rediscovered?

5. The Urim and Thummim just appear in the Bible record without discussion or description. Where do you suppose they came from?

A Visit from
God

TODAY WE SEND MESSAGES via landlines, cell phones, and the Internet. But God communicates differently.

God is creative in all things—including the way He makes His will known. Salted throughout the Bible are events in which God speaks, but the way in which He speaks differs widely. Voices from the sky, words from the wind, a hand from nowhere, flame and smoke—all are ways in which God has communicated.

God the Father is not removed from the day-to-day lives of His children. He is close at hand and involved so that every Christian believes that he can speak directly to God and be heard. That communication is called prayer. And God can speak directly to us, too, and does so, sometimes in unusual, even astounding ways.

The author of Hebrews summed it up when he wrote: "God, after He spoke long ago to the fathers in the prophets in *many portions* and in *many ways,* in these last days has spoken to us in His Son, whom He appointed heir of all things, through whom also He made the world" (Hebrews 1:1–2, italics mine).

Many portions, many ways—God has used scores of methods to make His words known, and the way He has done so reveals a powerful, caring God.

Is That You?

At a well in Samaria, Jesus meets an outcast woman. Breaking all social rules of His day, He begins a conversation. In the give and take of dialogue, Jesus tosses out a bite-sized nugget of truth: "God is spirit, and those who worship Him must worship in spirit and truth" (John 4:24). The Greek word for spirit is *pneuma,* from which we get words like pneumonia and pneumatic. Its basic meaning is a movement of air. It's the same word that would be used for wind or breath.

In that short sentence—just thirteen words in the original language—Jesus teaches a great truth: God is a spirit with no physical body. This makes sense, of course. For God to be omnipresent, He must be free from the confines of a body. In theology talk, we say that God is transcendent—beyond the boundaries of space and time.

While God is outside the limits of time and space, He can and has taken on physical form—and not just human form.

The Noise of God
Genesis 3

Our first hint that God has occasionally taken on human form is found in the garden of Eden. Adam and Eve have sinned, and the Creator has arrived on the scene. Usually we're so caught up in the sin and pending judgments in the scene that we overlook a little sentence that says a lot: "They heard the sound of the LORD God walking in the garden in the cool of the day" (Genesis 3:8). They *heard* God *walking.* The Hebrew word for sound is *qowl.* It is used many times in the Bible and is translated as "voice," "sound," or "noise." Only the context of the passage helps us know how to render the word. Every modern translation uses the word "sound" in this verse. The King James Version uses the word "voice" instead. Interestingly, the New King James Version (an updated version of the 1611 King James) switched to "sound." Now it may be that they heard the voice of God in the garden, too, but the key term here is "walking."

We're not told what they heard, but it was enough to get their attention. The sound of God strolling through the garden brought them fear and shame.

Did God appear physically to Adam and Eve? Most likely. The special relationship between the world's first couple and God was unique in many ways. It seems likely that God appeared in some physical form. This does not mean that God is confined to a body. Jesus told us otherwise and there are many Scriptures to prove His point. God can, however, take on a body when it suits His purpose.

Did God arrive in human form? We are not told what form He arrived in, but it was a form nonetheless. A human shape seems the best guess. What should have been a pleasant picture, a joyful fellowship, was ruined by sin. The sound of God coming now brought fear.

In Genesis 4 there is another dialogue between a human and the Lord. Cain, enraged at his brother, kills him. God asks the first murderer what he has done. The answer is the famous line, "Am I my brother's keeper?" One wonders if this, too, wasn't a face-to-face encounter. How did God speak to Cain? It may have been in a physical appearance.

Enoch is a famous man. He has a unique standing in Scripture. Little is known about him, but everything we do know tells us that he was godly. The most remarkable thing about Enoch is that he never died. Only two people can make that claim: Enoch and Elijah.

"Enoch walked with God; and he was not, for God took him" (Genesis 5:24). Only three people are said to have walked with God: Enoch, Noah, and Levi. Even among these great men, Enoch stands alone. So close was his walk with God that God simply took him to heaven.

The question is, How did Enoch walk with the Lord? Is this a mere euphemism, or did Enoch literally stroll side-by-side with God? Certainly the phrase means to be in agreement with God, to be pious and righteous, but it may mean more. God may have manifested Himself in some fashion, and it was with that manifestation that Enoch walked. There is no reason not to take this literally.

Another time when God came visiting in physical form was centuries later in the area that would become known as the Holy Land. The clearest Old Testament example of the Lord appearing in human form happens on Abraham's front porch. "Now the LORD appeared to him by the oaks of Mamre, while he was sitting at the tent door in the heat of the day. When he lifted up his eyes and looked, behold, three men were standing opposite him" (Genesis 18:1–2). What makes this passage so fascinating is Abraham's response to the visitors. He does four things. First he greets them by bowing; he offers to have water brought so they can wash their feet; he fixes them a lavish meal; and then he stands by in the posture of a servant to meet their needs.

In addition to providing us with a lesson on ancient hospitality, we also see God in a physical form. Four times the passage says "the LORD said." Further, Abraham refers to his primary visitor as Lord and also Judge. The conversation between God and Abraham makes it clear that it was none other than God Himself who stopped by, and He had feet to wash, and a mouth with which to eat and speak. This is God in human form.

What about the other two visitors? In Genesis 19 they are referred to as angels. Angel in Hebrew means messenger. These are two such beings that accompany the Lord on His visit.

Just a Peek

Sometimes only pieces of God are seen. In Exodus 24, God calls Moses, Aaron, and Aaron's two sons to come up on Mount Sinai. Seventy leaders were to join them. It was a time for God to confirm His covenant and give instructions to Moses about the tabernacle and the ark of the covenant. Only Moses would ascend to meet with God, but God does manifest Himself to the group.

"Then Moses went up with Aaron, Nadab and Abihu, and seventy of the elders of Israel, and they saw the God of Israel; and under His feet there appeared to be a pavement of sapphire, as clear as the sky itself" (Exodus 24:9–10).

What an amazing vision. Why only feet and pavement? No one has ever truly seen God. God is incomprehensible. In fact, we are told by none other than God Himself that no man can see His face and live (Exodus 33:20). Yet the Lord takes on a partial form for the leaders to see.

It happened again when Moses asked God to show him His glory (Exodus 33:18–23). Since such a thing would be fatal to Moses, God shelters him in the cleft of a rock and then, in some physical manifestation, passes by, allowing Moses to see only His back.

Perhaps the most startling manifestation occurred during the prophet Daniel's time (Daniel 5). The king was an arrogant party animal named Belshazzar. He threw a feast for one thousand of his nobles, and the wine flowed freely. During that celebration, Belshazzar had an idea. It was the worst idea of his life. The Jews were in captivity in his land. Belshazzar's father, King Nebuchadnezzar, had removed the holy vessels from the temple in Jerusalem and had them brought back to Babylon. Those vessels, which included cups, were reserved for the worship of God and God alone. Belshazzar thought it might be fun to drink his wine from them.

More is here than meets the eye. One reason ancient kings raided temples was to show their superiority over not only the people, but their gods as well. Belshazzar was showing his arrogance by using holy objects for common drinking. He was making a statement: "I am greater than the God of Israel." So he drank from them, as did his wives and concubines.

In one of the most unusual manifestations recorded in the Bible, a hand suddenly appears and begins to write on the white plaster wall.

Traditional site of Mount Sinai where Moses received the Law

"Mene, Mene, Tekel, Upharsin"—God had numbered the days of Belshazzar's kingdom. He had been weighed in the balances and found wanting. Belshazzar's kingdom would be divided and given to the Medes and Persians.

A hand, just a hand, scratching out a message in the plaster of the palace. The manifestation was substantial enough to be seen by the king and to leave a message on the wall. God made His point in an unforgettable way.

God by Any Other Form Would Still Be God

Through the centuries, God has chosen to appear in various forms, each appearance showing not only His presence, but His control over nature. Here's a short catalog of such manifestations.

Fire

Exodus 3 tells the story of Moses' call. He sees a bush burning but not being consumed. Making his way to the bush, Moses finds God waiting for him there. From the midst of this burning bush, God gives Moses his mission.

God continues to use fire as a representation of His presence. Mount Sinai is covered in smoke because "the LORD descended upon it in fire" (Exodus 19:18).

During the years in which the children of Israel wandered in the wilderness, a pillar of fire led them by night and a column of smoke by day. Scripture says that it was the Lord who went before them "in a pillar of fire" so that the people could travel by day and night.

Smoke

Where there's fire, there's smoke and that is certainly true for manifestations of God. Mount Sinai is the clearest example of this. When God was present on the mountain, the children of Israel at the foot of the mountain could see that the "smoke ascended like the smoke of a furnace" (Exodus 19:18).

And the holy smoke occurs also in the Book of Isaiah. Like all the major prophets, Isaiah receives a personal call. That call comes in the form of a vision in which the prophet sees God sitting on a throne in the temple that is filled with smoke (Isaiah 6:4).

Wind

Job, the man of great suffering, receives a lecture from God. It is a lecture meant to drive home the point that He, the Creator, is above all things and in control. The lecture comes through a voice from a whirlwind. Job hears God's stern voice come from the tumult of a storm (Job 38).

In a fashion opposite of Job's situation, Elijah, dejected, depressed, and angry, finds himself on Mount Horeb (the same place Moses first hears from God) and gets an unusual message. After complaining that he is the last faithful man left in the land, God makes an appearance. The wind blows hard enough to pick up rocks and dash them to the ground; fire appears and burns on the mountain; and the earth begins to shake violently. But God was in none of those things. Instead, He makes Himself known through a "gentle blowing" (1 Kings 19:12). Some translate the passage as a "still small voice." God can speak loudly with flashes of lightning and ground shaking intensity or He may whisper.

Light

The apostle John tells us that "God is Light" (1 John 1:5). In the Book of James, we find something very similar: "Every good thing given and every perfect gift is from above, coming down from the Father of lights, with whom there is no variation or shifting shadow" (James 1:17). Light comes closest to describing God's essence.

Cloud

The phrase "shekinah glory" is often heard in churches to refer to the appearance of God in the Old Testament. The word "shekinah" never appears in the Bible, but it is described on several occasions. The word itself first appears in ancient Jewish Targums. (Targums were translations and paraphrases of the Hebrew Scriptures into the common language of Aramaic.)

Shekinah means "dwelling" or "residence" and was used to describe a visual manifestation of God. The term was used to portray God's appearance at the tabernacle and the temple. At those events and others, a cloud is mentioned. For example, when the tabernacle is erected, "the cloud covered the tent of meeting, and the glory of the LORD filled the tabernacle" (Exodus 40:34).

Nearly six hundred years later, a similar event happens at the dedication of the temple in Jerusalem. "It happened that when the priests came from the holy place, the cloud filled the house of the LORD, so that the priests could not stand to minister because of the cloud, for the glory of the LORD filled the house of the LORD" (1 Kings 8:10–11).

Such manifestations are not limited to the Old Testament. On the Mount of Transfiguration, the disciples see a glowing cloud that envelops them. God's voice is heard from the cloud saying, "This is My beloved Son, with whom I am well-pleased; listen to Him!" (Matthew 17:5).

Voices from a Very Specific Nowhere

The Mount of Transfiguration is not the only place in which the voice of God is heard. A nearly identical phrase was uttered when Jesus was baptized (Matthew 3:17).

The phrase "God said" appears in the Bible nearly fifty times. The "LORD said" is used well over two hundred times. (LORD, set in small caps, is used by modern translators to translate the personal name of God, as opposed to "Lord" that translates the Hebrew *adonai*.) The fact that God speaks is clear in Scripture.

Sometimes we are told where the voice of God originates, such as the burning bush, a whirlwind, or a cloud. At other times, it is left a mystery. For example, when God spoke to Noah, was it a voice from heaven or did God take on some physical form? We don't know. Nonetheless, the voice of God has been heard through the centuries.

The Unique Moses

Moses is unique in many ways. His courage will always be remembered, as well as his determination to do what God called him to do. Granted, he was often reluctant and even fearful, but when the time came to step up to Pharaoh or step into the sea, Moses was there—all reluctance and fear put behind him.

But he is unique in another way. According to the accounts recorded in the Bible, Moses saw God in more ways than anyone else. While God showed Himself in many ways to many people, Moses holds the record for direct communication with God.

It is said of Abraham that he was a friend of God (James 2:23). God called King David a man after His own heart (1 Samuel 13:14). But of Moses it is said: "Thus the LORD used to speak to Moses face to face, just as a man speaks to his friend" (Exodus 33:11).

Moses first encounters God in a burning bush. From that bush came the voice of God and with it a command to return to Egypt with the message, "Let My people go." This was not just a plant or even a talking plant (as remarkable as that would be), but a visual manifestation of God.

Moses also saw "parts" of God. We've already mentioned the feet that stood on the sapphire paving stones and the back of God that passed before Moses.

The glory of God was something Moses experienced on several occasions, including his encounters with God on Mount Sinai and during the dedication of the tabernacle. God was present in a cloud, smoke, and fire, as well as trembling earth.

The voice of God rang in Moses' ears. Not only did Moses hear the voice of God, but he also carried on extensive conversations. God gave detailed instructions on the building of the tabernacle and the ark of the covenant. Many of Moses' writings are simply the records of God's dictated words.

Not only did Moses see manifestations of God in all these forms, but he also saw and spoke to Jesus on the Mount of Transfiguration. So Moses becomes one of only two people to see manifestations of God in both the Old and New Testament (Elijah was the other, and he was also on the Mount of Transfiguration).

Jesus—the Greatest Communication

What then is the clearest revelation of God? Jesus is the winner, hands down. Earlier we saw that God spoke in "many portions" and in "many ways." That same passage in Hebrews 1:1–2 tells us that it is Jesus who best reveals God: "God, after He spoke long ago to the fathers in the prophets in *many portions* and in *many ways,* in these last days has spoken to us in *His Son,* whom He appointed heir of all things, through whom also He made the world" (italics mine).

Jesus gives us His own testimony: "He who has seen Me has seen the Father" (John 14:9). He also said, "I and the Father are one" (John 10:30). This statement so enraged the religious leaders of Jesus' day that they picked up rocks and were ready to stone Him. When asked for which good work they planned to stone Him, they replied, "For a good work we do not stone You, but for blasphemy; and because You, being a man, make Yourself out to be God" (John 10:33).

To study Christ is to learn about God. Jesus—God in the flesh—is the most complete revelation of God possible in this world. It is Jesus who makes the Father known. As the apostle John said, "No one has seen God at any time; the only begotten God who is in the bosom of the Father, He has explained Him" (John 1:18).

More to Think About

1. How does God reveal Himself today? Does He show Himself differently in the twenty-first century than in the centuries before?

2. Nature is complex and much of it still beyond our understanding. Can God be seen in nature? If so, how?

3. Is there a reason why God appeared as fire, smoke, wind, and in human form? Is there something special in these symbols?

4. Each time God appeared, there was no mistaking His identity. How did those who saw these manifestations know that it was God they were seeing and not a natural phenomenon?

Places to Avoid

IN 1609 A CURIOUS, INDUSTRIOUS, brilliant Italian named Galileo turned his homemade telescope skyward and became the first man to see the moons of Jupiter. It made history. He learned that one of the five then-known planets had worlds of its own.

Today people speculate about life in space. They wonder if there could be life on other planets. The thought of life being somewhere other than Earth—that there might be inhabited places we cannot see—is just magnetic.

Centuries ago Robert Hooke did the opposite of Galileo and used a primitive microscope to gaze at a world too small to see with the unaided eye. Here was a whole new set of creatures to examine—microscopic organisms that were just as fascinating as planets and moons.

Other worlds do exist, including the worlds found in Scripture. Where are they? What are they like? They are unlike any physical world we know. While we can send men to the moon and look through microscopes and telescopes, we cannot see these other places of existence except through the lens of the Bible. Through the pages of Scripture, we catch a glimpse of an existence beyond the physical one we know . . . and that peek can be provocative, but also disturbing.

The Starting Line

The starting point for most of these worlds, at least for humans, is death (angels, as we will see, are in a different boat altogether). Most

CHAPTER TWELVE

people see death as an end of life: Consciousness ceases, awareness is gone, and nothing is left but oblivion. Christians know different: Death may be many things, but it is not the end of existence.

To understand death, we must first understand life. The human creation is the blending of the immaterial part of us (known as the soul) with the physical body. By God's design, the two were meant to be inseparable. Because of sin, death entered into the world. This death is both physical and spiritual. Through Christ, however, eternal life came into the world (1 Corinthians 15:22).

When death occurs, it is sad and upsetting to those left behind. Instinctively we know that death is not normal—that it is not something for which we are designed. Yet it is a reality that we all face.

But what is death? It is the forced parting of the soul from the body. Everyone knows what happens to the body. It is buried, entombed, or cremated. The soul, however, is a different matter.

No one knows the composition of the soul. It is spiritual in content, but what does that mean? We do know that the soul is real and the very essence of a person. Reasoning continues, physical sensations remain, and communication is possible. In other words, life continues on after the physical body ceases to function.

Where?

Some are surprised to learn that the Bible mentions more than one place—some of which are already present and others that will be in the future.

Theologians use the term "intermediate state" to describe the state of the soul after death. When a person dies, the immaterial part of him is parted from the physical body. The question is, Where does that immaterial part go? The answer isn't as simple as we imagine. We must first ask about time.

Jesus changed everything. His death, resurrection, and ascension not only changed the world we see, but the ones we don't. Prior to Christ's work, things operated differently in this world and the next.

The key to the problem is understanding the timeline. Imagine a horizontal line that represents time (just like the ones in history textbooks). The past is to the left of the present; the future to the right.

Somewhere along that line is our moment. Two thousand years ago, the pivotal event in history took place: Jesus died and was raised from the dead.

To the right of our moment in time are the Second Coming and the various judgments. A person's death on this side of Christ's resurrection is different than a death on the Old Testament side of the cross. Prior to the cross and Resurrection, all souls went to the same place (although very different areas with very different conditions). That place is called Sheol.

Sheol—One Word, Two Meanings

Sheol is a mysterious word. Its original meaning is unknown, yet the word appears sixty-six times in the Bible and is translated in various ways: grave, pit, and hell. Only the context of the word helps us understand which English word to use. The King James Version prefers to translate Sheol as hell, but that leads to confusion. Hell is something entirely different.

Often the word simply means the grave, referring to where the body would be laid. When Joseph's brothers sold him into slavery, they returned to their father and told him that his son had perished. Jacob is crushed and replies, "Surely I will go down to Sheol in mourning for my son" (Genesis 37:35). Jacob felt the news would drive him to his grave.

But for the majority of the time, the word means the abode of the dead. King David wrote, "For You will not abandon my soul to Sheol; nor will You allow Your Holy One to undergo decay" (Psalm 16:10).

Lazarus and What's-His-Name
Luke 16:19–31

Sheol was a place for both the righteous and the wicked. "The wicked will return to Sheol, even all the nations who forget God" (Psalm 9:17).

The clearest teaching of this is not found in the Old Testament, but in the New, and is taught by none other than Jesus. In Luke 16:19–31, Jesus relates an account of two men who die. One is righteous and the other wicked. Some have called this a parable, but it appears to be an account of an actual event. When Jesus taught in parables, He never used proper names. Here we are told that the righteous man was named Lazarus. The wicked man's name is unknown, although traditionally he is referred to as Dives.

This Lazarus should not be confused with the Lazarus Jesus raises from the dead. This Lazarus had a miserable existence: he was poor, ill, covered with sores, and always hungry. His life could not sink lower. In contrast, there was a rich man who had everything. Both die, and *both* end up in Sheol (called "Hades" in these verses—more on that later). But there's a difference: Lazarus is in comfort and the rich man is in torment.

The rich man "lifts up his eyes." This is interesting and revealing. All through the account, Jesus describes the souls of these two men in physical terms. Words like eyes, finger, and tongue are used. The soul is described as being capable of feeling pleasure and pain. This has caused some Bible students to assume that the soul receives another body in the next life.

The apostle Paul's words give credence to this idea: "For we know that if the earthly tent which is our house is torn down, we have a building from God, a house not made with hands, eternal in the heavens. For indeed in this house we groan, longing to be clothed with our dwelling from heaven, inasmuch as we, having put it on, will not be found naked. For indeed while we are in this tent, we groan, being burdened, because we do not want to be unclothed but to be clothed, so that what is mortal will be swallowed up by life" (2 Corinthians 5:1–4).

Paul may be saying that the soul does not continue on in a bodiless form, but is "housed" in a body God has prepared. This would agree with Jesus' use of bodily terms to describe Lazarus and the rich man.

The Bad Side of Town

When the rich man opens his eyes, he sees a world he could not imagine in his earthly life. He has full sensory capabilities, and for him, that is not good. He is in torment, and from that torment we learn several important things.

First, Sheol is a literal place for departed souls. Those souls are aware of themselves and their surroundings and have physical sensations.

They can also communicate. The rich man sees Abraham, recognizes him and Lazarus, and then makes two appeals: to be relieved of his suffering and to send Lazarus with a message to the rich man's family. Both requests are denied.

The reason the rich man is in such dire straits is not revealed, but some clues are given. When the rich man asks for some relief from his torment, Abraham says, "Child, remember that during your life you received your good things, and likewise Lazarus bad things; but now he is being comforted here, and you are in agony."

Then, when the rich man asks that Lazarus be sent back with a message to warn the rich man's family about their potential places in Hades, Abraham states, "They have Moses and the Prophets; let them hear them." From these two comments we can see that the rich man's crime was not his wealth, but his refusal to obey God's law as laid down in the books of Moses and the prophets.

The Good Side of Town

While the rich man was in torment, Lazarus was in comfort and peace. Jesus described Lazarus's place as in "Abraham's bosom." In this account, Lazarus says nothing. His physical sensations are not described. Abraham just states the fact that he was being comforted.

Why Abraham? Jesus is teaching in a Jewish setting. Abraham holds a unique place in Jewish history. He is the father of the Jews. Although not a perfect man, he was a righteous and faithful man, and his reward is great. The faithful Jew could expect an eternity of peace and comfort with Abraham.

In another New Testament scene, a different and intriguing term is used for the afterlife: "Paradise." While Jesus hung on the cross, one of the thieves crucified beside Him asks to be remembered when Jesus comes into His kingdom. Jesus' response is informative: "Truly I say to you, today you shall be with Me in Paradise" (Luke 23:43). Two important aspects jump out of that statement: time and place.

Jesus notes the time when the thief would be in paradise—that day! Even more important, it tells us that Jesus, too, would be in paradise that day. That day was crucifixion Friday, the afternoon Jesus died on the cross.

The word paradise is a "loan word." That means the term is not original to the Hebrew. Paradise is a Persian term and referred to the parks and gardens of the Persian kings. It is a beautiful expression that describes a serene, peaceful, comfortable place. Ancient Persian kings would honor certain individuals by allowing them to walk with them through their gardens. When Jesus tells the thief that he would be with Jesus in paradise, He is making the same magnificent gesture.

Sometimes it is useful to note what is *not* said. Jesus specifically used the word paradise and not heaven. Heaven is a word Jesus used many times in His ministry. The Lord's Prayer is just one example: "Our Father who is in Heaven, hallowed be Your name" (Matthew 6:9). The fact that He avoided the word He used so often before is significant. Jesus is being absolutely accurate. The thief was headed to heaven, but there was a stop to be made first. The thief would go where all the faithful went—paradise, also known as Abraham's Bosom.

Paradise is used only three times in the New Testament. First, in the passage about the crucified thief (Luke 23:42); then by the apostle Paul when he described a man he knew who "was caught up into Paradise and heard inexpressible words, which a man is not permitted to speak" (2 Corinthians 12:4); and lastly, in Revelation: "To him who overcomes, I will grant to eat of the tree of life which is in the Paradise of God" (Revelation 2:7).

Lazarus was in paradise, and paradise was the righteous side of Sheol. Note the past tense. Things changed when Jesus died. The apostle Paul makes an intriguing remark in his letter to the Ephesians. He wrote: "Therefore it says, 'When He ascended on high, He led captive a host of captives, and He gave gifts to men.' (Now this expression, 'He ascended,' what does it mean except that He also had descended into the lower parts of the earth? He who descended is Himself also He who ascended far above all the heavens, so that He might fill all things.)" (Ephesians 4:8–10).

It appears that after Jesus' death, but prior to His resurrection, He descended into Sheol/paradise and ministered to the righteous saints there. Then He lead them to heaven itself, where He would be and from where He would reign.

The Way It Used to Be

So what happened to the dead? On the Old Testament side of the cross, the souls of the departed went to Sheol. The righteous dead found themselves in paradise/Abraham's Bosom; the unrighteous discover that they have landed in a place of torment, just like the rich man in Jesus' account.

But why would there be torment now, if the final judgment has yet to occur? The final judgment has to do with the eternal habitation of the dead. Sin has already been judged. The purpose of the judgment is to allow everyone to confess that Jesus is Lord. Paul tells us that "for this reason also, God highly exalted Him, and bestowed on Him the name which is above every name, so that at the name of Jesus every knee will bow, of those who are in heaven and on earth and under the earth, and that every tongue will confess that Jesus Christ is Lord, to the glory of God the Father" (Philippians 2:9–11).

Paul makes an interesting choice in his words. He speaks of those "in heaven and on earth and under the earth." Under the earth? Sheol is always seen as under the earth—someplace unseen and unable to be visited by the living.

As It Stands Now

What happens to the dead on this side of the cross? Again, that depends on the relationship the person had with God. The believer is ushered into heaven. The righteous inhabitants of paradise were taken to heaven. Paul said, "We are of good courage, I say, and prefer rather to be absent from the body and to be at home with the Lord" (2 Corinthians 5:8). When a believer dies, he is immediately with the Lord in heaven. The unbeliever is a different matter. Sheol still exists, and the souls of those who reject Christ find themselves in the same place as the rich man until the final judgment.

Hades: Sheol by Any Other Name

Sheol is a Hebrew word and therefore doesn't appear in the New Testament; instead another word is used: Hades. There is much confusion about this word. In English, we tend to make Hades and hell synonymous, exchanging them freely and with little thought. However, there is a big difference.

Hades is the New Testament word for Sheol. It's the same place. Peter, for example, while giving his first sermon on the day of Pentecost, quotes an Old Testament passage from David. The passage is from Psalm 16:10: "For You will not abandon my soul to *Sheol;* nor will You allow Your Holy One to undergo decay." But when Peter quotes the phrase, he says, "Because you will not abandon my soul to *Hades,* nor allow Your Holy One to undergo decay" (Acts 2:27).

Hades and Sheol are the same place. However, Hades and hell are not.

The now serene valley of Hinnom was once used for child sacrifice. It became the symbol of hell.

Hell: A Valley to Be Avoided

If you could stand in Jerusalem during the time of Christ and look south of the city, you would see an acrid smoke rising in the air. Day and night the smoke continued upward, made by a fire that never went out. If you peered over the southern wall of the city, you would be looking down upon hell. Not the hell of eternal punishment, but the place where it got its name.

Hell is the word used by scholars to translate the New Testament word *gehenna,* and *gehenna* comes from the Hebrew *Ge-Hinnom,* which means "Valley of Hinnom." The valley is an actual place found directly south of Jerusalem. It is a place of some very unpleasant history, having been used by the Canaanites for pagan worship. It was there that parents would sacrifice their children to the god Molech. So pervasive was the religion that it continued on into Jewish times, seducing Canaanites and Jews alike.

In Jesus' day, the valley was used as the city garbage dump. What else would Jews do with a place associated with child sacrifice? Every unwanted and unclean thing went into that burning dump. Not just the refuse of the city, but dead animals and even the bodies of prisoners. It was a place of death and ugly decay; worms ate whatever wasn't being burned.

It was the place that Jesus used to describe hell.

The word Gehenna (hell) is found twelve times in the New Testament—eleven of those times it was uttered by Jesus. The only other appearance of the word is found in James 3:6, but that verse doesn't refer to hell as the place of future punishment. James had something else in mind. James 3 is about the power of the tongue to do evil. He says that the "tongue is a fire" that defiles the entire body and is "set on fire by hell (*gehenna*)." The picture is graphic: a tongue whose fire is lit by the vile burning of a garbage dump. His point is that the uncontrolled tongue is a repulsive thing.

The other eleven mentions of hell come from Jesus Himself and always in a very negative way. He goes so far as to call some of the religious leaders of His day children of hell (Matthew 23:15).

Hell is a place of future punishment. It is always referred to in a future sense as something that has not yet happened, but certainly will.

Technically, there is no one in hell at this moment. Hell is empty, but after the final judgment, that will change. While teaching about the future judgment, Jesus said, "Then He will also say to those on His left, 'Depart from Me, accursed ones, into the eternal fire which has been prepared for the devil and his angels'" (Matthew 25:41).

Notice several important points in this verse. First, hell was not prepared for humans, but for the devil and his messengers. However, those who reject Christ have the same end before them. "Prepared" is in the past tense, showing that hell already exists, but is empty until the future Great White Throne judgment. After that judgment, Satan and his minions and unbelievers through the ages share the same fate.

Also, Jesus refers to hell not by name, but by description. He calls it "the eternal fire." Literally, it is the "never-ceasing fire." Hell is often associated with flames. Of the twelve times the term is used, "fire" is used in half of the verses and implied in several more.

The Book of Revelation mentions a judgment that ends in a "lake of fire." The phrase is used six times and only in Revelation. The place is described as a fiery lake, burning with brimstone—a place of torment which is the "second death" (Revelation 20:6).

Revelation goes on to list all who will be cast into the lake of fire:
- the Beast
- the False Prophet
- the Devil
- death
- Hades (Sheol, now empty of believers)
- anyone whose name is not found in the Book of Life
- murderers, immoral persons, sorcerers, idolaters, and liars, along with those who are cowardly, unbelieving, and abominable

Some have made conjectures about where hell might be, but the truth is no one knows. Most likely, hell is not a place as we know it. It is real. It exists, but does so in a place beyond our ability to perceive. This is true for Sheol and heaven. The reality of existence does not depend on our ability to observe it. The entire subatomic world operates without our being able to see it, yet it is no less real.

Contrasts and Conflicts

Hell is described in the Bible. We've already seen references to a lake of fire burning with brimstone, but there's more. It is also described as being "outer darkness" (Matthew 8:12), where there will be the "weeping and gnashing of teeth." Mark reveals more unpleasantness about hell being a place "where their worm does not die, and the fire is not quenched" (Mark 9:48).

Some of these descriptions seem contradictory. How can there be darkness in everlasting fire? How can worms live in such conditions? The last one is the easiest to answer. They exist the same way the tormented lost do. Somehow, the body continues on despite the presence of fire. Hell is a place of torment for the lost—a torment that lasts for eternity. We cannot measure its heat, fix its location on a map, or describe its size. We simply know of its existence because Jesus gives us the facts.

Time-wise, because hell is a future punishment, it follows the resurrections. There are two resurrections—one for the righteous and one for the unrighteous. Jesus said: "Do not marvel at this; for an hour is coming, in which all who are in the tombs will hear His voice, and will come forth; those who did the good deeds to a resurrection of life, those who committed the evil deeds to a resurrection of judgment" (John 5:28–29).

Everyone is resurrected—the faithful to life and the unbelievers to judgment.

Abaddon

Another name is associated with death: Abaddon is a Hebrew term meaning "destruction" or "to perish." It is used seven times in the Bible—six times in the Old Testament and once in the Book of Revelation.

It is one of those words that either gets overlooked or quickly dismissed. In the six Old Testament references it is used as a place name. Three times it is associated with the word Sheol. For example, Job says, "Naked is Sheol before Him, and Abaddon has no covering" (Job 26:6). Twice in Proverbs is the phrase "Sheol and Abaddon."

Abaddon is also paired with other key words. Once it is coupled with "death" (Job 28:22), once with "grave" (Psalm 88:11), and once with "fire" (Job 31:12). Pretty negative company.

These few verses create a problem. If Abaddon is a place, then who occupies it? Is it different from Sheol? What we know is, like Sheol, Abaddon is always associated with death. In the verses where it appears with Sheol, it stands apart, indicating that it is somehow different. Just how it is different we are not told. Scripture reveals that God can see into Sheol and Abaddon and that neither place is satisfied. It is said that the dead go into Sheol, but the same is said of Abaddon.

The New Testament never mentions Abaddon as a place. The only occurrence of the word is in Revelation 9:11 where it is used as a personal name for an angel.

So what is it?

We are not told specifically, but we can make a small conjecture. Going back to Luke 16, we see the two compartments of Sheol. Sheol is the Old Testament catchall term for the abode of the dead. Lazarus resides in blessed comfort in Abraham's Bosom. This is the same place that Jesus speaks about from the cross when He says to the thief, "Today you shall be with Me in Paradise." As we have seen, this place has two names. But what was the name of the place in which the rich man suffered? Jesus did not say, but could it be Abaddon, whose very name means destruction?

There's a very good chance this is true. Both Lazarus and the rich man die and go to Sheol. Lazarus, however, is in a much better place. The rich man is in Abaddon. In Old Testament times, all the dead went to Sheol. The righteous dead went to Abraham's Bosom; the unrighteous to Abaddon.

Can we prove this? No. Since the Scripture doesn't state the matter plainly, we can only speculate. It does, however, answer many questions while keeping the fabric of Scripture intact.

Tartarus: The Overlooked Place

Humans are not the only beings that live through eternity. Angels, who are as real as your next-door neighbor, also have life. And like humans, some have sinned. Second Peter has a fascinating thought, "God did not spare angels when they sinned, but cast them into hell and committed them to pits of darkness, reserved for judgment" (2 Peter 2:4).

Angels are just as subject to God's law as humans. This passage does not state what sin the angels committed. (Although they are probably the sons of God mentioned in Genesis 6. All the other illustrations used in this chapter from 2 Peter are from the Book of Genesis.)

More interesting than what the angels have done is where they are. Every English translation says "cast them into hell." However, the word for hell (*gehenna*) is not in the verse. Instead, the passage reads "cast them into Tartarus." Tartarus is a Greek word that refers to a subterranean, gloomy realm where the unrighteous were kept in suffering. This is the only place in the Bible where the word is used. It appears these angels did something so hideous and criminal that they must be bound until their judgment.

Another verse supports this scenario in Jude 1:6: "And angels who did not keep their own domain, but abandoned their proper abode, He has kept in eternal bonds under darkness for the judgment of the great day."

It's hard to miss the similarities between Tartarus and Sheol. Both are places of bondage and gloom; both are temporary and will be emptied at some future date; and both are created by God.

Nothing else is revealed about Tartarus. All we know is that it is real and currently occupied by angels who have committed some grievous sin. The Bible's lack of revelation on this place is understandable. The place neither concerns nor involves humans. It is a matter between God and certain fallen angels. This is one of those cases in which we are reminded that the Bible tells us everything we need to know, but not everything there is to know. The curtain of mystery is still drawn on the topic.

What It All Means

In all honesty, we must admit that what we know about the intermediate state of the soul—that time between death and the Resurrection—is no more than a thimbleful of knowledge compared to our vast ocean of questions. God's word is purposely silent on some of these issues. We are not meant to understand all there is to know about hell, Sheol, Abaddon, and Tartarus. Instead, we are to focus on the One who delivers us from such places. Through Christ we find life and acceptance instead of judgment and punishment. That's what faith in Christ brings.

More to Think About

1. Hell is an unpleasant topic—one which many people avoid. Yet it is mentioned many times in the Bible. How does a belief in hell change our view of the world and of time itself?

2. Places other than heaven and hell are mentioned in the Bible but seldom discussed in the modern church. Why is that? Should there be more teaching about these places?

3. If the story Jesus tells in Luke 16 were a parable, would that change our understanding of Sheol?

4. It cannot be proved that the rich man's place of torment was the same place the Bible calls Abaddon. What difference would it make if they were not the same?

How the Bible Is Structured

The Bible is less a single volume and more a library of sixty-six books. These books form an encyclopedia of "God knowledge." Today many approach the Bible as if it's a novel or even a textbook. It is neither; instead it is a collection of books written more than fifteen hundred years ago, composed by more than forty authors in three languages on three continents. Like a jigsaw puzzle, each book fits in precisely the right place, unique from all the others, with a purpose in history and a current application.

Instead of seeing the Bible as a whole, we should see it in all its parts. Bible students should know the basic structure of the book that teaches them about faith. To understand the mysteries in the Bible, the Bible itself must first be understood.

The Bible is a structured book. The material contained in it hangs on a skeleton that shows a divine design. It is not an abstract collection of writings. It has a cohesiveness that could only come about from an orchestrated effort of a great Intelligence.

Two Parts of the Whole

The Bible is divided into two basic parts, but those parts are not mutually exclusive. One is the sword; the other, the hilt. Together they make a whole, and one interprets the other. The two parts are called the Old Testament and the New Testament.

Testament is a word that means contract or agreement. We use it today in legal matters, speaking of a last will and testament that contains the written directions a person makes for the disposal of his or her property after death. In one sense, the Bible is the same: It is God's written instruction about what should take place in our lives and in society in general. That instruction, however, is not a long set of commands. Instead, it contains historical accounts, letters, and love stories.

Testament also means covenant. A covenant is an agreement between people. The Old and New Testaments contain the agreement between God and humankind. It would be just as proper to refer to the Bible as the Old and New Covenants. Jesus brought a new covenant. At the Last Supper, Jesus said, "This cup which is poured out for you is the new covenant in My blood" (Luke 22:20). His death and resurrection brought a new agreement between God and humanity.

Within these two major divisions fall the books of the Bible.

Old Testament

The Old Testament has thirty-nine books and is divided neatly into five sections.

First, the law section which contains five books (often called by the Greek term Pentateuch, which means five books). In these books are the account of creation, the calling of Abraham as the father of the Jews, the Exodus, and the giving of the law.

Next are the twelve books of history. They begin with Joshua leading the people into the Promised Land and continue on through the conquest of Canaan, the reign of the judges and the kings, the capture and exile, the building and rebuilding of the temple, and more.

Poetry is the next section, and there are five books here also. The poetry section covers the story of Job through the great songbook called Psalms, the wisdom of Proverbs and Ecclesiastes, and the romantic work called the Song of Solomon.

The five major prophets follow the poetry section. These are called major because of the size of the books, not the importance of the prophet. Many of the great prophecies about Christ are found in the pages of Isaiah, Jeremiah, Lamentations, Ezekiel, and Daniel.

Following the major prophets are the twelve minor prophets. Again, the term minor refers to the size of the book (not the size of the prophet).

There's a pattern here: 5–12–5–5–12. There are 5 sections of 5 or 12 books.

New Testament

Like the Old Testament, the New Testament's twenty-seven books are divided into categories.

First are the Four Gospels that record the events of Christ's life. Each is written from a different perspective and highlights a different aspect of Jesus and His ministry.

The New Testament history book is found in the single volume of Acts, which records the first thirty years of the church.

Then come the Epistles. An epistle is a letter. These books were written to churches and contain the brass tacks of Christian living. Some deal with problems in the church and bad doctrine. All of them point to Christ.

The apostle Paul wrote the first section of letters. He was the most prolific writer of the group, penning thirteen letters. He may have, however, written fourteen. Hebrews contains no mention of its writer. Many think the apostle Paul wrote it; others think someone else put the pen to paper on that book. Most likely Paul was the writer.

The seven letters that follow are called the general Epistles, which is a catchall term for the various writers of those letters. The writers are James (one book), the apostle Peter (two books), the apostle John (three books), and Jude (one book).

The last book is Revelation, and it is a book of spectacular and sometimes mind-numbing prophecy.

Pieces of the Whole

Just as it is a mistake to see the Bible as a single book, it is also an error to see it as a collection of smaller writings. Like a steel bridge that is

The lower level of this wall dates to the first century and is from a synagogue in Capernaum.

composed of many pieces that are welded and riveted into one, so the Bible is a single unit made up of many lesser units. All these books are connected.

Genesis is reflected in the Gospel of John. Jesus quotes Psalm 22—a psalm that is a clear prophecy of His crucifixion—from the cross. The Book of Hebrews quotes scores of Old Testament passages and weaves them into a presentation of Christ's superiority. It is impossible to understand the Book of Revelation without understanding the Old Testament. Through prophecy and direct connection, all sixty-six books of the Bible tell one story, and it is the story of Jesus.

Fire from
Heaven

SOME STRANGE THINGS HAVE DROPPED from the sky. Man-made objects have left orbit and come crashing to the planet like the 143-ton Mir space station did in the spring of 2001. On June 30, 1908, a comet streaked through our atmosphere and exploded just above ground level in Tunguska, Siberia, laying waste to more than five hundred thousand acres of pine forest.

Through the pages of Scripture, we can travel back and see other things that have come from the sky (not man-made objects or even natural ones like the Tunguska comet, but supernatural ones). The most amazing of these heaven-sent objects is deadly fire.

The Bible records seven occasions in which fire descends from heaven. The most notable of these occurred in an area now known as the Dead Sea. Once a lush, well-watered paradise, it is now hot, smelly, and covered in salt. What happen to this place that was once home to several significant, thriving cities?

Sodom and Gomorrah
Genesis 19

It is hard to imagine that the sulfurous, salty Dead Sea was once considered a paradise, but it was. Today no extended cities are there, and few inhabit the area except for the occasional spa or factory. The Book of Genesis says, "Lot lifted up his eyes and saw all the valley of the Jordan, that it was well watered everywhere—this was before the LORD

CHAPTER THIRTEEN

destroyed Sodom and Gomorrah—like the garden of the LORD, like the land of Egypt as you go to Zoar" (Genesis 13:10).

Five cities—Sodom, Gomorrah, Admah, Zeboiim, and Zoar—were situated at the southern end of what is now called the Dead Sea. Only Zoar would survive the fiery destruction. After a split with his uncle Abraham, Lot set up house in Sodom, which proved to be a dangerous decision.

The names of the cities provide a nifty bit of foreshadowing. Sodom means "burning or scorching." Gomorrah means "submersion" or "heap," as in a heap of debris. Zoar, the city Lot fled to, can be rendered "little" or "insignificant." Today the names of Sodom and Gomorrah stand for wanton, aberrant behavior—a reflection on the activities of the once-thriving, evil townspeople.

Perhaps it was because of their success and the ease of their lives that the inhabitants of Sodom turned into the depraved people we find in the Bible. "Now the men of Sodom were wicked exceedingly and sinners against the LORD" (Genesis 13:13). God's patience reached its breaking point. The sin of the people, which included abhorrent sexual misconduct (the name of the crime sodomy comes from the name of the city), had become intolerable to God.

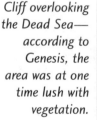

Cliff overlooking the Dead Sea— according to Genesis, the area was at one time lush with vegetation.

Genesis 19 tells the story of two angels sent to remove Lot from the city before its destruction. So evil were the citizens that they demanded access to the strangers, and no amount of pleading by Lot could control them. Banging on the door, shouting through the windows, the crowd was determined to take the newcomers by force. Attacking angels is never wise. Miraculously struck blind and supernaturally confused, the mob was thwarted. A short time later, they were obliterated in a fiery conflagration along with their city.

For reasons that are difficult to fathom, Lot resisted leaving the town, but the angels compelled him, dragging him and his family along.

Then the firestorm began.

"Then the LORD rained on Sodom and Gomorrah brimstone and fire from the LORD out of heaven" (Genesis 19:24). The air filled with acrid smoke as clumps of fiery sulfur fell upon animal, man, and every building in the area. An inferno followed. The area around the Dead Sea is known to be volcanic. Gases escaped from the ground and were ignited by the inferno.

"And He overthrew those cities, and all the valley, and all the inhabitants of the cities, and what grew on the ground" (Genesis 19:25). Four cities, jewels in the lush valley of the Great Rift, were destroyed by an inferno from the heavens. Gone were the people, the houses, and the public buildings. Even the vegetation in the area was destroyed. The number of dead must have been enormous.

Some scholars think the destruction was so intense that it closed off the outlet of the Jordan River. With no outlet, the river began to fill the valley until the lake known as the Dead Sea, the lowest body of water on earth, was formed. Centuries of evaporation have left the inland sea so dense with salt and other particulate matter that no life can live in its waters. Seven times saltier than the ocean, the Dead Sea is truly lifeless and remains a symbol of the high price of wanton sin.

But How Did It Happen?

It is impossible to determine conclusively how the sulfur (brimstone) and fire fell from the sky. What is clear is that this event was beyond nature. Some have attempted to attribute the destruction of the cities to volcanic activity or some other natural disaster, but the explanation doesn't match the text.

Several key points tell us that this was a divine act of judgment. Consider the timing: The rain of brimstone and fire did not start until Lot and his family were safely out of the way. The destruction was also precisely confined and controlled. There were five cities in the valley, but only four were destroyed. Zoar was spared because it was the only city to which Lot could flee. A natural disaster would not be so discriminating.

Where could so much sulfur and fire come from? It could only come from God. There have been great naturally caused explosions that have literally shaken the world—Krakatoa, a volcanic island in southwestern Indonesia, erupted on August 26, 1883, producing the loudest noise ever generated on Earth. It was heard three thousand miles away and produced tsunamis more than one hundred feet high. Thousands were killed. Still, there has never been anything in history to match the description found in Genesis. Sodom and Gomorrah were not victims of a natural disaster; they were the objects of God's judgment.

Job Loses It All
Job 1

Less spectacular than the demise of Sodom and Gomorrah is the fire from heaven that took Job's valued servants and belongings. The story of Job is tragic but revealing, showing that God is sovereign in all things. It is a lesson we learn through the life of Job.

The first chapter of Job describes a man who is "blameless, upright, fearing God and turning away from evil." We also learn that he is a man of great wealth with a wife, seven sons, and three daughters. His possessions included seven thousand sheep, three thousand camels, five hundred yoke of oxen (one thousand oxen), five hundred female donkeys, numerous servants and more. He was considered the "greatest of all the men of the east."

One day, all of those things and more were his; the next day, they were all gone. His animals were stolen, his servants were slaughtered, and his children were crushed to death.

In all this tragedy we find an interesting, puzzling phrase: "The fire of God fell from heaven and burned up the sheep and the servants and consumed them" (Job 1:16). What kind of fire could this be?

A Point of Clarification

The surviving servant bringing Job the bad news uses the phrase "fire of God" (the description is used only one other time in the Bible at an event we will see later). However, the first chapter of Job makes clear that the horrible troubles that fall upon Job are not the work of God, but of Satan. While it is true that God allows the testing, it is not He who sends the destruction. That weight rests squarely on the shoulders of Satan.

Why then the "fire of God" phrase? Perhaps for the same reason thunder was referred to as the "voice of God." Anything unusual and powerful was attributed to God. So it is here. To the servant's mind, from where else could such fire have come except from God. The Bible, however, carefully shows that it is Satan that wreaks the havoc in Job's situation.

Revealing Details

The temptation is to read "fire of God" as lightning. After all, it originates in the heavens and falls to earth. Many commentaries take this approach, but the details demand a different answer.

Notice the widespread death caused by the falling fire. The servant revealed that it killed sheep and servants. A few verses before this, we learn that Job had seven thousand sheep. No lightning strike could kill that many animals as well as a large number of servants. If the fire were lightning, then many repeated strikes would be necessary to kill thousands of sheep spread over a wide area.

One possibility is that the lightning started a fire that swept through grasslands, consuming the animals. This is a logical approach, but doesn't fit with the servant's account. The worker states that the death was caused by fire that came down from heaven, not a fire started by lightning.

Another detail that stands out deals with the extent of the destruction. Not only are man and animal killed, but they were also "consumed." The

Hebrew word '*akal* means "to devour" or "to eat." The fire did more than strike the living dead; it also consumed its victims.

When we put the details together, we have a fire that falls from the sky over an area large enough to hold seven thousand sheep and scores of servants, and continues to burn long enough to consume the bodies. This is no natural fire. Add to this the unusual fact that one servant was spared to deliver the message of destruction.

The exact nature of the fire is unknown. While it may have been the same type that fell upon Sodom and Gomorrah, it is impossible to know for sure. The Sodom and Gomorrah fire was accompanied by brimstone, something not mentioned here.

Could it be the result of natural causes like a meteor or a comet? Such things could cause widespread damage, and the heat generated by the impact would consume everything in its path. If this were an isolated incident, then such an interpretation would be tempting, but the event does not happen alone. It is the second in four successive calamities (slaughtered servants, stolen animals, and crushed children). It is the timing that indicates that something supernatural has occurred.

Don't Mess with Elijah
2 Kings 1:9–12

Elijah has the distinction of being the only person to see fire fall from heaven in two different situations. He is also the only human to call down such fire. In each case, Elijah stood opposite the supporters of the ancient cultic god Baal.

Baal was a regional god of fertility whose name means "lord." Often the name was followed by the name of a city or region: Baal-gad or Baal-hermon. The Phoenicians worshiped Baal with rites and sexual displays. Believing that it was Baal who would bring a good harvest, they felt compelled to please him, even to the point of sacrificing their children on fiery altars. This was not pleasing to God.

The Right Side and the Very Wrong Side
1 Kings 18

Elijah is considered the greatest Old Testament prophet. For most of his ministry, he stood against idol worship and proclaimed God with confidence. He faced an uphill job. King Ahab had followed his Phoenician wife's example and had become a worshiper of Baal. Jezebel, the king's wife, was a despicable woman who desired nothing more than to have every prophet of God killed. Elijah would stand for none of it.

Finally, Elijah proposes a showdown, a contest of the gods. He would pit his beliefs and life against those of the priests of Baal. He suggested that Mount Carmel be the place of the showdown. Ahab accepted his challenge.

The day came, and Elijah stood alone against 450 prophets of Baal and 400 prophets of Asherah (the female deity and Baal's consort). All Israel had been summoned to see the contest on Mount Carmel.

The test was simple: Each side would build a stone altar to be covered with wood to burn the sacrifice. However, no one was allowed to ignite the wood. That would have to be done supernaturally.

Baal was considered the god of the sky and fire. From the people's point of view, if any god could answer such a prayer as Elijah was suggesting, it would be Baal.

The prayers of the pagan prophets went up. To add power to their supplications, they danced and shouted and even cut themselves with knives, but Baal remained silent. The day wore on, tedious hour followed tedious hour, and still Baal remained as mute as his statues. No matter how much the prophets pleaded, no matter how deeply or often they cut themselves to show their dedication, nothing happened.

Finally it was Elijah's turn. He prepared his altar with twelve stones, one for each tribe of Israel. Then Elijah added an extra degree of difficulty: he soaked the offering, wood, and altar with water, until it trickled down and filled the trench surrounding the altar. No one could claim trickery here. Elijah had created an impossible situation. No man could light an altar so soaked with water. That, of course, was the point. (For additional comments about the water and altar, see chap. 15, "Wild Weather.")

His prayer was simple: "Answer me, O LORD, answer me, that this people may know that You, O LORD, are God, and that You have turned their heart back again" (1 Kings 18:37).

Then it happened. It came without the shouting and self-mutilation of the Baal prophets. It came without ceremony or tradition. It just came.

From the sky, fire descended and struck the altar, consuming not only the offering and wood, but also the water, the stone, and even the dust on the ground.

It's All in the Timing

As with other such miracles, the timing is important. Some might argue that by coincidence lightning struck and consumed the altar, but logic dismisses that idea. The fire that came from heaven was mentioned before the contest began as a condition of the showdown. Whichever god answered first would be declared the God of Israel.

Not only does fire descend from heaven, but it does so after Elijah has prepared the altar, made the sacrifice, covered it in water, and prayed. The text implies that the fire came the moment Elijah was done praying. Accuracy is also important. The fire struck the altar and nothing else.

What happened on Mount Carmel nearly three thousand years ago was a miracle in the truest sense. As in most cases involving heavenly fire, death was close by. Elijah killed every prophet of Baal and Asherah. At least 850 people died that day, not by fire, but by the man who called fire down to the altar. Jezebel and Ahab had sought to have every prophet of God murdered, but, instead, every prophet of Baal and Asherah was killed.

Fifty-One Plus Fifty-One

Mount Carmel was not Elijah's only experience with heavenly fire. After King Ahab is killed in battle, a new king arises—Ahaziah, the son of Ahab and Jezebel. He reigned only two years. His rule was cut short by a fall through the "lattice in his upper chamber." Most likely he fell through an upper window to the ground below. His injuries were severe and he feared death. Being the son of Jezebel and Ahab, he turns to Baal for advice, sending messengers to the city Ekron to inquire of Baalzebub. Baal-zebub, whose name means "lord of the flies," was the local god of Ekron.

On their way, the messengers meet Elijah who has a question from God for Ahaziah: "Is it because there is no God in Israel that you are going to inquire of Baal-zebub, the god of Ekron?" Then Elijah gives the bad news: The king's injuries would be fatal.

This was not what the king wanted to hear, so Ahaziah sends a captain with fifty men to seize the prophet. They find Elijah sitting on a hill and call to him: "O man of God, the king says, 'Come down.'"

Elijah's response is cryptic, but what follows is clear enough: "If I am a man of God," he says, "let fire come down from heaven and consume you and your fifty." And it did. Fifty-one men perished in a blaze.

But Ahaziah was not to be dissuaded. He sent another captain and fifty men. They delivered the same message. Elijah replied with the same words as before, and the "fire of God" came down and consumed the men.

A third set of men was sent, but this captain took a more respectful approach. With 102 dead bodies on the ground, we can understand why. His humility saved his life and the life of his men. Under orders of the angel of the Lord, Elijah came down from the hill.

The story ends with Ahaziah's death.

Details, Details

Again, fire from heaven is associated with death. This time, 102 men died because of a foolish king. Why fire? Ahaziah followed the pattern of his parents—placing his trust in Baal when it had been demonstrated that the Lord alone was God.

It's hard to understand why Ahaziah could not see the similarities between the fire on Mount Carmel and what happened to the first fifty-one men. The fire from heaven was a reminder of what had happened before. Still, he refused to see it.

As in the other cases of fire from above, we can see the accuracy that proves the miracle. The destructive fire struck just those fifty-one men. When another group arrived, the fire struck again, in the same place with the same result—an act hardly coincidental, but accurately fatal.

David's Sin
1 Chronicles 21

No king is better known than David. As a poet, musician, warrior, and political leader, he was a true Renaissance man. His name stands for integrity, honesty, and righteousness—most of the time. He was also a man of passion who could suffer lapses of logic and reason. His sexual indiscretion with Bathsheba is just one example. Another example, worse because of the number of deaths it caused, is the unfortunate, deadly census incident.

It's an unusual tale with dire consequences. As with Job, Satan is involved. "Then Satan stood up against Israel and moved David to number Israel" (1 Chronicles 21:1). This in itself is a great mystery, but the fact that it was Satan's idea speaks volumes about the nature of the task.

The census was a bad idea from the beginning. In Israel's unique situation, such an act was a sign of waning faith. David wanted a count of able-bodied warriors. In most cases, this would be wise, but Israel had a distinctive standing with God. Their strength was to be centered in God's might and direction, not in numbers of soldiers.

David assigned Joab to do the deed. Joab found the task unsettling and pleaded with David to skip the idea completely. This shows that David knew the act was one of disobedience. If Joab understood the act was evil in the sight of God, then why didn't David? "Why should he be a cause of guilt to Israel?" Joab asks (1 Chronicles 21:3). Later in the account we learn that Joab didn't finish the job because "the king's command was abhorrent" (1 Chronicles 21:6). He had had enough.

God was displeased with the census and the people of Israel paid for it. The crime was not theirs, but that of their leader. Still, they knew of it and tolerated the sinful behavior. Then as now, sin never exists in isolation: A person's sin can and does affect others. In this case, it led to the death of seventy thousand people from a plague.

Being a righteous man at heart, David realizes his transgression and his duty to repent. Interceding for his people, he buys a piece of property on which to build an altar for sacrifices to God. God accepts the offering and answers David "with fire from heaven on the altar of burnt offering" (1 Chronicles 21:26).

As in the other cases, fire descends from heaven to a specific spot at a specific time in response to a specific action of a person. No natural phenomena can explain such an event.

Fire in God's House
2 Chronicles 4–7

Solomon was David's son and successor. He was a man known for wisdom, wealth, and a great number of wives. It was Solomon who built the first temple. It was at that temple that another fire-from-heaven episode occurred.

The temple was a glorious structure meant to glorify God and serve as a spiritual focal point for the nation of Israel. Situated on Mount Moriah on the east side of Jerusalem, the temple became the center of worship for all Jews. David, since he was a man of war, was not permitted to build the structure, but was allowed to gather the material. It fell to Solomon to start and oversee the actual work. Work began in the fourth year of his reign (around 967 B.C.) and was completed around 960 B.C.

The work was staggering in size. Seventy thousand workers "carried burdens"; eighty thousand quarried stones. It took thirty-three hundred supervisors to watch over the project. The building was a work of art that stood ninety feet long, thirty feet wide, and forty-five feet high. Quality wood, fine stone work, gold plating, and detailed art were all woven into a building that was certainly one of the greatest wonders of the world.

Once construction was completed, the people gathered for the dedication. It was a remarkable affair. Priests went about their duties, music filled the air, and a sacrifice lay upon the altar that was outside the building. King Solomon voiced a magnificent prayer, and a cloud from God, representing His presence, filled and surrounded the temple. When Solomon had finished his dedication prayer, "fire came down from heaven and consumed the burnt offering and the sacrifices, and the glory of the LORD filled the house" (2 Chronicles 7:1). So intense was God's presence that the priest could not enter the temple.

This is one of the few times that fire from heaven is a good thing. Here it is a sign of acceptance, showing that the temple, the priestly activity, and the hearts of the people were pleasing and acceptable to God. Here, as with David, it is evidence of an offering freely given and freely accepted.

The Judgment of God

Unlike the fire-from-heaven episodes we've seen so far, this one has yet to happen. It's found in the cryptic Book of Revelation and deals with a time yet to be.

Revelation describes a thousand years of peace in which Christ reigns on Earth. It is a time of bliss—a time when the world is run as it should be. Satan is bound during that time. At the end of that millennium, Satan is released for a short period. A separating of the faithful from the pretenders occurs, with the latter following Satan in an armed rebellion against the reigning Christ.

Led by Satan, the armies surround "the camp of the saints and the beloved city [Jerusalem]." It is a futile act of desperation. Revelation 20:9 tells us the end of the story: "Fire came down from heaven and devoured them."

Fire from heaven, in most cases, was (and will be) a tangible sign of judgment. It's a judgment not made in private, but in public. It was rare. It was unusual. But according to the Bible, it was real.

More to Think About

1. While fire from heaven was mostly used as a sign of judgment, it was also used in two cases to show acceptance. How is it that such a thing can be used both in a positive and negative way? Are there other such acts of God?

2. Elijah experiences two episodes of fire from heaven. Is there some reason why this is so? What was special about Elijah?

3. Many have suggested that what happened to Sodom, Gomorrah, and the other cities of the plain was an unusual but natural phenomena. What response can be given to show otherwise?

4. Fire is a popular theme in the Bible. Are there other ways in which fire was used to impart a spiritual truth?

5. If the judgment events of Sodom and Gomorrah were repeated today, how do you think the world would respond?

Sin on the Slither

WHAT IS THE MOST IMPORTANT chapter in the Bible? Many would argue that it is Genesis 3. All of history hinges on the events described in the first few verses of that chapter. The universe itself was altered to such an extent that it will need to be destroyed and replaced by a new heaven and new earth (2 Peter 3:13).

The way people relate to one another, the conflict between nations, and the willingness of people to indulge in sin can be traced back to a single conversation at a particular location and a decision made in a moment. It was the most critical decision ever made by a human, but the idea began with someone far from human.

In Eden lived a man and a woman. The environment was perfect and pure. Gentle breezes wafted through trees adorned in supple green leaves. Overhead, an azure sky covered them in warmth and beauty. It was an idyllic world that was sullied in a single act of desire.

Every Sunday school student can recite the account of the serpent's deceit and Eve's gullibility. The overall picture is clear and unambiguous. It's the details that give us trouble.

The Players
Genesis 3

The cast of characters in this one-act play in Genesis 3 is small. Adam, the first man, is there. While the entire universe and everything in it was called into being by God's spoken word, Adam was formed and given life in a personal work of art as a sculpture, that only God could create. Adam names the animals and keeps the garden of Eden in shape. Intelligent, unique, and industrious, Adam represents the best man could ever hope to be: perfect in mind, body, and spirit.

Eve soon joins Adam. She, too, is handmade, but where Adam was taken from the dust of the ground, she was taken from Adam's side. His flesh gave rise to her flesh. Eve is the Grand Mother of all humanity.

Not only were they perfect in every sense—mind, body, soul, and environment—they were also perfect in what they did not have. They were faultless. They had no knowledge of sin. They had never seen it, never experienced it. They knew what everyone wishes to know: pure innocence.

All that humanity ever dreams of having, they had in abundance: peace, purpose, service, freedom from illness and decay, and no concerns about the future.

Eden was perfect; they were perfect—but that soon changed. A third character appears on the scene. He is the blemish on the face of perfection, the stain on an unadulterated world.

The Bible calls him "the serpent." But he is unlike anything found in nature today.

The Intrusion

"Now the serpent was more crafty than any beast of the field which the LORD God had made" (Genesis 3:1). Who was this serpent? What did he look like? How can he talk?

To find answers to these questions we must first rid ourselves of some erroneous ideas. In nearly every Sunday school room are pictures of Adam and Eve standing by a lush tree with an anaconda-size snake hanging on a branch. In Eve's hand is an apple. This is a picture that needs to be erased. What happened those many eons ago was far stranger.

In an uncharacteristic way, we are introduced to a creature that seems to be a bundle of contradictions. First, he is described as "the serpent." The word used here is *nachash,* and it has several meanings. In most cases, it is translated as "serpent." At the burning bush, when God tells Moses to throw down his staff, the staff is transformed into a *nachash.*

Yet the root of the word means something entirely different. It refers to an enchanter, someone who utters incantations and whispers magic spells. Perhaps the whispering of these ancient magicians sounded like a snake hissing because the word can also be translated "to hiss."

The root word could also refer to something shiny like bronze. In fact, it is translated that way in Genesis 4:22. The serpent could be referred to as the "shining one."

The passage also says that the serpent was craftier "than any beast of the field which the LORD God made." Was the serpent a beast of the field? In our culture we divide animals by physical characteristics. If an animal has hair, gives birth to its young, and nurses its babies, we call it a mammal. If it lays eggs and has feathers, we define it as a bird. The ancient Jews categorized animals by their habitat. If it swam in water, it

Artist rendering of the serpent in the garden

was fish; thus, a whale was a fish. If it flew in the sky, then it was a bird; thus, a bat would be considered a bird.

Another question is, Was the serpent a beast of the field or is the passage just telling us that the creature was shrewder than those animals? It's hard to say. If he was a beast, then he was like no beast we see today. Not only was he crafty—a term that implies human intelligence—but he possessed the ability to communicate and to think in the abstract. Although not stated, it appears that the creature planned the confrontation with Eve. He initiates the conversation with a question, an inquiry that twists God's words. "Indeed, has God said, 'You shall not eat from any tree of the garden?'" (Genesis 3:1). What is puzzling is how the serpent knows what God did or did not say. Was this an assumption on his part, or did he have some insight into the relationship between God and the first couple? The Bible shows God giving that statement to Adam, not the animals.

Eve was quick enough to note that the statement was incomplete. In Genesis 3:2–3, she says, "From the fruit of the trees of the garden we may eat; but from the fruit of the tree which is in the middle of the garden, God has said, 'You shall not eat from it or touch it, or you will die.'" The "touch it" part was an addition by Eve. At least she was being cautious.

It is here that we begin to see the evil side of the *nachash*. "You surely will not die!" It's one thing to be intelligent, but quite another to be evil. Not only does he say that God has lied (or at least doesn't know what He is saying), he goes on to attribute selfish motives to God. "For God knows that in the day you eat from it your eyes will be opened, and you will be like God, knowing good and evil."

Eve gave in. She did so, not just on the word of the serpent, but because she was attracted to the fruit for its beauty and its ability to make her wise. The irony is hard to overlook: Wanting to be wise, she did a very foolish thing. To make matters worse, Adam followed suit.

Then they realized they were naked. What the serpent achieved was enticing the first couple to give away the power of their innocence to embrace the weakness of sin. The pun here that we miss in our English translations involves the Hebrew word for "shrewd" (*awrom*) and the Hebrew word for "nude" is (*eyrom*). There is only a slight difference in the spelling. Wanting to be "shrewd," Adam and Eve learned that they were "nude."

Condemnation follows the act, and in the judgment we learn more about the *nachash*. "The LORD God said to the serpent, 'Because you have done this, cursed are you more than all cattle, and more than every beast of the field; on your belly you will go, and dust you will eat all the days of your life; and I will put enmity between you and the woman, and between your seed and her seed; He shall bruise you on the head, and you shall bruise him on the heel'" (Genesis 3:14–15).

The curse provides a few more clues about the nature of the serpent. The serpent is cursed more than all cattle, more than every beast of the field. This is revealing. If an evil force possessed the serpent, then why curse the creature and not the force?

The curse includes a transformation: "On your belly you will go," implying that prior to the curse the serpent was in some position other than on its belly. Perhaps it stood upright on two or more legs. We are not told, but the physical alteration is meant to be demeaning, forcing something "shiny" and "shrewd" to spend its days moving along the dirty ground.

The curse is severe and rightly so. Because of his guile and Adam and Eve's surrender to temptation, sin entered the world. What we see today is a result of the catastrophe that took place that dark day in the garden.

Why would the serpent be so inclined to ruin perfection?

The Traditional View

For centuries Bible students have assumed that the serpent is Satan in disguise. This was the belief of the ancient Jews and the early Church. The idea has much to commend it, but it raises more questions than it answers.

It is true that Satan is portrayed as a serpent in Scripture, but not often. Revelation 12:9 is one such passage: "And the great dragon was thrown down, the serpent of old who is called the devil and Satan, who deceives the whole world; he was thrown down to the earth, and his angels were thrown down with him." So he is called the dragon, the serpent of old, the devil, Satan, and a deceiver. Certainly some of those appellations would apply to the serpent in the garden. In fact, they fit like a well-tailored suit.

Some of those terms are repeated in Revelation 20:2: "And he laid hold of the dragon, the serpent of old, who is the devil and Satan, and bound him for a thousand years."

There's no doubt that Revelation sees Satan as a deceiver and tempter. Jesus had something to say about it, too, when speaking to the Pharisees: "You are of your father the devil, and you want to do the desires of your father. He was a murderer from the beginning, and does not stand in the truth because there is no truth in him. Whenever he speaks a lie, he speaks from his own nature, for he is a liar and the father of lies" (John 8:44).

The Bible also informs us that "Satan disguises himself as an angel of light" (2 Corinthians 11:14) and that "the devil has sinned from the beginning" (1 John 3:8). The behavior of the serpent certainly fits these descriptions, but not everything adds up.

A Fly in the Garden Soup

It well may be that the serpent is Satan in disguise, but we are left with some questions.

First, why does God curse the serpent and not Satan? Why isn't Satan's identity mentioned?

There are several Old and New Testament passages that mention the events in the garden of Eden. None of them mention Satan. Paul, fearing that the believers in Corinth might be led astray, wrote: "But I am afraid that, as the serpent deceived Eve by his craftiness, your minds will be led astray from the simplicity and purity of devotion to Christ" (2 Corinthians 11:3). Paul sticks with the Genesis term of serpent.

We must also ask how Satan used the serpent. Did he possess its body like the demons we read about in the New Testament? If so, then why is the *nachash* punished? Why does God direct His conversation to the serpent and not to the satanic possessor?

Who Was the Mystery Serpent?

If we assume that it was not Satan in the garden, then we must ask who it was. The Bible does speak of other intelligent creatures. Different types of angels—such as the living creatures with four faces and four wings found in Ezekiel 1 are mentioned—but there is no record of a walking, talking *nachash* anywhere else in the Bible. Genesis 3 stands alone in this regard.

The mystery will remain for now. The best we can do is follow the New Testament example of Paul (2 Corinthians 11:3) and call the serpent in the garden "the serpent."

The Bottom Line

Does it really matter? Yes and no. Yes, in the sense that as students of the Bible, we want to understand as much as we can, which requires study and a questioning mind. The passage appears in the Bible, and we are duty-bound to know as much as possible about it. On the other hand, there are things we are not meant to know. The apostle Paul speaks of a man who glimpsed heaven and "heard inexpressible words, which a man is not permitted to speak" (2 Corinthians 12:4). We are not told why those words were forbidden. We know of the event, but not the details. The same is true of the serpent: We know the fact of the temptation and its outcome, but the details are not revealed.

Likewise, John in Revelation 10:4 records, "When the seven peals of thunder had spoken, I was about to write; and I heard a voice from heaven saying, 'Seal up the things which the seven peals of thunder have spoken and do not write them.'" We don't know what he heard because we were not meant to know.

Perhaps the same can be said here. We do know that the event was real, that a serpent beguiled Eve, and she and Adam sinned. We also know that sin brought a curse upon each of them in particular and humanity in general.

What matters in this account is that the sins of the guilty have effects on the innocent, that personal responsibility cannot be laid at the feet of another, that sin always has a price, and that God loves us enough to pay that price.

More to Think About

1. The exact nature of the serpent remains a mystery. Does our not knowing certain details change what we do know? Does it make a difference to our doctrine if the serpent was not Satan or Satan-possessed?

2. As pointed out in this chapter, there are several occasions in the Bible in which information is withheld from the reader. Why are some spiritual matters kept secret?

3. When the serpent speaks, Eve doesn't appear to react to the fact that an animal can carry on a conversation. Why is that?

4. Why is it that Satan is never associated with the garden of Eden in the Bible? If Satan was the serpent (or in control of the serpent), then why doesn't the apostle Paul mention that in 2 Corinthians 11:3?

Wild Weather

TECHNOLOGY ENABLES US TO MONITOR, chart, and even predict what the weather will be like over the next few days. And scientists can show what the weather was like thousands of years ago from studying cores of glacial ice and tree rings. We know a great deal about the weather, but we can't do anything about it. We rise from our beds in the morning, look out the window, then take whatever comes our way. We have no choice. The weather is what it is.

That was certainly true in biblical days. The people of the Bible were farmers and ranchers. They were dependent on rain for water and the sun for warmth. If the rains failed to come, crops withered and livestock died. These concerns prompted idol worship in the days of the Old Testament, particularly to Baal, the god of fertility. Rain and crops were supposedly in his control, so everyone was dependent upon him for survival—or so thought the Canaanites. So important was weather and its affect on crops that the Canaanite people often sacrificed their children in hopes of pleasing a pagan god like Baal. The Bible is clear that weather is controlled by God and has often been used for some strange effects in His work.

Rain

Israel has a typically Mediterranean climate that varies according to altitude and location. Most rainfall occurs in the winter months of

November to February, with more rain falling in the north and west. Upper Galilee receives about forty inches of rain each year. Further south, the average drops to thirty inches. Around the Dead Sea, rainfall is rare—as little as one inch for an entire year. Biblical times were not much different—at least, not normally.

The word rain appears nearly one hundred times in the Bible. On several occasions, the rain is more than mere precipitation; it's a message from God. The first mention of rain in the Bible is actually a reference to the absence of rain. "Now no shrub of the field was yet in the earth, and no plant of the field had yet sprouted, for the LORD God had not sent rain upon the earth, and there was no man to cultivate the ground" (Genesis 2:5). Rain isn't mentioned again until the day Noah was commanded to enter the ark. During Adam's day, the garden was not watered by rain but by a mist (Genesis 2:6). Some scholars have speculated that the earth did not see true rain until Noah's day. If so, then rain would have been a unique experience, if an unpleasant one.

The Biggest: Noah

The Bible's presentation of the flood shows a global catastrophe. In fact, Jesus used the Greek term *kataklusmos* instead of the usual word for flood (Matthew 24:39; Luke 17:27; 2 Peter 2:5). *Kataklusmos* became our word "cataclysm." This was a flood like no other: "all the fountains of the great deep burst open, and the floodgates of the sky were opened" (Genesis 7:11). For forty days and nights, water fell unceasingly from the sky. We don't know how much water came down, but it was enough to cover the earth.

The current record for the most rainfall in a short period took place at Basse Terre, Guadeloupe, an island in the Caribbean. On November 26, 1970, a storm dropped 1.8 inches of rain in one minute! That's the equivalent of nine feet of rain in a single hour. In Cherrapunji, Meghalaya, India, 366 inches of rain fell in a single month—that's more than thirty feet of rainfall! As events like these are the result of natural forces, consider the deluge possible when the supernatural forces of God are applied. Then what we read in Genesis is not only believable, but also highly credible.

Rain, mixed with the "fountains of the deep," brought a flood of monumental proportions. So much so that the waters covered the highest mountains by fifteen cubits of water (approximately twenty-two feet). The ark came to rest in the mountains of Ararat. Today Ararat peaks at seventeen thousand feet. How tall the mountain was in Noah's day cannot be ascertained, but even if it were only half its current height, the flood would still be remarkable.

In early 1993, scientists claimed the discovery of a freshwater flood, presumably from a large lake seventy-five miles long and twenty-five hundred feet deep. The flood, which investigators say took place eighteen thousand years ago in the Altay mountains of Russia, began when an ice dam gave way, releasing water in a one hundred-mile-per-hour torrent. Other such floods have been discovered in various places of our planet. There is even evidence that our planetary neighbor Mars once had water in abundance, enough to scar its now-dry surface.

Noah's flood exceeded all of these; it lasted far longer, was far deeper, and covered the whole planet. Some have doubted the flood was global, but even a casual reading of the account shows that a worldwide flood was described. All but eight people died in the deluge. It was the first time in Scripture that a natural phenomenon was used as judgment against sin.

Not every supernatural rainstorm was so destructive or widespread.

Elijah's Cloudburst
1 Kings 18:41–45

An abundance of rain can be used as a tool of punishment, as can an absence of rain. Famine was common in biblical times. Abraham and Jacob both traveled to Egypt to escape food shortages. Similar events occurred during the days of David and Elijah. Sometimes, the famine arose because of sin. This was certainly true for a drought that occurred during the reign of the wicked King Ahab and the godly prophet Elijah. Elijah stood before Ahab and gave the dire prediction: "As the LORD, the God of Israel lives, before whom I stand, surely there shall be neither dew nor rain these years, except by my word'" (1 Kings 17:1). Then Elijah skipped town. According to the Book of James, Elijah's prophecy was carried out to the letter: "Elijah was a man with a nature like ours, and he prayed earnestly that it would not rain, and it did not rain on the earth for three years and six months" (James 5:17). Rains were needed every year. A single year of insufficient rain could be disastrous; three and one-half years would have been devastating. Yet, because of Ahab's persistence in doing wrong, his nation suffered. Drought was one of the promised results of forsaking God to worship idols: "Do not turn away and serve other gods and worship them. Or the anger of the LORD will be kindled against you, and He will shut up the heavens so that there will be no rain and the ground will not yield its fruit; and you will perish quickly from the good land which the LORD is giving you" (Deuteronomy 11:17). So severe was the drought, Elijah himself had to be preserved through miraculous feeding.

To end the drought, God told Elijah to deliver a new message to Ahab: Rain would come soon. But before that could happen, Elijah would have a face-off with 450 prophets of Baal and 400 prophets of Asherah to see whose god would send fire to consume an offering. In that confrontation, fire came from the dry heavens and consumed Elijah's offering, wood, altar, and the very dust of the ground even after the altar had been soaked in water, a very precious commodity at the time.

God had answered Elijah's prayer. This was a slap in the face of Baal and the people who had cried out to Baal. God proved who was really in charge of all things. The false prophets of Baal and Asherah were slain.

Then Elijah climbed Mount Carmel. Crouching down on the ground and putting his head between his knees, he sought the Lord to bring rain. We are not told how long he stayed in that position, but he refused to rise even to check the horizon for clouds. Instead, he sent his servant to climb the rise and peer out over the sea. The servant came back with a negative report: the sky was clear. Six more times the servant would walk from Elijah to farther up the mountain until he could see the deep blue of the Mediterranean and the hot, dry azure sky above it. On the seventh trip, the servant saw something different: In the distance was a small cloud hovering above the horizon—a cloud no bigger than a man's hand.

That was what Elijah was waiting for. He needed no further evidence of answered prayer.

Elijah rose and sent the servant with a message: If Ahab didn't want his chariot to get bogged down in the rain and mud, then he had better leave quickly. Did this conclusion come from just the sight of a tiny cloud? No, Elijah had received word that rain would be sent; all he needed was to wait for the first sign. Things happened quickly. Rain, miraculous rain, came. A storm of wind, black clouds, and sheets of glorious water fell from God's heaven to the parched earth.

Samuel's Storm

Nine hundred and thirty years before Christ, another event of supernatural rain occurred, this time with the prophet Samuel. An old man, he had anointed Saul as the first king of Israel. It was something the people had wanted, but Samuel strongly opposed. Reluctantly, he submitted to the will of the people and, under God's direction, appointed Saul as king. In a message to the people, Samuel demonstrated his innocence in all matters, ending his message by saying, "'Is it not the wheat harvest today? I will call to the LORD, that He may send thunder and rain. Then you will know and see that your wickedness is great which you have done in the sight of the LORD by asking for yourselves a king.' So Samuel called to the LORD, and the LORD sent thunder and rain that day; and all the people greatly feared the LORD and Samuel" (1 Samuel 12:17–18).

What makes this remarkable (and therefore a cause of fear for the people) is the timing of the storm. Wheat was gathered around the end of June to early July—a time when rain was very rare; in fact, it would have been considered remarkable. But because of Samuel's prayer, rain and thunder came. The people saw it as a sign from God.

Hail

Joshua 10:11

Other things fall from the sky. While rain can be destructive, causing flash floods, erosion, and crop loss; hail can be worse. Most hail is no larger than raindrops, but it can be larger . . . much larger. Hailstones have been reported to weigh in excess of two pounds. A sudden hailstorm can injure crops, kill livestock, and even damage buildings. On April 14, 1986, large hailstones in Bangladesh killed ninety-two people. Hail has been known to fall in such quantities that the ground is covered several inches thick.

The psalmist said, "Fire and hail, snow and clouds; stormy wind, fulfilling His word" (Psalm 148:8). As with rain, hail has been used as a tool against evil. Moses stood before Pharaoh, the world's most powerful man in his day, and made a promise no man could fulfill: "Behold, about this time tomorrow, I will send a very heavy hail, such as has not been seen in Egypt from the day it was founded until now" (Exodus 9:18). And it happened. At the command of the Lord, Moses raised his hands and the sky erupted in ominous, rolling thunder, piercing bolts of lightning, and a hailstorm such as had never been seen in Egypt. Barley and flax were severely damaged; animals and humans injured. So relentless was the hail that Pharaoh summoned Moses and pleaded for relief. Moses walked outside the city and raised his hands, and the hail stopped as quickly as it started—as though a switch had been thrown.

The successor to Moses, Joshua, knew something about hail too. In Joshua 10:11 is the strange account of a battle that went bad for the enemy. In a confrontation with a coalition of Canaanite kings, Joshua brought his battle skills to bear and drove off the offending army, but the battle wasn't over. As the army fled, "large stones" fell from the sky killing more men than the hand-to-hand battle had. The passage is even more intriguing since the Lord Himself is said to have thrown the stones.

Hail is mentioned as future punishment in the Book of Revelation. Frightening, gruesome pictures are painted of "hail and fire, mixed with blood" cascading down on the ground, killing a third of the trees, grass, and earth (Revelation 8:7). Even more terrifying is Revelation 16:21: "And huge hailstones, about one hundred pounds each, came down from heaven upon men; and men blasphemed God because of the plague of the hail, because its plague was extremely severe."

Hail is a natural occurrence in the world, but none of these accounts can be classified as natural. Their size, degree, destruction, timing, and accuracy show their supernatural origin.

Wind

Wind is another force beyond the control of men. Its sweet breeze can cool a hot day, carry seeds to germinate in fields, clear the air, and more. It can also knock down buildings, run ships aground, and stir up sandstorms. Wind appears in the Bible frequently—more than 145 times. God used wind to diminish the flood (Genesis 8:1) and to divide the Red Sea (Exodus 14:21–22). It was a powerful wind that destroyed the house of Job's children, ending their lives (Job 1:18–19).

Paul's Travels

Some winds have earned their own names. At the end of the apostle Paul's ministry, he was taken by ship to Rome as a prisoner. In Acts 27, we are told of the difficult weather Paul and his shipmates endured. Paul warned the crew to dock in a safe harbor and to winter there, avoiding the driving wind. His words fell on deaf ears. Pushing their luck, the crew voted to continue on toward a sheltered harbor on the south side of the island of Crete. Once there, they would sit out the winter.

They should have listened to Paul. A wind so fierce that it carried its own name, Euraquilo, came screaming off the island, pushing the ship away from land with such force that the crew could do nothing but hang on and ride out the storm. The meaning of Euraquilo is uncertain. Some scholars think it is the equivalent of "northeaster"—the storms that often savage the East Coast of the United States. The word is a compound term, combining two Greek words "wind" (*euros*) and "wave" (*kludon*). In other words, Euraquilo was a wind-driven storm much like a hurricane.

Battered by uncontrollable wind and sea surges, the creaking ship was blown away from Crete and south of a small island called Clauda. The ship carried 266 passengers, some crew, and some prisoners. They battled the storm for fourteen days until, wearied by lack of food and great exertion, they ran aground on the island of Malta, south of Sicily.

While Paul and the others survived, there was no doubt that the wind was the winner. Was this wind a tool in the hand of God?

Moses and the Miracles

Wind played a significant role in the miracles of Moses.

One of the ten plagues leveled against Pharaoh and the Egyptians was swarming locusts. Millions of the insects descended on the land, eating what crops had survived the previous plagues. They covered the ground so that it could not be seen. No Egyptian could take a step without crushing the insects underfoot. The bugs filled their houses, covered their streets, and crawled on the walls of their temples, palaces, and pyramids. "There had never been so many locusts, nor would there be so many again" (Exodus 10:14). Pharaoh called for Moses and Aaron, pleading for an end to the plague. It was granted, but how does one get rid of countless millions of insects. Fire? Water? No. Wind.

"So the LORD shifted the wind to a very strong west wind which took up the locusts and drove them into the Red Sea; not one locust was left in all the territory of Egypt" (Exodus 10:19). One day the land was covered in locust; the next day, they're gone. Locust can control almost any force by their sheer number, but wind was too much for them. God chose the most efficient manner to rid the land of the pests.

Wind played an important role in one of the greatest miracles in the Bible. Moses was leading upwards of a million people out of Egypt. Before them was a large body of water called the *Yam Surph*. No one is certain exactly which body of water this was. The term means Reed Sea (*surph* is Egyptian for "reed"). Whether this is the body of water we now call the Red Sea or another is impossible to determine.

The details of the parting of the Red Sea are fascinating. The people are in a near-panic because the Egyptian army is pursuing them. Each moment that passes brings the Hebrews closer to death. Before them lay an obstacle too great to cross. They cry out for help, and Moses turns to God. God's answer is short and to the point: "Why are you crying out to Me? Tell the sons of Israel to go forward." At God's instruction, Moses raises his staff, and something strange begins to happen: "Then Moses stretched out his hand over the sea; and the LORD swept the sea back by a strong east wind all night and turned the sea into dry land, so the waters were divided" (Exodus 14:21). The Israelites cross the body of water on dry land. That's an important detail. Had the seafloor remained soft, the people would never have made it across in time. The sea is also said to have been like a wall on either side of them. This is remarkable. How does wind divide waters and hold them in place, yet allow the moving of men, women, and children across the area without impeding their journey? Wind of that magnitude would crush people, yet they walk across safely. This was no normal wind.

Sailors are familiar with wind-driven waves. When the wind reaches high speeds, it can push water along in great piles of waves. Rogue waves have been known to swamp ships with the destructive force of a tsunami. Here, God divides a large body of water and holds it in place by the power of wind. When the Egyptians arrive on the scene, they charge after their prey. At that moment, the wind stops, the waters crash in, and the entire army is drowned.

As with all miracles involving nature, the timing is important. Not only does God divide the sea, but He also holds it in place until His people are safely across, and then uses it to destroy the Egyptians.

Elijah's Whirlwind Trip

Everything surrounding Elijah was impressive. He could call fire from heaven, have the dead raised, and more. His exit from this planet was no different.

Elijah's ministry had come to an end, and the mantle (literally) was being passed to his successor, Elisha. It's a poignant moment as the two men walk along, both knowing that separation is near. There is a strong bond between the two men, and Elisha is as loyal to Elijah as a man can be. As they travel, something remarkable appears before them: a fiery chariot and horses. "As they were going along and talking, behold, there appeared a chariot of fire and horses of fire which separated the two of them. And Elijah went up by a whirlwind to heaven" (2 Kings 2:11). The term whirlwind is often used to describe a storm. It is the same word that would be used to portray a hurricane. Hurricane or storm, it took Elijah into God's arms, and he was no more.

Storms on the Water

Sudden storms are not unusual on large bodies of water. The Sea of Galilee is situated seven hundred feet below sea level and surrounded by mountains and hills. When an air mass moves from the Mediterranean over the coastal plains, it can be funneled through ravines where it encounters warm air rising from the inland sea. When that happens, powerful storms are created. Fishermen who work the sea know that such storms can come quickly and viciously.

It was such a storm that Jesus and the disciples faced early in the Lord's ministry. While Jesus slept in the rear of the boat, a storm descended on the disciples, some of whom were seasoned fishermen. It didn't take long for them to realize that the end was near. We can hear the fear in their voices as they woke Jesus and cried, "Save us, Lord; we are perishing!" (Matthew 8:25). Few things are as frightening as facing

The tranquil Sea of Galilee can turn fierce in a very short time.

angry nature. The wind and waves had cowered the disciples and would have done the same to anyone else. The storm was described as a *megas seismos*. *Megas* means "big, enormous," but *seismos* is the word normally used for "earthquake." Literally, it means "a shaking." The boat was being tossed about like a cork—its hull shaking from the force of the storm. There is no doubt that the disciples thought they had seen their last hour.

But Jesus was in the boat. Rising from His sleep, He first rebukes the disciples for their lack of faith, and then rebukes nature itself. Suddenly the tumultuous sound of wind and waves and the trembling of the boat came to an abrupt stop, replaced by stillness and eerie calm. The disciples are more than amazed. Such things cannot happen. They may not have understood the physics of meteorology or comprehended the effects of warm air encountering moist cold air, but they did know that such storms did not simply cease to be. Yet Jesus had made that very thing happen.

Jesus would later prove His mastery over weather again on the same sea (Matthew 14:22–32). After feeding the five thousand, Jesus sends His disciples away in the boat while He stays behind to rest and pray. The disciples were having a rough trip. The wind was contrary and the sea stormy. In the wee hours of the morning, Jesus starts out across the water, literally walking on its surface. It's one of the greatest pictures in the Bible: A peaceful Jesus walking through a tumultuous storm unaffected. Peter, feeling a moment of confidence, steps out into the storm, walking toward Jesus, but once outside the boat, he does a very human thing: he looks around and realizes that he is doing the impossible. The wind is too high and the waves too strong. He begins to sink. Jesus comes to his rescue.

Then, while the storm still raged, Jesus stepped into the boat. The wind immediately ceased.

Weather has been both a tool of God and evidence of Christ's deity. It has been used to thwart man's sin and display God's power. Although we must take whatever weather comes our way, we can know that God—who can control the wind, water, rain, and hail—can also care for us.

More to Think About

1. In the Old Testament, severe weather was used as judgment against sin. Jesus on the other hand, stopped storms. What does this say about Christ's ministry and purpose? Some verses to consider: John 3:17 and 12:44–50.

2. What makes supernatural weather special is its source, timing, accuracy, and purpose? Can the same be said for other miracles?

3. Jesus said, "But I say to you, love your enemies and pray for those who persecute you, so that you may be sons of your Father who is in heaven; for He causes His sun to rise on the evil and the good, and sends rain on the righteous and the unrighteous" (Matthew 5:44–45). Why do the evil benefit from good weather? Why do the good suffer in bad weather?

4. From April 3 through April 4, 1974, 148 tornadoes ripped through the southern and midwestern states, causing tremendous damage. A series of monsoons swept through Thailand in 1983, killing ten thousand people, infecting one hundred thousand people with diseases and causing more than $400 million in damages. Were these an act of God? Is God responsible for such tragedies?

The Ark of the
Covenant

NO OBJECT IS MORE VALUABLE, more sought after, more debated, more maligned, or more coveted than the golden chest known as the ark of the covenant. It has been the subject of countless books and documentaries. Men have invested thousands of dollars to search for it, and claims of discovery have been made through the years, yet it has never been seen. If every story is to be believed, then the ark is in Ethiopia, or in a cave at a place known as Jeremiah's mountain, or under the Dome of the Rock in Jerusalem, or in Egypt, or it has been destroyed. But not every story told by scholar, treasurer hunter, or archaeologist can be correct.

Although the location and condition of the ark remain unknown, we do know a great deal about the mysterious object itself. No other article in the Bible is so detailed in description as the ark and the tabernacle in which it resided. Its very design comes from the Almighty through Moses to the most gifted craftsman among the Israelites.

From above the ark the voice of God would speak audibly to Moses. Its presence represented the very attendance of God. The ark was there when the people left the wilderness, crossed the Jordan, and entered the Promised Land. It was there when the walls of Jericho fell. It was in its place when Solomon finished the temple. The ark was at the heart of holiness. Then it disappeared, never to be seen again.

No archaeological discovery would be more important or valuable. The worth of the ark is inestimable, although its value does not come from the gold that plated its interior and exterior, but from its place in history, the people who touched it, and what it carried. The gold would be secondary except to the greediest of men. To see the ark is to see a device unlike anything else in history.

The Biggest Little Box

The word ark has confused many. The Hebrew word is 'aron which means nothing more than "box" or "chest" and should not be confused with the ark associated with Noah, which translates a different word (tebah). Basically, the ark was a container to hold and carry certain holy objects. The same Hebrew word is used to describe a coffin. "So Joseph died at the age of one hundred and ten years; and he was embalmed and placed in a coffin ['aron] in Egypt" (Genesis 50:26). Jehoiada the priest made an offering box to receive money. He did so by taking a chest ('aron) and boring a hole in its lid (2 Kings 12:9). The word ark, therefore, is not significant, but the ark itself is.

Boxes such as the ark are not unique. A similar chest was found in the tomb of the Egyptian boy-king Tutankhamen. It's very likely that the craftsmen who built the ark learned their trade while in Egyptian captivity.

Construction

The construction of the ark is one of the things that make it unique. It was designed by the Lord, but built by man. A select group of craftsmen were chosen. They included Bezalel and Oholiab. These men were handpicked by God to build the world's most amazing object. They were also given a creative boost by God, who acknowledged, "In the hearts of all who are skillful I have put skill, that they may make all that I have commanded you" (Exodus 31:6). Bezalel and Oholiab lead a team of God-gifted craftsman.

Size

The "blueprints" of the ark are recorded in Exodus 25 and are given to Moses directly by God. The details are amazing and the size very specific. The ark was to be measured in cubits, the distance between a man's elbow and the tip of his finger. This unit of measurement varied from person to person, but scholars agree that a cubit was equal to 16 to 22 inches in length with 18 inches being the preferred figure. Assuming a cubit to be 1.5 feet in length, then the basic dimensions of the ark were 3.75-by-2.25-by-2.25 feet. If the large cubit is used, then the ark would 4.58-by-2.75-by-2.75 feet. It wasn't much larger than a travel trunk or a good-sized hope chest.

Heavenly Pattern

The ark was fashioned after a pattern God described. Moses, while on the mountain with God, may have actually seen what God wanted built, and the Lord may have allowed Moses to see into heaven. "See that you make them after the pattern for them, which was shown to you on the mountain" (Exodus 25:40). The ark, as well as the tabernacle and other furnishings, were patterned on objects in heaven. Moses and his craftsman were not to deviate or elaborate, but replicate.

Putting It Together

Just as the size was specifically given, so was the list of materials. Exodus 25:10–21 spells out the two basic building materials: acacia wood and gold.

Acacia wood would form the box itself and the poles used to carry the holy chest. Acacia wood (also called *shittim*) comes from a large thorny tree with rough and gnarled bark. The wood is orange-brown, hard-grained, and repels insects. Many species of acacia grew in the desert of Sinai, in southern Palestine, and in Egypt, so the material was abundant. Since the ark would be carried great distances, it had to be durable. A more fragile wood could not withstand the extreme weather and travels that the ark would undergo.

The second significant material was gold. "You shall overlay it with pure gold, inside and out you shall overlay it, and you shall make a gold molding around it" (Exodus 25:11). Everything was to be plated in gold—the exterior of the box, its lid, and its interior. The thickness of the gold is not given, but most likely it was a thin layer similar to gold leaf. Gold is heavy, and since the ark was to be carried by four priests, the precious metal could not have been very thick.

Some have wondered where the gold came from since a nomadic people like the Israelites could not be expected to mine it from the earth. The Bible has the answer: It came from their Egyptian neighbors. Before they left Egypt, they were to follow God's instructions: "But every woman shall ask of her neighbor and the woman who lives in her house, articles of silver and articles of gold, and clothing; and you will put them on your sons and daughters. Thus you will plunder the Egyptians" (Exodus 3:22). It was from those items that the gold came to build the ark and other tabernacle furnishings.

The ark was to be carried on wood poles made of the same material as the ark itself. These poles were also overlaid in gold. Rings were to be set in the feet of the ark for the poles, so that when carried upon the shoulders of the priests, the ark would be high above the heads of the people. Once the poles were set in the rings, they were never to be removed.

God then describes something called a "mercy seat." The Hebrew term is *kapporeth* and means simply "lid." It was to be placed on top of the ark to seal in its contents. It was on this lid that the priest would later sprinkle blood on the Day of Atonement for the forgiveness of the sins of the people.

But the mercy seat was more than a slab of gold. It supported the image of two cherubim. The western world's idea of the word cherub is far removed from its biblical definition. Today's image of a cherub comes from paintings of angels portrayed as cupid-like bare-bottomed babies. In the Bible, a cherub is a mighty, powerful angel. It was cherubim that God stationed as sentries to protect the garden of Eden (Genesis 3:24). Most scholars believe that Satan, a fallen angel, was a cherub (Ezekiel 28:12–19).

These cherubim's golden images were bowed with faces turned down toward the mercy seat, their wings raised and extended over the lid. With an angel on each end, their wings would touch over the middle. The sculptured angels were to be of one piece with the mercy seat—a delicate job requiring expert craftsmanship.

Many artistic renditions have been made of the ark. Some show winged sphinx-like creatures on the mercy seat. This representation is highly unlikely. While the Israelites would certainly have been familiar with the sphinx and similar statues that adorned Egyptian buildings, there is no reason to assume that they would use such an image on a device designed by God. In fact, to do so would have been offensive to God. Instead, they would have depicted human-like figures with extended wings. The author of Hebrews calls them "cherubim of glory" but gives no further details (Hebrews 9:5). Exactly what these creatures looked like is unknown. Ezekiel's visions show the beings as having four faces—that of a man, bull, eagle, and lion (Ezekiel 1:5–11). John mentions similar creatures in Revelation 4. Did the cherubim on the ark have four faces? Possibly, but since no further description is given, we may never know.

An Ark by Any Other Name

The ark is mentioned many times in the Bible, but not always by the same name. Twenty different references to the ark can be found. For example, "ark of God" is used thirty-four times, such as 1 Samuel 3:3: "The lamp of God had not yet gone out, and Samuel was lying down in

A cart similar to this may have been used by the Philistines to return the captured ark.

the temple of the LORD where the ark of God was." It is also referred to as the ark of God's strength (Psalm 132:8) and as the ark of His might (Psalm 78:61, NIV).

Contents

The term ark of the covenant comes from the ark's contents. The ark was meant to hold something and, indeed, held several very important things. The author of Hebrews itemizes the three contents: "a golden jar holding the manna, and Aaron's rod which budded, and the tables of the covenant" (Hebrews 9:4).

Stone Tablets

The tablets of stone—the tables of the covenant—are the ark's most famous and valuable contents. When Moses was on Mount Sinai, God gave him two stone tablets that had been written upon by the very finger of the Lord. These were the second set of tablets God had given Moses, the first having been destroyed by Moses when he descended the mountain and saw the golden calf being worshiped by the people. Moses recounts the event in the Book of Deuteronomy: "At that time the LORD said to me, 'Cut out for yourself two tablets of stone like the former ones, and come up to Me on the mountain, and make an ark of wood for yourself. I will write on the tablets the words that were on the former tablets which you shattered, and you shall put them in the ark'" (Deuteronomy 10:1–2).

Imagine the importance and value of those tablets. They were the "legal" documents between God and His people. They were the written covenant inscribed by the very Creator Himself. So precious were those objects that God required that they be carried around in the golden ark. There they remained until the ark disappeared.

Aaron's Budding Rod

Aaron and his family were selected by God to be priests. This decision, as well as the leadership of Moses, was challenged by a group of 250 people lead by Korah, Dathan, and Abiram. Moses turned the matter over to the Lord. As part of the deciding process, Moses commanded that one almond rod from each of the twelve tribes of Israel be placed inside the tabernacle—each rod having been engraved with the name of one of the tribes (with the exception of the rod for the tribe of Levi where Aaron's name was engraved instead). God promised to make the rod representing the chosen tribe sprout. The next morning, Moses went into the tabernacle and discovered that Aaron's rod had sprouted, budded, blossomed, and borne ripe almonds—all in one night. The rod displayed every stage of an almond tree's growth and maturity, even though it was previously a dead stick. The purpose was to put an end to the grumbling of the people. Aaron was God's choice to be priest and his family after him. That decision was final.

This rod, which represents the chosen priesthood, was also included in the ark.

Golden Jar of Manna

The author of Hebrews tells us that the ark also carried a golden jar holding an omer of manna. An omer is equivalent to two dry quarts. Manna was the mysterious food that God used to feed His people during their wilderness wanderings. It would appear on the ground in the morning, but could not be kept overnight except on the day before the Sabbath when it would keep for two days before turning rancid. While the Book of Exodus records the collection and preservation of the manna, only the Book of Hebrews tells us that it was kept in the ark (Exodus 16:33–34 and Hebrews 9:4). Apparently the manna remained fresh throughout the centuries.

Book of Law

The book of the law accompanied the ark. Interestingly, it seems that it traveled with the ark, but not on the inside of the chest. "It came about, when Moses finished writing the words of this law in a book until they were complete, that Moses commanded the Levites who carried the ark of the covenant of the LORD, saying, 'Take this book of the law and place it *beside* the ark of the covenant of the LORD your God, that it may remain there as a witness against you'" (Deuteronomy 31:24–26, italics mine). This book would have been the entire law, not just the Ten Commandments. The passage is interesting because of where it places the book—"beside the ark of the covenant." Most likely, the law was set next to the ark when it was in the tabernacle and carried by a priest when the people moved.

Only Tablets Remained in Solomon's Day

Nearly five hundred years later, Solomon finished the first temple, and the ark was placed in the inner sanctum called the Holy of Holies. But things were missing. During the centuries, the golden jar of manna and Aaron's rod had disappeared. Only the two stone tablets of the Ten Commandments remained (1 Kings 8:9). What happened to the items is another mystery surrounding the ark.

More Than an Inventory

Why are the details of these objects so important as to be recorded in Scripture? Nothing in the Bible is there by accident. Each of the items is a reminder of the past, but also representative of what God will do in the future. Each of the three items in the ark, as well as the ark itself, is symbolic of Christ. The manna shows God's provision for His people, and Jesus is our provision for salvation: He is the bread of life. Jesus uses manna as an illustration of Himself, then says, "I am the bread of life; he who comes to Me will not hunger, and he who believes in Me will never thirst" (John 6:35). He shows that He is the "bread which came down out of heaven" (John 6:41). As manna sustained the Israelites in the wilderness, so Christ is our sustainer. Without Him, we starve spiritually. Also, manna was food provided by God. It was unearned. The people did not make it, plant it, or grow it; they simply picked it up. That is the definition of grace—a gift received that was unearned and undeserved.

The stone tablets held the law of God. They were a call to obedience and righteousness and were written by the finger of God. The tablets laid out our relationship to Him and to one another. It was the blueprint of proper living.

The rod of Aaron represents Jesus as High Priest. Scholars have long known that Aaron was a type of Christ, representing Christ as our priest in heaven. But there's more. The rod of Aaron was dead, yet it came to life. The symbolism is hard to miss: Christ died for us, but was raised from the dead, showing us the complete fulfillment of our promised eternal life and resurrection. If we want to know what we will be like, then we need to look to Him. The apostle John said, "Beloved, now we are children of God, and it has not appeared as yet what we will be. We know that when He appears, we will be like Him, because we will see Him just as He is" (1 John 3:2).

One other thing to note about this odd collection of items: They were carried *inside* the ark (with the exception of the book of the law). They were under the lid called the mercy seat. It was upon this lid with its angels that the high priest would sprinkle blood once a year to atone for the sins of the people. All these things were under the blood, just as we are saved under Christ's blood. Christ's sacrifice changed everything. We are not under the law, the law is under Christ. We are not dead, but alive like Aaron's rod because of Christ's death. And we have the bread of life, which is Christ—something we didn't earn or even deserve, yet it was given to us anyway.

Transporting the Ark

"When the camp sets out, Aaron and his sons shall go in and they shall take down the veil of the screen and cover the ark of the testimony with it; and they shall lay a covering of porpoise skin on it, and shall spread over it a cloth of pure blue, and shall insert its poles" (Numbers 4:5–6).

During the wilderness years, the Israelites traveled many miles over the Sinai Peninsula, taking all that they owned with them, including the sacred items such as the tabernacle and its furnishings. That meant moving the ark. God was very specific about the way the ark was to be transported. Its design included gold-plated wood rings on the ark's feet and poles to fit into those rings.

A particular family was charged with the transportation of the ark and other tabernacle items (Numbers 3:29–31). Members of the Kohath family (Kohathites) were the designated movers. It was an important responsibility since certain, unchanging rules applied.

Bible illustrators are fond of showing the ark in all its golden, gleaming glory being carried on its poles by four priests. In reality, the people never saw the ark. It was either in the Holy of Holies in the tabernacle or covered with several layers of material. Aaron and his sons would lower the veil that separated the Holy Place from the Holy of Holies and cover the ark with it. They would then drape a layer of "porpoise skin" over the veil to protect it and the ark. The word which is translated as "porpoise skin" is difficult to determine as the meaning of the word has been lost to us. No one knows precisely what animal it refers to. It is doubtful that it means the skin of a dolphin or porpoise, but refers to some other animal. The porpoise would be considered an unclean animal since it has fins, but no scales (Leviticus 11:9–12). Such a skin would never be used in the tabernacle.

Only after the ark had been completely covered could it be moved.

The Power of the Ark

The power of the ark is as amazing as its construction. The ark was instrumental in several miracles.

The Jordan Rolls Back

The first miracle of note happens at the Jordan River as Joshua, Moses' successor, leads the people into the Promised Land. The forty years of wandering had come to an end. Camped on the east side of the Jordan, the people could look across to the land that God had promised their parents decades before. But there was a problem: They had to cross the Jordan. Although today the great river is smaller than it was in ancient times (water taken from the Sea of Galilee and the river itself has diminished the volume that flows through the land), in Joshua's day, the river ran at a dangerous speed. To make matters worse, it was the flood season and the river was swollen with early rains and water from the melting snow of the mountains in the north. Leading a large group of people across the fast-moving water was suicide, but God had a plan.

"This day I will begin to exalt you in the sight of all Israel, that they may know that just as I have been with Moses, I will be with you" (Joshua 3:7). This is the beginning of Joshua's leadership. Joshua loses no time. God's instructions are spread to the people, who may have wondered at the strangeness of them.

First, they were to follow the ark. Normally, the ark traveled in the midst of the people, not at the head. When encamped, the ark was at the center; when on the move, it remained in the middle of the traveling throng. Also, the people were used to following the column of smoke and pillar of fire; now they were to follow the ark.

Something else was different. Normally, Kohathites carried the ark, but for this event, it was to be borne by priests. So there has been a change in position (from the middle to the front of the people) and a change of personnel (Kohathite bearers to priests).

There is another mysterious command: "However, there shall be between you and [the ark] a distance of about 2,000 cubits by measure. Do not come near it, that you may know the way by which you shall go, for you have not passed this way before" (Joshua 3:4). Two thousand cubits is nearly a mile. Why such a distance? The verse explains the primary reason: a better view. Joshua leads a group that numbers in the hundreds of thousands, perhaps as many as two million people. The ark, even with four priests and a bright blue covering, was tiny by comparison. By providing such a distance between the Israelites and the ark, the people would be able to see the path they were to follow much more easily, and since that path included crossing a rapidly flowing river, it was important for them to see the miracle unfold.

The miracle was to occur in a specific fashion. The people were to keep the proper distance, while the priests carried the ark before the people and marched into the Jordan. This was a tremendous act of faith on the part of the priests: To march into a rapidly churning river while carrying a heavy gold box was madness, but they knew the command had come from God. It was their time to literally step out in faith.

And so they did.

With the people a mile behind them, the courageous priests came to the edge of the river and without hesitation stepped into the flow, ready to take whatever came their way. They had been told that a miracle would happen, but first they had to step into the river. When the first priest's foot left dry ground and touched the wet surface, the impossible happened. The roaring of the river changed. The southbound waters continued on their journey toward the Dead Sea, but the waters careening from the north stopped and began to pile up behind an invisible dam created by God. The piling of water occurred sixteen miles north at a city named Adam. One can only wonder what those people thought when the water ceased to flow and piled up!

Now it was the people's turn. Like their parents forty years before them, they crossed on dry land created by a miracle of God. The rules of nature were suspended. The priests stood steadfast in the middle of the Jordan while the people passed them on either side. Four men who served God and the people stood like statues in a place that had a short time before been covered in tumultuous water. Hours passed, but there they stood until the last person in line had made it up the west bank of the Jordan, the heavy ark always on the priests' shoulders.

Once the last person had crossed, the priests carried the ark up the bank and into Canaan, the Promised Land. Only then did the waters begin to flow again.

As with all miracles, there are those who seek a purely rationalistic explanation. Some have said that this was no miracle at all, but the result of a natural phenomenon. They cite an earthquake that took place in the region on December 8, 1267, in which the banks of the Jordan collapsed, damming the river for ten hours. On July 11, 1927, something similar happened, blocking the river for twenty-one hours. More than three hundred people died in that quake, and one thousand buildings were damaged. It is not beyond reason to believe that God could have used a natural event to achieve His purpose, but that, too, would be a miracle.

A naturalistic approach does not explain how the waters came to be dammed up at the precise moment the priest set foot in the Jordan; how Joshua knew when such an event would happen; how the waters remained in remission long enough for hundreds of thousands of people to cross; or why no earthquake is mentioned in the passage. It is not enough to dismiss a miracle by suggesting an event that explains only one aspect of the wonder. If a miracle is going to be dismissed, then each part of it must be shown to be false.

Jericho Falls

The ark was also present at the first battle of the Promised Land. Jericho was one of the oldest inhabited cities in the world. In Joshua's day, it was a walled stronghold considered impenetrable. Joshua undertakes a very unusual attack. Calling for the priests, he orders them to take up the ark and march around the city. Seven priests were to carry shofars—trumpets made from rams' horns. For six days, the warriors, priests, and bearers of the ark marched around the city of Jericho, once each day. On the seventh day, they marched around the city seven times, blew the horns, shouted in unison, and the walls of Jericho tumbled. The ark was present at the great collapse.

The Plague on the Philistines

One of the most interesting events surrounding the ark has to do with a people never meant to see it. The Philistines were a mysterious people. Very is little known of their origin. We do know that they were aggressive and fond of war. For centuries they were the enemy of Israel, so that the Old Testament is filled with accounts of battles between the Philistines and Israel.

In 1 Samuel 4, we read of how the Philistines attacked and defeated the Israelites at Ebenezer, killing about four thousand men. Shocked by their loss, the surviving army and elders sent for the ark, which was being kept in the city of Shiloh. Shiloh served as the religious center before Israel was a united nation with its capital in Jerusalem. It was there that the tabernacle found its first home. The ark of the covenant was brought to the battle site, and the armies cheered so loudly that the Philistines heard it and wondered what was going on. Hearing that the ark had come into the camp of Israel, they were terrified. They had heard of the ark, yet their leaders convinced them that if they didn't fight, they would become slaves to the Hebrews—something no Philistine could tolerate. So they fought one of the bloodiest, deadliest battles in history. Thirty thousand Hebrew foot soldiers died that day. Those who were not killed fled for their lives. It was the harshest kind of defeat: The Philistines had not only won the battle but had taken the ark as booty.

The ark of covenant was in the hands of Israel's most despised enemy. Nothing could be more disheartening. It was as if God Himself had been captured. The Philistines rejoiced over their victory. They had taken God captive . . . or so they thought.

It was one thing to defeat the army of Israel, but quite another to assume God had also been defeated. In an act of religious pride, the Philistines carted the ark back to Ashdod, one of their five great cities. There they placed it next to a statue of their god Dagon. From the waist up Dagon had the torso of a man; below were the fins of a fish. Placing the ark next to their "triumphant" god, the Philistines called it a night.

The next morning they entered the temple of Dagon and found the statue toppled from its perch, lying face down on the floor. Puzzled, they returned the icon to its place. The next morning they returned to find the statue overthrown as before, but this time its head and hands had been cut off. It is at this point that they began to understand that they had made a grave mistake in taking the ark.

Dagon was not the only one to suffer. A plague broke out upon the people of Ashdod. The epidemic was both painful and embarrassing. Perhaps carried by the mice that also overran the land, the disease causes the eruption of "tumors." Often the translators of the Bible are put in a delicate situation. Certain terms and descriptions are offensive and so often the true meaning of the word is hidden behind a more genteel term. The Hebrew word translated "tumor" is 'ophel and should be rendered "hemorrhoid." The disease went beyond the general discomfort associated with that condition: This was a punishment meant to make a point. The text says that God "ravaged them." The condition was severe enough that the people of Ashdod came to a quick decision: Get rid of the ark. They sent it to their neighbors in Gath—something Gathites didn't appreciate since the plague came with the ark, so they sent the ark on to Ekron, another one of the Philistine's famous cities. The plague grew worse. For seven months the people of Ekron put up with tumors that ravished their bodies and mice that devastated their crops and carried disease. Only one thing could be done: Send the ark back where it belonged.

Under advice of their religious leaders and diviners, the Philistines decide to return the ark and to make a guilt offering. When asked what the offering should be, they were told by their priests to make five golden mice and five golden tumors, one for each of the afflicted cities. A new cart was made and hitched to two milk cows that had never been yoked. This was to be a test. If the cows went to the land of Israel, then they would know that the plague was from God. If the cows returned home with the cart, then they were to assume that the plague was a coincidence.

So they loaded the ark on the cart, placing a box of five golden mice and five golden tumors next to it, and let the cows loose. Contrary to their nature, the cows left their land and their suckling calves behind and carried the ark to Beth-shemesh, a town about fifteen miles from Jerusalem.

The Ark Comes Home

The people of Beth-shemesh were overjoyed to see the ark. They cut up the cart and used its wood to make a burnt offering to the Lord, sacrificing the cows that had brought the ark home. But their enthusiasm gets the best of them. Some of the men looked inside the ark. Perhaps their intentions were good. Maybe they wanted to see if the tablets of Moses were still there. We don't know their motivation, but we do know that they did the forbidden. Only the priests were to deal with the ark, and even they were not allowed to touch it. These men of Beth-shemesh did and a large number of them died. Many translations list the number as 50,070. Others say the number was much smaller—just 70 men.

The number discrepancy comes from the way the Hebrew number system works. Unlike our Arabic number system—in which we have different symbols for numbers as well as zero for a placeholder—the ancient Hebrews used letters for numbers. The first letter of the Hebrew alphabet is Aleph and equals the number one. The next letter is Beth and equals two. Small marks were written above the letters to indicate multiples of ten. Sometimes these tiny marks can be misread, especially when the manuscript is very old. Most likely, 70 men died and not 50,070, since that would include not only the city's population but also a large area around it. Still, the large number cannot be ruled out entirely.

Tragedy in the Midst of Celebration
2 Samuel 6:6–7

After the Philistine incident, the ark came to rest in the house of a man named Abinadab in Kiriath-jearim (also known as Baale-judah).

With a procession of thirty thousand men, King David took possession of the ark and began the eight-mile journey back to Jerusalem where the ark would eventually be placed in the tabernacle. It was a loud and happy affair. "David and all the house of Israel were celebrating before the LORD with all kinds of instruments made of fir wood, and with lyres, harps, tambourines, castanets and cymbals" (2 Samuel 6:5). This was an exciting day; the ark of God was on its way to its new home. What could be better?

Perhaps it was David's enthusiasm or an inattention to detail, but the celebration came to a tragic and sudden stop. The rules about moving the ark were very specific: Only Levites were to carry it, and that included Kohathites and priests but no one else. The ark was carried by the gold clad wood poles and nothing else. In this incident, all those rules were disregarded.

The ark was placed on a cart, not carried by priests. The passage implies that the ark was laid out in full public view; and despite the fact that tens of thousands marched alongside it, danced before it, and sang praises, the ark was still treated disrespectfully. That's when the tragedy occurred. As the ox-pulled cart moved along the rough terrain, the cart shifted, and Uzzah, whose name means "strength," reached out and took hold of the ark to steady it. The act cost him his life.

The tendency here is to think the ark had some magical or even technological element to it that struck Uzzah dead, but the passage says otherwise: "And the anger of the LORD burned against Uzzah, and God struck him down there for his irreverence; and he died there by the ark of God" (2 Samuel 6:7). Nothing is said of lightning coming from the ark or any other such thing. Uzzah is "struck down" by God because of his "irreverence." The word means an error or fault, but the way it is used here implies that Uzzah did more than make a mistake. His death is the direct result of God's punishment. Did Uzzah simply react as any man would, trying to save the ark from tumbling off the cart? Not likely. There is more to the story. It was not an act of reflex but of irreverence. Irreverence is the condition of the heart. We are too far removed from the incident and know too little about the man to say what was in his heart, but God's response tells us something. Uzzah did what he knew he should not for reasons of his own, not for the welfare of the ark.

David's response is anger. His understanding of what happened was inadequate. All he knew was that a man near the ark had been struck dead. So angry and frightened was David that he refused to take the ark to Jerusalem. Instead, he placed it in the home of Obed-edom, a descendent of Levi. Why a Levite? Because only Levites were allowed to transport and care for the ark. It appears David knew the proper way of treating the ark but ignored it until Uzzah's death.

Obed-edom, the new caretaker of the ark, is enormously blessed during the three months that he has possession of the ark, which David notices. Just as Uzzah died for his irreverence, Obed-edom is blessed for his reverence. This blessing inspired David once again to bring the ark to Jerusalem. This time, he takes a more respectful approach. The differences are subtle in the text, but significant in action.

"And so it was, that when the *bearers* of the ark of the LORD had gone six paces, he sacrificed an ox and a fatling. And David was dancing before the LORD with all his might, and David was wearing a linen ephod. So David and all the house of Israel were bringing up the ark of the LORD with shouting and the sound of the trumpet" (2 Samuel 6:13–15). Instead of a cart, there were "bearers," meaning that the correct approach was taken in moving the ark. In fact, 1 Chronicles 15:26 states, "Because God was helping the Levites who were carrying the ark of the covenant of the LORD, they sacrificed seven bulls and seven rams." Instead of leaving God out of the procession, they rightfully included Him and followed His direction on the manner in which the ark was to be transported.

The ark made it to Jerusalem where, years later, it would be placed in the temple of Solomon. There it would remain until it mysteriously disappeared.

An Electric Contraption?

An increasingly popular theory is that the ark was an electrical device, more specifically, a capacitor. Capacitors, first discovered in 1745, are simple devices that can hold an electrical charge. They are composed of two pieces of conductive material (like metal) separated by a nonconductive material (like air, wood, and other substances). Gold is an excellent conductor of electricity, but wood is not, making the ark a perfect capacitor. With gold on the outside and inside, separated by a layer of wood, the ark could pick up a static charge from the hot, dry air and release it if properly grounded. To do this, the circuit must be closed between the inner gold layer and the outer. Some have suggested that the cherubim served as terminals, discharging electricity between their outstretched wings. This idea seems all the more plausible since ancient Jewish tradition says the ark flashed lightning. From there it is only a small step to thinking that Uzzah was electrocuted when he touched the ark and that the voice of God was little more than electrostatic discharge.

It is quite possible that the ark could have acted as a capacitor by storing electricity it gathered from the air, but it is never shown as such in the Bible. No mention of electrocution or anything similar is mentioned in the Bible. Some have suggested that the ancient Jews would have thought the electrical discharge a miracle and therefore mistakenly assumed the capacitor was a device of God. However, the modern capacitor was discovered in 1745. If Moses had led the people to build the chest to store and discharge electricity, then he invented the electronic device more than thirty-one hundred years before "modern" researchers did. Would a people that advanced be so gullible? Not likely.

Whether the ark could accumulate and store a charge is unknown, but we do know that it was not a topic of Scripture and certainly not the power of the ark.

What Happened to the Ark?

The most frequently asked question regarding the ark is, Where is it? The answer is simple: No one knows. The location of the ark, if it still exists on Earth, remains an inscrutable mystery. Where could it have gone? Several possibilities exist and each one seems plausible and doubtful.

Captured by Egyptians?

"Now it happened in the fifth year of King Rehoboam, that Shishak the king of Egypt came up against Jerusalem. He took away the treasures of the house of the LORD and the treasures of the king's house, and he took everything, even taking all the shields of gold which Solomon had made" (1 Kings 14:25–26).

Shishak attacked the southern kingdom of Judea, conquering 156 cities and laying siege to Jerusalem. King Rehoboam bought off Shishak with a large tribute of gold and valuables, including gold taken from the temple and palace. The question is, Did Shishak actually plunder the temple? The Egyptian account of the conflict is recorded on the temple of Amon in Karnak, Egypt. Interestingly, Jerusalem is not mentioned.

Shortly after the attack, the Bible records the presence of the golden lamp stand, altar of incense, and the table of showbread (2 Chronicles 13:10–11). Why would these objects still be present if Shishak had successfully plundered the temple? And if those items continued to exist, there's a very good chance that the ark remained safely in place (with all due respect to Steven Spielberg and *Indiana Jones*).

Still in Use in 622 B.C.

Centuries later, the ark is mentioned by King Josiah, grandson of the wicked King Manasseh. At the age of twenty, King Josiah began a purification campaign, removing idols from the land. Then he ordered that the temple be repaired and the holy objects returned (2 Chronicles 35:3). It is assumed that priests had hidden them during King Manasseh's evil reign.

Captured by Babylonians?

Beginning in 605 B.C., the Babylonians began an assault and deportation of Jews from the southern kingdom of Judah. The young man Daniel and others were taken in the first wave. Two additional attacks occurred until 586 B.C. In that year, the walls of Jerusalem were breached, many Jews were slaughtered, and the temple was looted and destroyed. The articles in the temple were removed and taken back to Babylon. Was the ark taken too? It's hard to say. Both the Babylonians and the Persians who conquered the Jews in 539 B.C. make no mention of the ark. Under the Persians, about five hundred thousand Jews were allowed to return home. Cyrus, king of the Medo-Persian empire, allowed the resettled people to take temple items back with them. A careful list was kept. The ark was not mentioned. While many suppose the ark was taken from Jerusalem, it is doubtful. It appears that the ark was gone before the Babylonian invasion.

The Ethiopian Connection
1 Kings 10:1–43

The most intriguing and romantic theory regarding the ark's disappearance involves the Ethiopian royal known as the queen of Sheba. The story is recorded in oral and written traditions of the Ethiopians. A thirteenth-century document called the *Kebra Nagast* is one of the oldest such records. It tells a story worthy of Hollywood, complete with foreign intrigue, seduction, a sexual tryst, theft, and conspiracy.

According to the account, the queen of Sheba, having heard of King Solomon's greatness, travels from her homeland of Ethiopia to Jerusalem, armed with gifts of enormous wealth and difficult questions to test the king's world-renowned wisdom. There she sees the grandeur of Solomon's palace and the temple and experiences firsthand the unrivaled intellect of the great king. Duly impressed she says, "It was a true report which I heard in my own land about your words and your wisdom. Nevertheless I did not believe the reports, until I came and my eyes had seen it. And behold, the half was not told me. You exceed in wisdom and prosperity the report which I heard. How blessed are your men, how blessed are these your servants who stand before you continually and hear your wisdom. Blessed be the LORD your God who delighted in you to set you on the throne of Israel; because the LORD loved Israel forever, therefore He made you king, to do justice and righteousness" (1 Kings 10:6–9).

Quite a compliment coming from a woman who possessed extreme wealth and power. She then gives him gold, spices, precious stones, trees, and more. The total weight of gold came to 666 talents. A talent is roughly seventy-five pounds. Therefore the queen brought nearly fifty thousand pounds of gold.

The *Kebra Nagast* departs from the scriptural account by stating that Solomon seduces the queen through an act of trickery. Returning home, she discovers she is pregnant and gives birth to Menelik. Years later, the boy, wondering about his father, travels to Jerusalem. Solomon is overjoyed to see him and, after a visit, sends the young man home with great riches. He also sent him with company. Feeling it unfair that he, the king, should have to send his own flesh and blood on a long and dangerous journey home, Solomon demands that other Jewish leaders send one of their sons. They do so.

It's on the journey back that young Menelik makes a surprising discovery: Some of his new companions have brought something else with them—the ark of the covenant. Elders, feeling that Solomon was departing more and more from the faith and allowing idol worship to flourish in the land, decided that the ark was in danger. With the help of the temple priests, they smuggle the holy object out of the country. Unable to turn back, Menelik continues his journey. To this day, the Orthodox Church of Ethiopia maintains that they have the ark in Axum, Ethiopia, where they protect it from the public. No one is allowed to see it; consequently, it is impossible to verify the claim.

As long as the temple priests were part of the conspiracy, the stealing of the ark would be the prefect crime. Since only one person a year is allowed to see inside the Holy of Holies and that person was a conspiring priest, then no one would know if the object were there or not.

As with all theories of the ark's location, this one cannot be confirmed. It is just one story among many, but there is some evidence to make it credible.

A Forever Mystery

The ark of the covenant was a mysterious object in biblical days and it remains so now. Will it ever be found? Since no one knows what happened to it, we are left to sift through the various theories and scant evidence and then take our best guess. The ark may have been destroyed, caught up to heaven, hidden near Jerusalem, or taken to Ethiopia. Despite persistent claims, the ark remains lost.

Perhaps that's how it should be. The ark represented the presence and power of God to His chosen people. It was not an object for the world, but for a select nation. Now Christ is the center of every believer's attention. No box of gold can replace that. Christ is Savior to all people. As the apostle Paul said, "He is the image of the invisible God, the first-born of all creation. For by Him all things were created, both in the heavens and on earth, visible and invisible, whether thrones or dominions or rulers or authorities—all things have been created through Him and for Him. He is before all things, and in Him all things hold together. He is also head of the body, the church; and He is the beginning, the firstborn from the dead, so that He Himself will come to have first place in everything" (Colossians 1:15–18).

Christ is our ark—a living, breathing ark. Not one confined to just a few, He is available to the whole world every day. Not hidden behind a curtain, not tucked away in a tabernacle or temple, He reigns in our hearts. That makes Him more precious than anything.

More to Think About

1. The ark has been missing for many centuries. If it were discovered tomorrow, how would that change the world? How would it change you?

2. The ark is just one Old Testament symbol of Christ. Why did God use so many symbols in the Bible?

3. Why would God choose to speak to Moses from above the ark? Considering that He had spoken to Moses from a burning bush and from the top of Mount Sinai, why switch to the ark?

4. Many have tried to make the ark into something it is not (a communication device to speak with aliens, a giant capacitor, etc.). What response can be given to people who hold such views?

Bad Guys of the Gospels

At the end of every movie is a long list of names—the credits—that recognize all the actors, directors, writers, and workers who had a hand in making the film. It also helps the viewer know who did what. Such things are important to us.

Reading through the Gospels, we discover some characters that need a little defining. Jesus' ministry didn't take place in a vacuum; it took place in the small outlying communities and the large cities of His day. In the course of Jesus' ministry, He encountered thousands of people. Many of those listened and responded to the message He brought; others remained ambivalent; and many others opposed Him. Some of those in the opposition were powerful and influential. Ultimately, such men put Jesus on the cross.

They went by names like Pharisees, Sadducees, and scribes. Their influence is unmistakable. One cannot understand the work of Jesus without knowing a little about these groups.

Stone steps leading from the traditional site of Caiaphas the high priest—Jesus may have walked the steps.

Pharisees

Jesus gave a dire warning: "Watch out and beware of the leaven of the Pharisees and Sadducees" (Matthew 16:6). Unflattering words. Leaven was yeast used to make bread rise. It was known for its ability to permeate dough and affect it completely. It was also a symbol of sin. Jesus, who befriended the sinner, the outcast, and the unwanted, would not tolerate those who professed themselves to be spiritual leaders.

The most troublesome group was a tight-knit assembly called the Pharisees. They opposed Jesus at every point, at first formulating questions they assumed to be unanswerable and then allowing their hatred to lead them into a conspiracy that resulted in the Crucifixion.

One thing is certain about Jesus: He gathered a crowd who listened to His teaching and sought miracles. Jesus was a celebrity, and celebrities draw attention from fans. They also attract dangerous people. Some loved Jesus and followed Him faithfully. Others despised Him and conspired to have Him hung on a cross.

John the Baptist spoke the truth without reservation and he was no friend of the Pharisees: "But when he [John] saw many of the Pharisees and Sadducees coming for baptism, he said to them, 'You brood of vipers, who warned you to flee from the wrath to come?'" (Matthew 3:7). Hardly kind words, but accurate ones.

Jesus had a few things to say about the Pharisees too: "But woe to you, scribes and Pharisees, hypocrites, because you shut off the kingdom of heaven from people; for you do not enter in yourselves, nor do you allow those who are entering to go in. Woe to you, scribes and Pharisees, hypocrites, because you devour widows' houses, and for a pretense you make long prayers; therefore you will receive greater condemnation. Woe to you, scribes and Pharisees, hypocrites, because you travel around on sea and land to make one proselyte; and when he becomes one, you make him twice as much a son of hell as yourselves" (Matthew 23:13–15).

But who were these people? There were several religious and political groups in Jesus' time, but two are the most noticeable: Pharisees and Sadducees. Another group, the scribes, was closely associated with the Pharisees.

In short, they were a group that was religious but not spiritual. Frederick Buechner said, "The trouble oftentimes with religious people is that they try to be more spiritual than God Himself." That sums up the Pharisees.

The word Pharisee means "separatists." Their goal was to remain separate from all legal contamination and to live a life that was governed by the smallest aspect of the Mosaic law and traditions. They kept themselves from any legal pollution, distinguishing themselves from the common people. They lived by every nuance of ritual. They were true holier-than-thou people.

On several occasions they complained when Jesus healed on the Sabbath. All they could see was that a rule had been broken. In the process, they missed the miracle that stood before them. Jesus laid out their problem: "Neglecting the commandment of God, you hold to the tradition of men" (Mark 7:8).

Their real problem boiled down to their effort to be holy by avoidance. They sought to be righteous by avoiding contamination rather than by seeking the God they chose to please. They also insisted that others do the same. The Pharisees made sin an external thing, not an internal one. This view made them intolerant of others who did not agree with them. That included Jesus. So extreme was their separation that they resorted to conspiracy, lies, perjury, and more to put an end to Christ's ministry.

Sadducees

The Sadducees were another group that opposed Jesus at every turn. In many ways, they were the tricksters of the New Testament, often coming to Jesus with questions so finely crafted that they knew He could not answer them. They were wrong. After one such question, Jesus stated the truth about them: "Is this not the reason you are mistaken, that you do not understand the Scriptures, or the power of God?" (Mark 12:24). He then went on to say, "You are greatly mistaken" (Mark 12:27).

In a confrontation with the Pharisees and Sadducees, Paul plays them against each other. In the process we learn something about the Sadducees: "For the Sadducees say that there is no resurrection, nor an angel, nor a spirit, but the Pharisees acknowledge them all" (Act 23:8). If the Pharisees were the religious conservatives of the day, then the Sadducees were the religious liberals, denying the existence of angels and the Resurrection.

Their doctrine was based on the Torah (the first five books of the Bible), and they denied all other Old Testament writings. They claimed that resurrection was not taught in the Torah and was, therefore, a false teaching. Jesus taught that there was a resurrection and that He Himself would be resurrected. He also taught the reality of angels. Those teachings put Jesus at odds with the Sadducees.

The Sadducees were wealthy, influential, and often bad-mannered. The ancient historian Josephus wrote, "The Sadducees are, even among themselves, rather boorish in their behavior, and in their conversation with their peers are as rude as aliens." They were a proud and arrogant lot who somehow thought they were better than other people.

Odd Bedfellows

The Pharisees and Sadducees were not the best of friends. They stood on opposite ends of the religious spectrum, but they were more alike than they realized. Both were caught up in their own self-importance, allowing their traditions to blind them to Christ. Their arrogance kept them from seeing the One they should have been the first to recognize.

Jesus' ministry was an uphill battle against these groups. Their hatred for Him reached the point that forged an alliance—something that no one could have imagined. Together they orchestrated the death of Christ.

Hatred makes for odd bedfellows.

A Mass o'
Miracles

THE BIBLE IS A MASS OF MIRACLES. Almost 140 supernatural events appear in its pages. Some miracles are universal in scope (creation), some are violent (fire from heaven), others are motivated by compassion (Jesus' feeding of the five thousand), and some are just plain puzzling (the healing aspects of aprons and handkerchiefs taken from the apostle Paul). Miracles remain an interest to many. Television shows that investigate possible miracles come on our screens every year.

Debunkers also flourish, attempting to show that miracles are nothing more than the misguided beliefs of unthinking people. Some of their attempts to explain away acts of God stretch a person's power to believe more than the miracle itself.

What exactly is a miracle? A biblical miracle is a supernatural event, rooted in God's power and presence, that achieves a useful purpose. It is an act that cannot be explained by the laws of physics and chemistry.

Miracles of biblical proportions are rare today. That is not to say that they no longer happen, only that they are not the standard for daily life. God is still in power. He has not diminished in any area or by any degree. In truth, even miracles in the Bible were rare. We often think that they happened frequently because we see and read the Bible as a single book, forgetting that it covers many centuries of time.

Most miracles were used to authenticate a message. In Jesus' case, His miracles proved that He was the Son of God. However, some of His miracles were done in private, not meant to be seen by others and were motivated by love alone. The disciples became apostles after Christ's ascension and followed His command to be witnesses in Jerusalem, Judea, and the rest of the world. As they went out, their message was authenticated by the miracles that were worked at their hands.

The Bible records thirty-five miracles worked by Jesus during His earthly ministry but alludes to many more. Verses such as "Jesus was going throughout all Galilee, teaching in their synagogues and proclaiming the gospel of the kingdom, and healing every kind of disease and every kind of sickness among the people" (Matthew 4:23) appear several times in the Gospels. The specifics of those miracles are not recorded. It is possible that Jesus worked hundreds of miracles and what we have is just a representative sample. The apostle John said it best: "And there are also many other things which Jesus did, which if they were written in detail, I suppose that even the world itself would not contain the books that would be written" (John 21:25).

Still we have nearly three dozen recorded miraculous events by Jesus, some given in great detail. The exact order of the miracles is impossible to determine. The events of the Gospels do not match up chronologically. This is not to say that one or more of the Gospels is wrong. Ancient Jews were not as bound to linear thinking as contemporary Western society is. Content, subject matter, and significance mattered more than event order. Matthew mentions twenty works; Mark numbers eighteen; Luke records twenty; and John shows only seven. They are grouped below under the type of miracle (conquering nature, illness, demons, or death) Jesus performed.

Nature

There are nine recorded miracles in which Jesus shows His authority over nature itself. The range of these miracles is stunning. Substances are changed, the weather altered, a little is made into a lot, and the laws of physics are ignored:

- turns water to wine (John 2:1–11)
- catches numerous fish (Luke 5:1–11)
- stills the storm (Matthew 8:23–27; Mark 4:35–41; Luke 8:22–25)

- feeds the five thousand (Matthew 14:14–21; Mark 6:34–44; Luke 9:12–17; John 6:5–13)
- feeds the four thousand (Matthew 15:32–39; Mark 8:1–9)
- walks upon the Sea of Galilee (Matthew 14:24–33; Mark 6:45–52; John 6:16–21)
- gets the temple tax money in a fish's mouth (Matthew 17:24–27)
- condemns a fig tree (Matthew 21:18–19; Mark 11:12–14)
- catches numerous fish again (John 21:1–11)

Illness

The most frequent miracle performed by Jesus involved the healing of natural illnesses (sixteen miracles are recorded as such). These should be separated from "healings" of the demon-possessed. (Often a demon-possessed person showed physical afflictions from paralysis to blindness. Because of that, miracles over demons are sometimes lumped together with miracles over natural afflictions of the body.)

- heals a nobleman's son (John 4:46–54)
- heals Peter's mother-in-law (Matthew 8:14–15; Mark 1:29–31; Luke 4:38–39)
- cleanses the leper (Matthew 8:2–4; Mark 1:40–45; Luke 5:12–14)
- heals the paralyzed man (Matthew 9:2–8; Mark 2:3–12; Luke 5:18–26)
- heals a lame man in Bethesda (John 5:1–9)
- restores the withered hand (Matthew 12:9–13; Mark 3:1–5; Luke 6:6–10)
- restores the centurion's paralyzed servant (Matthew 8:5–13; Luke 7:1–10)
- cures the woman with the issue of blood (Matthew 9:20–22; Mark 5:25–34; Luke 8:43–48)
- restores sight to two blind men (Matthew 9:27–31)
- restores sight to a blind man (Mark 8:22–26)
- heals man born blind (John 9:1–7)
- heals man with dropsy (Luke 14:1–4)
- heals ten lepers (Luke 17:11–19)

- heals blind Bartimaeus (Mark 10:46–52; Luke 18:35–43)
- heals Malchus's ear (Luke 22:49–51; John 18:10)

Demons

Demonic possession was a fearful thing. Often the possessed suffered greatly both physically and mentally. The impact on the family and community could be profound. On seven occasions it is recorded that Jesus cast out one or more demons from an individual:

- heals the demoniac in a synagogue (Mark 1:23–28; Luke 4:33–35)
- heals a blind and mute possessed man (Matthew 12:22; Luke 11:14)
- throws demons out of a man/two men in the country of the Gerasenes/Gadarenes (Matthew 8:28–34; Mark 5:1–20; Luke 8:26–39)
- heals a mute demoniac (Matthew 9:32–33)
- heals the daughter of the Syrophoenician woman (Matthew 15:21–28; Mark 7:24–30)
- heals demon-possessed boy (Matthew 17:14–18; Mark 9:14–29; Luke 9:38–42)
- heals possessed, crippled woman (Luke 13:10–13)

Death

The one force over which man has no control is death. Paramedics in the field or doctors in hospitals can make heroic efforts, but at some point every person faces the transition from this life into the next. Jesus, however, showed His deity and power by raising three people back to life.

- raises the widow's son at the village of Nain (Luke 7:11–15)
- raises Jairus's daughter (Matthew 9:18–25; Mark 5:22–43; Luke 8:41–56)
- raises Lazarus (John 11:17–44)

Miracles Fleshed Out

Most miracles in the Bible happen at the command of the miracle worker. When Peter and John went to the temple to pray, they saw a man who had been lame from birth. He asked them for alms, but they gave him something far more valuable—health. They did so with no magical incantations or waving of hands. Peter simply reached down, took the man by the arm, and, as we might expect of a rough-and-tumble fisherman, yanked the poor fellow up to his feet. His terror only lasted a moment, for instead of collapsing back to the hard stone pavement, his legs supported him—a totally new sensation for the man.

Often Jesus healed with a touch, and on several occasions—like the healing of the nobleman's son in Cana, Galilee—He simply healed at a distance. "Jesus said to him, 'Go; your son lives.' The man believed the word that Jesus spoke to him and started off" (John 4:50).

This seems the norm for miracle working. No flourish and no tools. On some occasions, however, an object or substance is involved, and the miracle is forever associated with a thing as well as the person who brought it about.

Spit and Healing

Of the thirty-five miracles worked by Jesus, eighteen of them deal with healing physical ills. Of those, five involve Jesus' healing of the blind. Three times Jesus did something very unusual—He healed with spit.

Case Number 1 in John 9:1–7. "As He passed by, He saw a man blind from birth." The fact that his blindness was congenital prompted a theological question from the disciples. "And His disciples asked Him, 'Rabbi, who sinned, this man or his parents, that he would be born blind?'" It was a natural question for the day. The ancient Jews believed that all severe illness was punishment for sin. This mind-set posed a problem when a child was born with a birth defect: Who is to blame? The child had not yet had opportunity to sin, yet it is afflicted. Are the parents at fault?

Jesus' response corrected that misconception: "It was neither that this man sinned, nor his parents; but it was so that the works of God might be displayed in him." Then with the proclamation, "I am the Light of the world," Jesus healed the man of his blindness, but did so in a very unusual way. Instead of working the miracle by simple command or a touch, Jesus spat on the ground and made mud of the spittle and dirt.

This has caused much debate. Why bother with this act? Wouldn't it be simpler to just touch the man's eyes and pronounce him healed? Yes it would, but Jesus wasn't after simplicity.

Jesus made the mud and then smeared it over the closed lids of the man's eyes. Some have supposed that Jesus did this to help the man focus his faith on the miracle. Others have suggested that the man's eyes were matted shut and Jesus was merely removing the matter so he would be able to open his eyes. This seems unnecessary because Jesus sends the man to wash his eyes in the pool of Siloam (a collection of water south of the temple).

A simple answer is found, not in the miracle but in the day of the week. It was the Sabbath and Jewish law prohibited the "work" of mud making. Such an activity would have annoyed the religious leaders, which it did.

The pool to which Jesus sent the blind man to wash

Another clue to Jesus' unusual technique is found when the man is sent to the pool of Siloam to wash. Sending people away to complete a miracle was not a normal pattern for Jesus. The man left the presence of Jesus, still blind, but now with mud on his eyes. In a sense, he was blinder than when he asked for help. Somehow, perhaps with the aid of friends or family, he made his way to the water and scrubbed away the mud. Eyes that had never seen suddenly began to work. The first image he saw was probably his own reflection in the pool. He was a man whose life had been marred by inability; suddenly he was whole, given sight by the only one who could give it to him. His joy is unimaginable. It is easy to picture him dancing around the pool, shouting, "I can see! I can see!" One minute he was a beggar; a few minutes later, he was a man with a future.

For the first time in his life, he saw buildings and people. But the one person he most wanted to see was not there. Jesus had sent him away. Where was the One who had made him whole?

It is here that we find the real answer to Jesus' strange behavior. By Jewish law, Jesus had broken the Sabbath. Not the Sabbath of the Bible, but the one that had been made ridiculously rigid by tradition. Under traditional Sabbath regulations, a doctor could deliver life-saving care, but not treat non-life-threatening disease. For example, a man who cut his hand could use a piece of cloth to stop the bleeding, but was forbidden to use it as a bandage. The religious leaders would have been happier if Jesus had waited a day to perform the miracle, but Jesus didn't come to conform to man's tradition; He came to meet spiritual needs. He fulfilled Isaiah's prophecy that the Messiah would open blind eyes (Isaiah 42:7).

The once-blind man is called before the Pharisees, the enemies of Christ. They question him repeatedly about his healing, and he answers honestly. When asked, "Where is He?" all the man could say is, "I don't know." He had never seen Jesus. He was blind when they met, and he was blind when, on Jesus' instruction, he went to wash in the pool. Scripture shows the Pharisees' inquisition as being grueling and difficult, but the man held firm.

What most readers miss is that although it appears the man is on trial, it is the Pharisees who are being tried. Even when presented with a verifiable miracle—such as a man born blind now made whole—they cannot see the power of God. All they can see is that someone broke the Sabbath. The Pharisees were blinder than the blind man had ever been. They continue to refer to Jesus as a sinner. While the blind man's affliction was not the result of sin, the spiritual and intellectual blindness of the religious Pharisees was self-inflicted.

The story comes full circle when, unable to withstand the man's logic, the Pharisees resort to demeaning his integrity, saying, "You were born entirely in sins." Then they "put him out" (John 9:34). It's a small phrase, but it carries great meaning. They did more than put him out of the building; they cast him out of the synagogue, out of religious life. He was no longer welcome to worship, to hear the reading of the scrolls. He was cast out because he chose to stand up for Jesus. First his blindness made him different from others, then his new health made him a *persona non grata*. Yet the story isn't over. Jesus, upon hearing the man had been expelled, found the man and asked him a question: "'Do you believe in the Son of Man?' He answered, 'Who is He, Lord, that I may believe in Him?' Jesus said to him, 'You have both seen Him, and He is the one who is talking with you.' And he said, 'Lord, I believe.' And he worshiped Him" (John 9:35–41). Jesus is in the business of taking in the outcasts. That's good news for all of us.

So why the spit, mud, and pool? The miracle was not in the substance, but in the Savior. There was nothing magical in the mud, nothing special in the spit, and nothing supernatural in the pool of Siloam. They were tools in the hands of Jesus—tools meant to drive home a point. Some people are physically blind from no fault of their own, but some are intellectually and spiritually blind by choice. By mixing mud, Jesus challenged the tradition of His day and showed the Pharisees for the myopic stooges they were. While they could offer nothing but scorn, Jesus offered sight and, more important, eternal life. The Pharisees may have cast the man out of the synagogue, but he fell right into the loving arms of the Savior.

Case Number 2 in Mark 8:22–25. Spit was also used in a miracle at Bethsaida, a town on the northeast shore of the Sea of Galilee. Jesus is seeking some time alone as He's just fed the four thousand. Leaving the area by boat, Jesus and the disciples come to Bethsaida and are immediately asked to work another miracle. People bring a blind man to Jesus and ask that He touch him. Jesus does, but first he does something interesting: He leaves town with the man in tow. Leading him by the hand, Jesus takes him past the outskirts of the town. This was to be a private miracle, something Jesus did on only two other occasions (Mark 5:35–43 and 7:31–37).

Once outside the village, Jesus turns His attention to the man. "After spitting on his eyes and laying His hands on him, He asked him, 'Do you see anything?'" Again we see the odd practice of spit being applied to the eyes. Jesus does the same thing with a deaf man who had trouble speaking (Mark 7:31–37). After placing his fingers in the deaf man's ears, Jesus spits and then touches the man's tongue. Here in Mark 8, Jesus applies the saliva to the man's eyes.

Why the application of saliva? No crowd is there to see the act, except his disciples. And unlike the man born blind, this man is not sent off to wash. Also, when Jesus lays hands on the man and asks if he sees anything, the man replies, "I see men, for I see them like trees, walking around." These men were most likely the disciples and perhaps other travelers, but why do they look like trees? Only after a second laying on of hands by Jesus (and this is the only time Jesus touches twice to heal) is the man able to see correctly. Why were two touches needed?

This is one of the most mysterious passages of the New Testament and as such must be handled carefully. A casual reading would make us think that Jesus didn't get it right the first time or that Jesus was uncertain about the outcome. We know this can't be true. Jesus raises the dead, heals at a distance, works miracles in an instant, and controls the weather and demons. It would be silly to assume that Jesus is struggling here.

If not that, then what? The general suggestion is that Jesus is forcing the man to focus his faith on his unseeing eyes, but that doesn't hold up. In no other healing (or any other miracle for that matter) does Jesus ask the recipient to focus on his affliction. What about the raising of the dead? The dead can't focus on their problem.

The answer must be elsewhere. Unfortunately, we have nowhere else to look. Only Mark records this miracle, and he does so with no explanation. Why Jesus uses saliva on the man's eyes and why the miracle takes place in two stages is without answer. An "I don't know" answer is always hard to give, but at times we must simply admit that no answer is forthcoming.

Some have suggested that the ancient Jews thought spittle was a treatment for eye disease and blindness. This is true, but it fails to explain why Jesus would resort to an action that He knew had no benefit itself. A healing would take place, but not because of folklore; it would come because of the directed power of Christ. The answer may be far simpler than we suspect. Since we do not know the cause of the man's blindness, we do not know the condition of his eyes. Could Jesus have been cleaning the eyelids of debris left by the disease? Is the second stage of the miracle more a touch-up than an extra supernatural effort by Jesus?

Still, the miracle is recorded. It is there for our benefit. The "two stage" miracle explanation may be as simple as preparing the man for full sight. Jesus, who knows the heart of all men, may have felt that this seeker needed an extra step of preparation.

Whatever the actual reason for Jesus' action, we know that Jesus felt compassion on all men who searched Him out, and that the way He works is varied and interesting, even if we don't understand the underlying motives.

Sneaky Faith

One of the saddest stories in the New Testament is also one of the most uplifting. It is an account that is sandwiched in the middle of another event. First, a synagogue ruler named Jairus approaches Jesus with an urgent request: his twelve-year-old daughter is dying. His emotional plea was heard, and Jesus began to make His way to the ruler's house. The crowd around Jesus was enormous and moving was difficult, but the entourage continued forward like a tide of humanity.

A new player appears. She is a woman who for twelve years has suffered from menstrual hemorrhage. She had been losing blood as long as Jairus's daughter had been alive. The doctors of the day could offer no help. All her work and money and time had been spent in seeking a cure. The disease must surely have left her weak and frail. She no longer had hope.

Even worse, a menstruating woman was considered to be unclean. Not only was she unclean, but anything she touched would also be considered ceremonially defiled. So strict were the rules on this matter that men were to avoid their wives during this monthly occurrence. This woman had been "unclean" for twelve years. She could not touch her husband, prepare meals, or carry out the very duties that gave first-century women dignity and a place in society. The illness that had ravaged her for more than a decade had isolated her from family and friends.

This loneliness drove her to a desperate act. As an unclean woman, she should not have been part of the crowd, but somehow she made her way to Jesus, pushing past the men and women who had come to see Him. But how should she approach Jesus? Could she just walk up and ask for a moment of His time? Perhaps if Jesus were alone or just surrounded by His disciples she could approach, but not with scores of people surrounding the Messiah and especially not with the synagogue official walking beside Him. Jairus would know her; he would be aware of her problem.

She had only two options: give up and walk away or run the risk of faith-driven boldness. She chose the latter. Once in range of Jesus, she reached out not for His sleeve or collar, but low to the ground, to the area of His outer garment, a square piece of clothing with tassels on the end. Leaning forward, bending down, her faith and hope stretching far beyond her reach, the woman touched the hem of Jesus' garment.

Immediately Jesus stopped.

Instantly she understood she had been healed.

The rapturous joy of her healing was suddenly paralyzed by a simple question from Jesus. "Who touched me?" The disciples were confused; Jairus's anxiety grew; and the woman was awash in terror. She had been found out.

Peter asked the natural question: "Master, the people are crowding and pressing in on You." In other words, "Lots of people have touched You."

Then we are given an insight not found in any other miracle: We are told that Jesus sensed something physical happening during a miracle. "Someone did touch Me, for I was aware that power had gone out of Me."

It was time to face the music. Scripture is detailed in its description. "When the woman saw that she had not escaped notice, she came trembling and fell down before Him, and declared in the presence of all the people the reason why she had touched Him, and how she had been immediately healed" (Luke 8:47). She had to face Jesus, reveal her intent, and do so in front of the crowd, some of whom must have been wondering if they were not now ceremonially unclean.

Jesus had other concerns, her concerns. In a tone that was saturated with love, Jesus said, "Daughter, your faith has made you well; go in peace."

But how did this miracle work? Was there power in the garment Jesus wore? The woman had not touched Jesus. The only physical contact she had was with the hem of His garment. Could the very clothes Jesus wore be imbued with miraculous power?

The short answer is no, although there is some merit to the idea. For centuries people have believed that physical objects could carry spiritual powers. There's a long tradition surrounding objects like the Spear of Longinus, the spearhead that was used to pierce Jesus' side while He hung on the cross. Legends of health and power are associated with the cup Christ used at the Last Supper, often referred to as the Holy Grail.

But is there a biblical precedent for objects carrying the power to heal? Believe it or not, there is, but not in the miracles of Jesus. Jesus makes clear that the "power" left Him, not His clothing. Even clearer is the statement that the woman was made well not by the garment she touched, but by the faith placed in Him.

Still, the unusual miracle was associated with an ordinary object: Jesus' outer garment.

Aprons and Sweatbands

The strangest event of miracles involving inanimate objects occurred in one of the greatest cities of the ancient world and is associated with the greatest missionary ever. The apostle Paul had traveled to Ephesus and spent two years working by daylight and teaching by moonlight. It is during this time that the Bible records an odd event: "God was performing extraordinary miracles by the hands of Paul, so that handkerchiefs or aprons were even carried from his body to the sick, and the diseases left them and the evil spirits went out" (Acts 19:11–12).

Can handkerchiefs and aprons cast out demons and heal the sick? While objects like the staff of Moses, the ark of the covenant, and others have been integral to certain miracles, this is the only account in which items taken away from a person perform miracles.

Ephesus was a city of great importance and influence in the Roman kingdom, serving as the capital of Asia. Today, the remains of the city can be seen near Izmir in Turkey.

Ephesus was an ancient city when Paul arrived. First inhabited fifteen hundred years before Christ, it came into the Roman empire in 133 B.C. In Paul's day, it had a population of about five hundred thousand people. The city was important enough that the Roman governor resided there.

Ephesus was an important and influential city. This library was built by Julius Caesar a few decades after the apostle Paul ministered there.

The city was a cultural center (with a twenty-five-thousand-seat theater). It was also a religious center with a faith based on the worship of Diana (the temple of Diana was one of the seven ancient wonders of the world). It was a city filled with occultic practices—so much so that Paul wrote to the believers of Ephesus: "For our struggle is not against flesh and blood, but against the rulers, against the powers, against the world forces of this darkness, against the spiritual forces of wickedness in the heavenly places" (Ephesians 6:12).

In the middle of all this was the apostle Paul, bringing the message of Christ—certainly not an easy ministry considering how steeped the city was in idol worship. It was late A.D. 53, and Paul was on his third missionary journey. He would work in Ephesus for more than two years, teaching the gospel regularly and supporting himself as a tent maker.

Paul had been to Ephesus before and was familiar with the uphill battle that he faced. While in Ephesus, he wrote to the church in Corinth: "For we do not want you to be unaware, brethren, of our affliction which came to us in Asia, that we were burdened excessively, beyond our strength, so that we despaired even of life; indeed, we had the sentence of death within ourselves so that we would not trust in ourselves, but in God who raises the dead" (2 Corinthians 1:8–9).

Despite the prevalence of the occult, hatred, and riots, Paul persevered, teaching six days a week. Each day, from about 11:00 A.M. until 4:00 P.M., the people of Ephesus closed up their shops and went home. They would reopen their business around 4:00 P.M. and work until 9:30 that evening. It was during the hiatus that Paul would teach in the hall of Tyrannus, lecturing for five hours.

Miracles and healings were abundant. Acts 19:11 uses the phrase, "extraordinary miracles." It may seem redundant, but it's not: These miracles go beyond all previous miracles. God's power was evident even to the point that common objects became conduits of His grace.

Two such objects are mentioned: aprons and handkerchiefs. These were not handkerchiefs and aprons as we think of them. Most likely, the handkerchiefs were sweatbands worn by Paul as he made tents during the heat of the day. The other item was also associated with his work.

While working his craft, Paul would have worn a leather apron for protection as he drew the rough tent material over his legs.

But how did leather aprons and sweatbands carry miraculous power? For decades, televangelists have offered water, prayer cloths, and more to those who would financially support their efforts. Is this verse a justification of such things?

The answer comes in the understanding of the purpose of miracles. Miracles authenticated the miracle worker, showing that his message was true and that he had been called to do the work at hand. Ephesus was a city caught up in magic, but as the Gospel spread, many gave up their occult practices to embrace faith in Christ. So much so that a bonfire was built fueled by books of magic. These were the books of incantation for which Ephesus was famous. So many books were burned that the sum of them totaled fifty thousand silver coins. No one knows the exact value of those coins, but it was an enormous amount.

In a town where magic was considered commonplace, greater signs would be needed. Miracles worked in Ephesus would truly have to be "extraordinary miracles" just to be noticed. But no one outshines God. Paul's ministry was authenticated by the many miracles he worked. Those miracles softened hearts calloused by occult practices. The very real God had replaced the artificial Diana.

So powerful was Paul's ministry that even objects he touched became tools that testified to the greatness of God. The effort was successful. Acts 19:10 reports that "this took place for two years, so that all who lived in Asia heard the word of the Lord, both Jews and Greeks."

Not So Common

What is common in the hands of man is uncommon in the hands of God. Miracles that involve common objects like handkerchiefs and aprons (or in other cases, a burning bush, a mountaintop, salt, a wooden staff, and more) or common substances like spit become things beyond our realm when used by the Creator.

The same can be said of people. There is no one "common" in the kingdom of God. The gospel has gone out from churches made of the finest materials, designed by the greatest architects, and located in the best communities. It has also gone out from churches made of mud and old boards nailed to studs. The message is the same, and the eternal results are the same. Common or spectacular, God can use it all.

More to Think About

1. Jesus often did the unexpected. We have detailed accounts of what occurred, but not why it occurred. Why is that? Is there a lesson to be learned from what we don't know, as well as from what we do?

2. One reason Jesus may have spit in the eyes of the blind man was to show the superiority of faith over superstition. The ancient Jews believed that spittle from a firstborn son could cure blindness. If Jesus was indirectly addressing that idea, then what was Jesus teaching by His actions? Did the fact that the spittle did not completely heal the man (and that Jesus had to touch him again) mean anything?

3. The handkerchief and apron incident took place in a highly cultic area. Does God alter His methods based on the situation? Should Christians do the same?

4. The story of the woman with the hemorrhage is tied together with the account of Jairus. This is rare in the Gospels. Why were these two accounts arranged this way?

The Unrecognizable
Jesus

PEOPLE CHANGE. A QUICK LOOK THROUGH the family album proves that. As we grow older, our bodies change, our hair grows white, and our face takes on a different look. Occasionally we encounter people we have not seen in years and barely recognize them, and they us. That's to be expected. It is the course of life.

In the Bible are several events where a person goes unrecognized for a time, and that person is Jesus. It's a puzzle. After His resurrection, Jesus appeared to many people, and some did not recognize Him even though they knew Him very well. Why? What about Jesus had changed?

The Mystified Mary
John 20:11–18

The Gospel of John records an unusual event. Mary Magdalene has made her way to the tomb of Jesus (the other Gospels show that she was accompanied by other women). It is barely dawn, and Mary is pressing forward to the tomb to finish preparing Jesus' body for burial. This work was normally done before a person was entombed, but the rapidly approaching Sabbath—a day upon which no work could be done—made that impossible. She had left home early, no doubt having been awake in her grief all night. She had no idea how she would move the stone or what the Roman guards would say to her, but she went anyway.

Mary Magdalene loved Jesus perhaps like no other. She supported Him financially from her own funds (Luke 8:2–3) and had been one of Jesus' followers. When Jesus was crucified, Mary was at the foot of the cross. She saw it all: His brutalized body, the actual act of crucifixion, and Jesus' last breath. While she loved Jesus, she was also indebted to Him for she was one of the "women who had been healed of evil spirits and sicknesses" (Luke 8:2). Seven demons had occupied her body until Jesus came along. All this made her a woman of profound love and immense gratitude. Now she had the awful task of treating the corpse of Jesus—except there was no corpse.

In a panic, she raced back to town to inform Peter and John. The two men raced, literally, to the tomb and found it empty. Their confusion was understandable. Their thoughts spun in their minds like leaves in a tornado, but there was no making sense of it. Jesus was gone. There was nothing for them to do but return home.

Mary couldn't go home. Her emotions froze her in place outside the opening of the grave: "But Mary was standing outside the tomb weeping; and so, as she wept, she stooped and looked into the tomb." Perhaps she was looking for a clue as to what might have become of her Lord's body. This time the tomb was not empty. Two angels were inside, and they make an announcement that must have rocked her mind and heart: "Woman, why are you weeping?"

The answer was honest and heartrending. "Because they have taken away my Lord, and I do not know where they have laid Him."

Mary did not understand. The concept of the Resurrection was beyond her, as it is beyond many today. If Jesus was not in the tomb, then someone must have moved Him. It was a logical conclusion, but an erroneous one. Her error would not last long.

Perhaps hearing something behind her, she turned to see Jesus. There He stood, alive, vibrant, no longer beaten down, no longer drained of strength. It should have been a moment of great joy; instead it was a moment of confusion. Mary did not recognize Him. After years of seeing Him, after traveling many miles with Jesus, Mary could not see Him for who He was.

Jesus started a conversation: "Woman, why are you weeping? Whom are you seeking?"

Then comes the odd twist. John records, "Supposing Him to be the gardener, she said to Him, 'Sir, if you have carried Him away, tell me where you have laid Him, and I will take Him away.'"

The gardener? Why does Mary make this profound mistake? Why is she unable to see that the man who stood before her was none other than Jesus?

Recognition comes quickly, though. With a single word, Jesus revealed Himself to the grieving woman: "Mary." The response was immediate and overwhelming: "Rabboni!" she cried. Rabboni was the Aramaic term for teacher. With that, she seized Jesus, probably around the feet, unwilling to let go. Now she has seen Him, heard Him, and touched Him. It was no dream. Jesus was alive.

The question remains, however. Why did Mary not recognize Jesus? It wasn't distance; they were close enough to carry on a conversation and near enough for her to wrap her arms around Him. It wasn't darkness; she had gone to the tomb a little after daybreak and returned. There was enough light for her to see into the tomb. What then? What was different about Jesus? The passage doesn't say, but we do know that the problem isn't Mary's alone.

A Long Walk with a Stranger
Luke 24:13–32

Mary was not the only one who had trouble recognizing the resurrected Savior. Two disciples walked from Jerusalem to the small town of Emmaus, seven miles away. Stunned by the events of the Crucifixion, these two believers discussed all that has happened. It will take them two to three hours to make the journey, and every moment of the trip would be filled with talk of Jesus.

As they walked the dirt road, someone joined them. We know who it is because the Bible tells us that "Jesus Himself approached" and traveled with them. Jesus asked what the conversation of the day was and they told Him. Actually, they asked a revealing, ironic, almost humorous question: "Are You the only one visiting Jerusalem and unaware of the things which have happened here in these days?" Was Jesus unaware of what had just happened in Jerusalem? Jesus was aware, all right. No one knew better than He what had occurred and what it meant.

But there's a twist in this tale too. Luke records a key fact: "But their eyes were prevented from recognizing Him." Odd. Prevented? The Greek word *krateo* means "to restrain," or "to hold back." What isn't said is who or what is holding their perception at bay. It gets even stranger when we factor in Mark 16:12: "After that, He appeared in a *different form* to two of them while they were walking along on their way to the country" (italics mine). This is the same event as the one recorded in Luke. What different form did Jesus take? Does this mean that there was a material change in His appearance or simply that He seemed different to the disciples?

A tomb similar to what Jesus may have been laid in after His crucifixion

For the rest of the journey, Jesus gave a Bible lesson about the Christ, His suffering, and how it related to what was foreshadowed throughout the Old Testament. The two listened carefully, hanging on every word. Later they would ask, "Were not our hearts burning within us while He was speaking to us on the road, while He was explaining the Scriptures to us?"

The men invited Jesus to stay with them and enjoy a meal. After some coaxing, He agreed. Then more mystery followed. Luke notes that "He took the bread and blessed it, and breaking it, He began giving it to them." This is strange because it was the host's job to break the bread, not the guest's. But this breech of protocol achieved something useful and revealing: "Then their eyes were opened and they recognized Him; and He vanished from their sight." There are two key words in this verse. The first is the word for "opened" (*dianoigo*). The Greek is an intensive word combining "completely" with "open." The word open is often used to show a gate that has been swung wide. The next important word is "recognized" (*epiginosko*). It means to know something fully and completely, to know something well. What we're left with is the understanding that the two disciples had their understanding thrown wide open.

Their new knowledge is too much to contain. After traveling the seven miles from Jerusalem to Emmaus, they turn around and make their way back to Jerusalem. They had one goal: Share the news with the disciples.

What triggered that sudden insight? Could it be the way in which Jesus broke bread? As followers of Christ, could they have broken bread with Jesus before? This would explain why Jesus assumes the role of host in someone else's house. This is indeed the answer. "They began to relate their experiences on the road and how He was recognized by them in the breaking of the bread."

There's another aspect to this. After Jesus broke the bread, He would have handed some to the two men. That bread would have been held in hands that bore the marks of crucifixion. The teaching on the road, the breaking of the bread, and the sign of the scars were enough to break down the barriers to understanding.

An Unexpected Guest
Luke 24:36–45

That evening, Jesus appears for a third time. The two Emmaus disciples were excitedly telling the other disciples all that had happened to them—how Jesus joined them on the trip, taught them, broke bread with them, and then disappeared. Sometime during the story, Jesus showed up—through locked doors.

The reaction is understandable: "But they were startled and frightened and thought that they were seeing a spirit." "Startled" is too soft a term. "Terrified" would be better. Terrified and frightened by Jesus' sudden appearance? Why? They thought they were seeing a ghost. It seems odd, but many of the disciples thought it was easier to believe in ghosts than in the Resurrection. Once again, Jesus is unrecognized and has to prove who He is and what He is (that He's not a spirit that has come to haunt the disciples). He showed the scars on His feet and hands and insisted that they touch Him to see that He has substance. He even ate some fish to drive home the point that He is alive.

One other point of interest is that Jesus also "opened their minds to understand the Scriptures." The word for "opened" is the same strong word used with the eye-opening realization of the two Emmaus disciples.

Breakfast with Jesus
John 21:1–14

Another time the disciples failed to recognize the resurrected Savior occurred one dawn while seven of them were fishing from a boat in the Sea of Tiberius (Galilee). In the long passage is this short verse: "But when the day was now breaking, Jesus stood on the beach; yet the disciples did not know that it was Jesus" (John 21:4). This event may be less mysterious than the others. While Jesus may have looked different that cool morning by the lake, it is more likely that the insufficient light of dawn and the distance from the boat to the shore was the real cause for their inability to identify Him.

The reverse of this is interesting: If darkness and distance are the reasons the disciples could not recognize Jesus that day, then it is all the more spectacular to note that He recognized them.

The Big Question: Why?

Two primary possibilities may explain why people had trouble recognizing the resurrected Savior, but let us first dispense with the idea that the disciples and followers were just making a mistake—that if they looked a little closer they would have easily recognized their Lord. Since the puzzlement occurred several times, it is far more likely that something about Jesus had changed.

New and Improved Body?

Jesus' resurrection was physical. That is a cardinal truth of Christianity. Jesus still has His body today. Yet, that body seemed different in some ways. He could appear and disappear as He did with the Emmaus disciples. He appeared suddenly in a closed and locked room. In other ways, however, His body seemed quite normal. Jesus was touched and examined. He ate food on several occasions, and Mary was able to cling to Him.

The apostle John wrote an intriguing verse: "Beloved, now we are children of God, and it has not appeared as yet *what we will be*. We know that when He appears, *we will be like Him*, because *we will see Him just as He is*" (1 John 3:2, italics mine). This verse only makes sense if we understand that Christ's resurrected body is somehow different from the way it was before His death. In that change (of which we have no details) is a promise to the believer: We, too, will be changed.

Paul speaks about having a different body in his letter to the church in Rome: "And not only this, but also we ourselves, having the first fruits of the Spirit, even we ourselves groan within ourselves, waiting eagerly for our adoption as sons, the redemption of our body" (Romans 8:23). He mentions the redemption—the buying back—of our bodies.

He says something similar but with more detail in his first letter to the church in Corinth: "Behold, I tell you a mystery; we will not all sleep, but we will all be changed, in a moment, in the twinkling of an eye, at the last trumpet; for the trumpet will sound, and the dead will be raised imperishable, and we will be changed" (1 Corinthians 15:51–52).

A change is coming for every believer. The bodies we now have will be altered into something like Christ's. No more death, sorrow, or pain—

that's the promise (Revelation 21:3–4). For that to happen, there must first be resurrection.

Jesus may very well have appeared to Mary, the two on the road to Emmaus, and the disciples in His glorified body—a body so different as to be hardly recognizable. Yet, Jesus was recognizable. A single word, "Mary," gave her all the information she needed to properly identify the man she first thought was the gardener. The simple act of breaking bread revealed Jesus to the Emmaus disciples.

Another, More Brutal Possibility

Much of Jesus' life was alluded to in the Old Testament, centuries before it occurred. Micah 5:2 told us that the Messiah would be born in Bethlehem. Isaiah 7:14 informed us that the Christ would be born of a virgin. The list is long and detailed. The most descriptive prophecies, however, deal with Jesus' death on the cross. Centuries before crucifixion was used, it was described. Some of these passages, as well as what we read in the New Testament, give us another possibility as to why Jesus was difficult to recognize after the Resurrection. It is a reason based in cruelty and brutality.

Psalm 22 and Isaiah 53 give graphic detail about a man being brutalized. Jesus even quotes Psalm 22 from the cross. These passages include descriptions of what Jesus experienced:

- Weakness: "I am poured out like water."
- Dislocation of the joints: "All my bones are out of joint."
- Incapacitation: "My heart is like wax; it is melted within me."
- Exhaustion: "My strength is dried up like a potsherd."
- Dehydration: "My tongue cleaves to my jaws."
- Impalement: "They pierced my hands and my feet."
- Hyperextension: "I can count all my bones."

Another passage that sheds light on why Jesus was difficult to recognize is in Isaiah 50:6—"I gave My back to those who strike Me, and My cheeks to those who pluck out the beard; I did not cover My face from humiliation and spitting."

We know that the temple guards and later the Roman guards beat Jesus without mercy. That beating included striking His face with a reed.

A reed could be ridged and sharp on the end. Those same guards also pummeled the Lord's face with their fists. The Isaiah passage remarks that His beard was plucked out. That was a form of torture that lead to great pain and scarring.

Jesus may have been difficult to recognize because He still bore the marks of His torture. This idea is not a pleasant one. No one likes to imagine the Savior being abused by men He was about to die for, but it happened. And it left marks that we will see someday.

More to Think About

1. Those who saw Jesus after the Resurrection often responded with surprise and even fright. Considering the number of times that Jesus spoke of His resurrection, why do you suppose His followers were so taken aback when Jesus did exactly what He said He would?

2. Considering the nature of the Resurrection, would you have responded differently than the disciples?

3. Of the two possibilities for why Jesus wasn't quickly recognized after His resurrection, which one do you think is more likely correct?

4. Jesus still bore scars from the Crucifixion after rising from the grave. Why is that? Is it important that those scars remain?

5. The Resurrection is the cornerstone of Christian faith, but how important is the suffering Jesus endured? Several Old Testament passages foretell the brutal treatment Jesus would receive. Why are those verses included in the Bible?

The Wrong-Way
Prophet

SEVENTY-ONE PERCENT OF OUR PLANET IS COVERED with ocean, totaling more than 322 million cubic miles of water. The average depth of these oceans is an astounding sixteen thousand feet. In these waters live animals unseen by men, creatures yet to be identified and studied. The mysteries of the sea are as deep as the oceans themselves. Some animals are microscopic while others, like the blue whale, can reach lengths of one hundred feet and weigh three hundred thousand pounds. The enigmatic oceans have long been a source of wonder and fear.

2 Kings 14:25; Jonah; Matthew 12:39–41

It is in one such ocean that one of the strangest events recorded in the Bible happens. The account is recorded in a tiny book in the section of the Old Testament called the "minor prophets." In the Book of Jonah is the fascinating story of a man called by God to a great task, but who makes every effort to avoid the assignment. One dynamic and unexpected turn follows another. Supernatural events are sprinkled throughout the account, making it one of the most intriguing and mysterious in the pages of Scripture. Jonah lives through one mind-numbing event after another.

The account, at just forty-eight verses, can be read in a few minutes. But the set of verses contains: rebellion, fear, supernatural storms, a unique and mysterious creature, and miracle upon miracle. (No less than ten miracles are in the book—one for every 4.8 verses.)

Jonah the Man

Jonah has been called the "reluctant prophet." He was more than reluctant; he was as disobedient and unbending as they come. He is described as "Jonah the son of Amittai." Translating this phrase straight to English, his name would be "Dove the son of Truth." The word dove is used about fifty times in the Bible and, in most cases, relates to sacrifice. Most of all, doves were seen as gentle creatures. Ironically, Jonah was neither gentle nor sacrificial.

The story begins when God issues a straightforward call to Jonah: "Arise, go to Nineveh the great city and cry against it, for their wickedness has come up before Me." Jonah had a problem with that call, but not because he was afraid. Still, he had good reason to be fearful: The people of Nineveh had a terrifying reputation, known for such things as decapitating their enemies and piling their heads into bloody pyramids.

But Jonah flees the call of God because of religious differences. In Jonah's day there were only two types of people in the world (at least from a Jewish perspective): Jews and Gentiles. Jonah was Jewish; the people of Nineveh were Gentiles. Jonah, knowing God would not send him if there were no chance of repentance and forgiveness, chose to opt out of God's command.

Here's where the story turns ironic. The Bible tells us that Jonah went down to Joppa, found a ship, and paid for passage to Tarshish. (Herodotus, the ancient Greek historian, tells us that Tarshish was a city in Spain.) In other words, Jonah left a Jewish city to travel to a Gentile town and paid fare to a Gentile sea captain so that he could flee God's commission by sailing on a Gentile ship. And why does he do this? So he won't have to preach to a Gentile city.

Did Jonah really believe that he could sail to a spot where God could not find him? Some scholars have suggested that Jonah believed that God was confined to the physical area occupied by Israel. But what Jonah really wanted to do was remove himself as far from Nineveh as possible.

If he could get far enough away, then God would have to send someone else to deliver the message.

It was a simple plan. It was also a foolish one. No one can outrun God.

Miracle Number One: The Storm from Nowhere

Unexpectedly, the sky grew dark, the wind changed from a breeze into a screeching gale, and the waves of the calm Mediterranean turned vicious. This sudden storm was of such intensity that it terrified the experienced sailors on Jonah's ship and pounded the vessel until the crew was certain that all was lost.

In desperation, they jettison their cargo, which meant that they would receive no pay for the voyage and may owe the owner for the lost goods. But none of that would matter if they were dead. The terrified men worked feverishly to keep the boat afloat. Still, it was not enough. The wooden vessel creaked and groaned under the burden of crashing waves. Against the screaming, unrelenting wind they cried out to their gods, Baal and Ashtoreth, but no help came.

Where was Jonah through all this? He was asleep in the hold of the ship. While the crew struggled for their lives, the prophet snoozed. The captain of the vessel, perhaps trying to cover all his bases, woke Jonah and demanded that he pray to his God. Maybe Jonah's God would have mercy on them since Baal and Ashtoreth remained silent.

Miracle Number Two: Casting Lots

In the meantime, the crew stayed busy. Knowing that their combined efforts and experience could not overpower the strange storm, they sought divine guidance the way many ancient people did. The sailors cast lots—flat stones or some form of dice most likely—which all pointed to Jonah. The next step was obvious: Confront their passenger. Steadying themselves with whatever they could find to hold on to, the angry and frightened crew fired question after question at the prophet. "Tell us, now! On whose account has this calamity struck us? What is your occupation? And where do you come from? What is your country? From what people are you?"

The last three questions are intriguing. Had Jonah disguised himself? Was he no longer dressed like a Jew? Jonah follows the path that so many have followed—one deception leading to another. Now there could be no more lies. Jonah had to step up to the truth.

"I am a Hebrew," Jonah said, "and I fear the LORD God of heaven who made the sea and the dry land."

The words cut through the storm and into the hearts of the sailors. They had heard of this God, and they knew that the storm was Jonah's fault. Then an unexpected, interesting twist: "What should we do to you that the sea may become calm for us?" What should we do to you?

Jonah knew: "Pick me up and throw me into the sea. Then the sea will become calm for you, for I know that on account of me this great storm has come upon you." Was Jonah being heroic? Sacrificial? No. The prophet doesn't volunteer to throw himself overboard for the sake of the crew. In fact, he insisted that they do the dirty deed. They must seize him and toss him over the rail. From Jonah's perspective, he drowns either way.

Miracle Number Three: New Prayers

But these sailors were noble: They continued to fight the sea, rowing toward land, hoping to find a secluded harbor or a place to beach the boat. The craft would be lost and there would be damages to pay, but they thought that better than sacrificing Jonah. Then they prayed. These pagan sailors prayed to the God of Israel, leaving behind Baal and other pagan idols. They said, "We earnestly pray, O LORD, do not let us perish on account of this man's life and do not put innocent blood on us; for You, O LORD, have done as You have pleased." Sometimes, belief comes from disaster.

Despite their brave intentions, rowing proved impossible. The storm intensified, and their hopes poured over the side like the seawater running from the deck. Amid the screeching wind, the creaking, popping boat, and the pounding surf, a decision was made. Jonah had to go, and he had to go right away.

Did the men linger on the pitching, yawing boat, before they finally heaved the prophet over the edge and into the pounding sea? Did Jonah see a sleek, dark form just below the water, closely pacing the ship?

Splash.

Miracle Number Four: The Appointed Fish

One moment Jonah is on the deck of a rolling ship; the next, immersed in the cool water of the Mediterranean; and then, blackness. Not the blackness of unconsciousness or death, but the ebony darkness of a fish's gullet.

Death would have been preferable, but God had other plans. Jonah lived for three days and nights in the stomach of that fish. No one knows the type of fish that God used for this unique mission. The best we can do is speculate with the few clues we're given. The Old Testament word for fish is *dag* and refers to that which swam in the sea. The Greek language of the New Testament has more than four hundred different names for fish; Hebrew has only one. To the ancient Hebrew mind, anything that swam in the sea was a fish, whales included.

In Matthew 12:40, Jesus used Jonah as a sign of His own death and resurrection. In doing so, He used the Greek term *ketos* to refer to the fish that swallowed the prophet. Translations like the New American Standard render the word as "sea monster." It's possible that the fish may have been unique in all of history, specially created for this one event. Jonah 1:17 states that God "appointed" the fish, meaning that He had prepared or prearranged the fish's presence. At some time in the past, God had made this fish for this express purpose, or, at least, God chose this creature from all the creatures that swam in the sea.

Was it a whale? Of the seventy-five species of whales, there are several kinds large enough to swallow a man. Toothed whales hunt for food, like squid, fish, and, in some cases, seals. Baleen whales filter sea water for small fish and plankton. Any number of whales would be able to swallow a man. In this unusual situation, God could have appointed a whale to the task.

Was it a whale shark? Perhaps. A whale shark is the largest known fish in the sea, reaching a length of fifty feet and weighing in excess of eighteen thousand metric tons. The creatures are generally harmless, although some have been known to ram boats. The whale shark, how-ever, is a "filter feeder," straining its food through a large mouth and catching plankton and small fish in its gill rakers. To swallow something as large as a man would be contrary to its nature, but not impossible for a fish especially appointed to the task. Also, some of the 350 species of sharks—some harmless, some deadly—could have ingested Jonah. The tiger shark, which can reach lengths up to thirty feet, will swallow just about anything and has the ability to turn its stomach inside out to empty things it can't digest. Considering Jonah would later be released from the fish's belly and deposited on dry land makes this last feature especially interesting.

Whatever creature was used, it had to swallow Jonah whole, sustain him for three days, swim to a specific spot, and be able to regurgitate the prophet onto the beach. No matter what the specifics may be, the mira-cle is amazing.

Miracle Number Five: Switching Off a Storm

Within moments of Jonah's ejection from the ship, the storm stopped. There came a stillness, an eerie, unnatural quiet. Only God can start and stop a storm on cue. What an amazing thing to see. These maritime experts had endured storms before, but none like this one that came on suddenly and stopped within moments. Then the sailors did what their hearts compelled them to do: There, on the deck of the battered wooden ship, the weary and battered seamen made a sacrifice and voiced a solemn vow to the Lord God.

Miracle Number Six: A Pitiful Prayer and Survival

From the belly of the creature, Jonah prayed. What else would a man do? Yet, there is something unusual about this prayer. At first it seems noble, poetic, and even powerful. It honors God, alludes to life after death, and shows hope in despair. But there is no admission of guilt, no repentance, and no commitment to obedience. It's a pretty prayer, but an impotent one. All that Jonah offers God is that which he has done in the past; he makes no offer to answer God's call to go to Nineveh.

Even in his hellish situation, Jonah took a shot at those God was trying to reach. "Those who regard vain idols forsake their faithfulness," Jonah said. He was speaking of the idol-worshiping people of Nineveh. His hatred for them remained. He could not see how God could love and change a people like those in Nineveh. Jonah had not changed.

Fortunately for the people of Nineveh (and for Jonah), neither had God.

"Then the LORD commanded the fish, and it vomited Jonah up onto the dry land." There is an overlooked miracle here. At God's command, the creature beaches itself and vomits up the prodigal prophet. This is not normal behavior. From time to time, whales infected with illness will beach themselves on shore, but this one does so because God commands it to do so.

Why bother with a fish? At first glance, using a fish as a vessel seems an awkward way of doing things. But that fish becomes Jonah's lifeboat, keeping him alive in an ocean where he would surely have drowned. It also becomes Jonah's mode of travel back to shore. Another angle on the fish involves the god of the people of Nineveh—Dagon. Dagon was portrayed as a hybrid of man and fish, having a fish's tail and a man's head

Ocean view from Joppa, the city from which Jonah set sail

and torso. Even in God's punishment of Jonah, He was making a state-ment. The fish was more than a convenient tool; it was an unmistakable message.

As Jonah staggered away from the shore, he left behind him the body of the dying fish, but he took with him his bigotry, hatred, and resentment.

Miracle Number Seven: God of the Second Chance

Again the Lord said to Jonah, "Arise, go to Nineveh the great city and proclaim to it the proclamation which I am going to tell you." Jonah went—not out of loyalty, love, compassion, or a noble vision, but because he had no other choice.

After more than a month of travel along the ancient trade routes, Jonah stood upon a hill overlooking the vast city of Nineveh. He could see its high walls with its towers and the Tigris River that flowed by it to the west. There they were—the people of Nineveh, known the world over for their cruelty in decapitating their prisoners and burning alive men, women, and children and for worshiping their pagan gods: Dagon, Nabu, Asshur, Adad, and Ishtar. Evil people. Wicked people. Pagan people. What did God want with them? Jonah was a patriot, faithful to his own people and country, and now he gazed down upon the enemy.

More than a million people lived in or around the city. It would take Jonah three days to walk across it, and the thought of it galled him. They deserved divine punishment. But first, he had a message to deliver. God had revealed what it was that he was to say. He would say it, leave town, and watch the destruction as we might watch a movie.

Jonah's message was short: "Yet forty days and Nineveh will be over-thrown." Overthrown in Hebrew is *haphak,* meaning, "to tip on end, turnover, upend." Nineveh would be not just destroyed, but demolished.

What a sight Jonah must have been after three days in a fish's belly. Walking through the streets of the city, crying out a message of destruc-tion, he quickly gathered attention.

But then something happened that Jonah didn't expect—something he could never have anticipated. People listened. People responded. From every age and rank, they heard the message and believed. The king issued a proclamation that required the wearing of rough sackcloth against bare skin and sitting in ashes to show their sorrow and contrite hearts. There was to be a city-wide fast. Not even the animals were allowed to eat or drink.

How could such repentance come about? Nineveh had been having a rough time of late. In 765 B.C., a sever famine struck the area. Two years later in 763 B.C., the people saw a total solar eclipse—a frightening thing for ancient pagan people—and another famine swept through the land in 759 B.C. Then Jonah arrived on the scene with a message of doom. Jonah was surprised at how quickly the people repented. God had been at work in their hearts.

Jonah did not bring a message of hope. He did not proclaim repentance or grace. He offered only destruction, yet the people turned to the God whom Jonah said would destroy them. The people listened; they personalized the message, taking it to heart; they humbled themselves with fasting and sackcloth; and they repented with heartfelt emotion.

God is the God of second chances. Jonah got a second chance, and now the people of Nineveh were given a new opportunity to make good. That was God's desire. But it was far from what Jonah wanted.

Miracle Number Eight: A Plant with a Purpose

Jonah prayed another prayer, and this one was more unusual than the first. Unlike the prayer adorned in pleasantries that he prayed while inside the fish, this one vented emotional steam. Jonah unleashed his frustration on God. He minced no words, spared no emotions, and concealed none of his feelings. Scripture says that when God relented and spared the people of Nineveh, "it greatly displeased Jonah and he became angry." Jonah saw God's forgiveness of the Ninevites as something wicked. And this made Jonah angry. Actually, the word for angry is translated as "hot." Jonah was furious. He argued with God, saying, "Was not this what I said while I was still in my own country?"

Why was Jonah stomping around in the dust of Nineveh's streets? Why was he shaking his fist at God? Two reasons. First, he still hated the Ninevites. Second, he could now be considered a false prophet. His reputation had been sullied. He had proclaimed Nineveh's doom, and now it wasn't going to happen.

Jonah continued to unload on God, blaming Him for the whole event: "Therefore in order to forestall this I fled to Tarshish, for I knew that You are a gracious and compassionate God, slow to anger and abundant in lovingkindness, and one who relents concerning calamity" (Jonah 4:2).

Sounds comical, and it would be if it weren't such a serious event.

What was left for Jonah to do? "Therefore now, O LORD, please take my life from me, for death is better to me than life." Strong, heated, manipulative words. God responded with a simple question: "Do you have good reason to be angry?"

But as far as Jonah was concerned, the conversation was over. He headed east of the city. East? His home was west, so why would he head east? Perhaps that was the best place to see the city. Also, to move west would mean crossing the Tigris River. So, east of Nineveh he built a shelter for himself and waited. He had prophesied that the end would come in forty days, so he was determined to linger and see it happen. Could the people remain faithful for forty days? Jonah doubted it.

Then God appointed a plant to grow near the small shelter Jonah had made for himself. This is the second time God "appointed" something to do His will and He will do it twice more.

Miracles Numbers Nine and Ten: A Worm and a Wind

A worm, appointed by God, attacked the plant and killed it. Next a hot and vicious wind, called a sirocco, assaulted the depressed prophet, and he mourned the loss of the plant that would have provided some shelter for him. Again, Jonah begged for death.

It was then that God asked a question similar to the one He had asked days, even weeks before, but this time He added a twist: "Do you have good reason to be angry about the plant?"

It was an unusual question, but Jonah's response is even stranger: "I have good reason to be angry, even to death."

God then drives the point home saying, "You had compassion on the plant for which you did not work and which you did not cause to grow. . . . Should I not have compassion on Nineveh, the great city in which there are more than 120,000 persons who do not know the difference between their right and left hand?" The last phrase meant that there were a great number of children in Nineveh. Why wasn't Jonah concerned about the children?

There the account ends. It is the most abrupt ending of a book in the Bible, concluding with God having the last word. We have no idea what happened to Jonah. Did he come to grips with God's plan or did he carry his resentment to the grave? No one can say, but his life was an example of the power of hate and the greater power of God's forgiveness.

More to Think About

1. Is the story of Jonah too much to believe? What would you say to someone who thinks that there are just too many coincidences for this story to be true?

2. In Luke 11:29–32, Jesus mentions Jonah and the Ninevites, stating that the Ninevites would judge Jesus' generation. What similarities exist between Jesus and Jonah? What differences?

3. Jonah was a man filled with faults. How is it that God would call upon such a man to undertake such an important mission? Is there more here than the message to the citizens of Nineveh?

4. Jonah refuses to change his attitude despite the storm, the great fish, and other events. Why does he remain so angry?

5. The Book of Jonah ends abruptly with no resolution. Why is the ending so sudden?

Afterword:
There 'Tis

TOGETHER WE HAVE EXPLORED just a few of the fascinating mysteries contained in the Bible. We have investigated ancient giants, examined unusual miracles, followed enigmatic people, and seen how God can work in mysterious ways. The nineteen topics of this book are just a cursory look at what lies in the pages of Scripture. Many more mysteries await you. All that is required is the desire to know more of God and His work.

Each time we open our Bibles, we join the many millions of people through the ages who have searched for meaning and direction in their lives. As we read, as we study, we peer into the revealed mind of God. What greater adventure can there be? Einstein is quoted as saying that he wanted to think God's thoughts *after* Him. With the Bible, we think God's thoughts *with* Him.

The mysteries of the Bible will continue to be examined and some debated. Not every idea or opinion is represented in these pages, nor were they meant to be. No book can hold all that is written on any biblical subject. That is the way it should be. The search is as important as the discovery; the journey as noble as the destination.

Still, as fascinating as these subjects are, they are mere oddities if we fail to apply the underlying truth to our lives. What is that underlying truth? Jesus, of course, said it best: "I came that they may have life, and have it abundantly" (John 10:10).

That is a truth we can live with—eternally.

Here is the greatest mystery of all: a perfect God loves imperfect humans. The apostle Paul said, "But God demonstrates His own love toward us, in that while we were yet sinners, Christ died for us (Romans 5:8)." Think of it: The infinite sacrificing for the finite; the perfect for the defective; the pure for the contaminated—motivated by a love too pure to fathom. It is this love that connects you to the distant past that you've just read about. The people mentioned are real, the events actual historical occurrences, and the presence and power of God was a reality then as it is now.

What does it all mean? Do the amazing events have some purpose beyond being the record of unusual occurrences? Yes, they do. They are messages that are written in broad strokes yet specifically enough to be applied to every person . . . to you.

Not far from where I live are a set of radio telescopes once used in the SETI project. These large radio dishes rise above the sandy soil of California's Mojave desert, their faces pointed skyward, all in hopes of hearing something special, something indicative of intelligent life. SETI was the anacronym for the now defunct government program Search for Extra-Terrestrial Intelligence. (The program is now run by private funds.) Despite millions of dollars and thousands of hours of searching, the effort came up empty. Yet, an intelligence *is* out there, and He's not waiting for us to find Him.

Over countless centuries God has reached out to His creation: humankind. Through creation, through prophets, through events, God has made Himself known. The author of Hebrews said, "In these last days [God] has *spoken to us in His Son*, whom He appointed heir of all things, through whom also He made the world" (Hebrews 1:2, italics mine). Christ is and shall remain the greatest and most complete revelation of all. He is the center of Scripture. Christ in the beginning. Christ through the middle. Christ to the end.

It is my hope and prayer, that this book has created or renewed in you an interest in the God of the Bible, and that your future will hold many more adventures in the pages of Scripture. After all, it was written with you in mind.

No wonder the psalmist uttered,

> Let them give thanks to the Lord for His lovingkindness,
> and for His wonders to the sons of men! (Psalm 107:8)

Grace and peace,
Alton Gansky